Lecture Notes in Computer Science 16757

FoLLI Publications on Logic, Language and Information

Subline of Lecture Notes in Computer Science

More information about this series at https://link.springer.com/bookseries/558

Patricia Johann · Ruy de Queiroz
Editors

Logic, Language, Information, and Computation

32nd International Workshop, WoLLIC 2026
Lima, Peru, August 3–6, 2026
Proceedings

Springer

Editors
Patricia Johann
Appalachian State University
Boone, NC, USA

Ruy de Queiroz
Universidade Federal de Pernambuco
Recife, Brazil

ISSN 0302-9743 ISSN 1611-3349 (electronic)
Lecture Notes in Computer Science
ISBN 978-3-032-33485-5 ISBN 978-3-032-33486-2 (eBook)
https://doi.org/10.1007/978-3-032-33486-2

This Springer imprint is published by the registered company Springer Nature Switzerland AG
The registered company address is: Gewerbestrasse 11, 6330 Cham, Switzerland

Preface

This volume contains the papers presented at the 32nd Workshop on Logic, Language, Information and Computation (WoLLIC 2026) held online August 3–7, 2026, hosted by the Peruvian Computer Society (SPC) and the Universidad Nacional de Ingeniería (UNI), Lima, Peru. The WoLLIC series of workshops started in 1994 with the aim of fostering interdisciplinary research in pure and applied logic. The idea is to have a forum which is large enough in the number of possible interactions between logic and the sciences related to information and computation, and yet is small enough to allow for concrete and useful interaction among participants.

For WoLLIC 2026 there were 17 submissions. Each submission was reviewed in a single-blind process by at least 3 program committee members. The committee decided to accept 9 papers. This volume includes all the accepted papers.

We would like to thank all the people who contributed to making WoLLIC 2026 a success. We thank the Program Committee and all additional reviewers for the work they put into reviewing the submissions. We thank the invited speakers and the tutorialists for their inspiring talks, the Steering Committee and the Advisory Committee for their advice, and the Local Organizing Committee (especially Ernesto Cuadros-Vargas) for their great support. Finally, we thank all the authors for their excellent contributions.

The help provided by the EasyChair system created by Andrei Voronkov is gratefully acknowledged. We also would like to acknowledge the scientific sponsorship of the following organizations: Interest Group in Pure and Applied Logics (IGPL), Association for Logic, Language and Information (FoLLI), Association for Symbolic Logic (ASL), European Association for Theoretical Computer Science (EATCS), European Association for Computer Science Logic (EACSL), the Brazilian Logic Society (SBL), and the Peruvian Computer Society (SPC).

August 2026

Patricia Johann
Ruy de Queiroz

Organization

Program Committee Chair

Patricia Johann	Appalachian State University, USA

General Chair

Ruy de Queiroz	Universidade Federal de Pernambuco, Brazil

Steering Committee

Samson Abramsky	University College London, UK
Agata Ciabattoni	Vienna University of Technology, Austria
Anuj Dawar	University of Cambridge, UK
Helle Hvid Hansen	University of Groningen, The Netherlands
Juliette Kennedy	University of Helsinki, Finland
Ulrich Kohlenbach	Technische Universität Darmstadt, Germany
Dexter Kozen	Cornell University, USA
Daniel Leivant	Indiana University Bloomington, USA
Leonid Libkin	University of Edinburgh, UK
George Metcalfe	University of Bern, Switzerland
Lawrence Moss	Indiana University Bloomington, USA
Luke Ong	University of Oxford, UK
Valeria de Paiva	Topos Institute/Pontifical Catholic University of Rio de Janeiro, USA/Brazil
Elaine Pimentel	University College London, UK
Ruy de Queiroz	Universidade Federal de Pernambuco, Brazil
Andre Scedrov	University of Pennsylvania, USA
Alexandra Silva	Cornell University, USA
Thomas Studer	University of Bern, Switzerland
Renata Wassermann	Universidade de São Paulo, Brazil

Advisory Committee

Johan van Benthem	University of Amsterdam, Netherlands and Stanford University, USA
Joe Halpern	Cornell University, USA
Wilfrid Hodges	Queen Mary University of London, UK
Angus Macintyre	University of Oxford, UK
Hiroakira Ono	Japan Advanced Institute of Science and Technology, Japan
Jouko Väänänen	University of Helsinki, Finland

Program Committee

Patricia Johann (Chair)	Appalachian State University, USA
Sandra Alves	University of Porto, Portugal
Zena Ariola	University of Oregon, USA
Clément Aubert	Augusta University, USA
Pierre Cagne	Appalachian State University, USA
Silvia Ghilezan	University of Novi Sad, Serbia
Makoto Kanazawa	Hosei University, Japan
Tobias Kappé	Leiden University, The Netherlands
Dexter Kozen	Cornell University, USA
Ugo dal Lago	Università di Bologna, Italy
Sonia Marin	University of Birmingham, UK
Valeria de Paiva	Topos Institute, USA
Daniela Petrişan	IRIF, Université de Paris, France
Peter Selinger	Dalhousie University, Canada
Alex Simpson	University of Ljubljana, Slovenia
Ana Sokolova	University of Salzburg, Austria
Georg Struth	University of Sheffield, UK
Janis Voigtländer	University of Duisburg, Germany

Additional Reviewers

Justus Becker
Filippo De Bortoli
Liam Chung
Erich Grädel
Christoph Haase
Wiebe van der Hoek
Louwe Kuijer
Bas Laarakker
Adrienne Lancelot
Étienne Miquery
Paaras Padhiar

Invited Speakers

Marianna Girlando	University of Amsterdam, The Netherlands
Delia Kesner	Université Paris Cité, France

Contents

Model Comparison Game and n-Bisimulation for Conditional Logic

Xiaoxuan Fu[1] and Zhiguang Zhao[2](✉)

[1] China University of Political Science and Law, Beijing, China
xfuuva@gmail.com
[2] Taishan University, Tai'an, China
zhaozhiguang23@gmail.com

Abstract. In this paper, we refine the notion of bisimulation for conditional logic proposed in [1] by defining n-bisimulation, and define a model comparison game for conditional logic. The definition of n-bisimulation characterizes semantic equivalence up to depth $\leq n$, and the winning strategy of the duplicator in the model comparison game matches the notion of n-bisimulation.

Keywords: Model comparison game · conditional logic · bisimulation

1 Introduction

Conditional logics [3, 6–8, 11] study the reasoning about sentences of the form "if φ, then ψ". In [1], the concept of bisimulation for conditional logic is studied thoroughly. In particular, Baltag and Cinà [1] give four criteria for a good notion of bisimulation, and two of them are structurality and closure under unions and relational composition. Structurality means that the definition of bisimulation should not use information of formulas, except for the propositional variables conditions in the basic case. Closure under unions guarantees the existence of a largest bisimulation, and closure under relational composition guarantees that the notion of bisimulation is transitive.

Game semantics [5, 9, 10] use zero-sum games with two players to characterize logical concepts such as truth, model similarity and consistency. In particular, a model comparison game is designed to characterize the similarity of two given models. In this game, one player claims that the two models are similar, and the other player claims that they are different, and the winning strategy of the first player corresponds to the similarity between the two models.

In the present paper, we further refine the definition of bisimulation for conditional logic by defining the so-called n-bisimulation, which captures semantic equivalence for formulas of depth $\leq n$, and provide a model comparison game corresponding to n-bisimulation between two models and their semantic equivalence for formulas of depth $\leq n$. We also show that our definition satisfies the two criteria mentioned above.

The structure of the paper is as follows: Sect. 2 gives the preliminaries on conditional logic. Section 3 defines n-bisimulation for conditional logic. Section 4 gives the n-rounds model comparison game for conditional logic. Section 5 gives some discussions.

P. Johann and R. de Queiroz (Eds.): WoLLIC 2026, LNCS 16757, pp. 1–13, 2027.
https://doi.org/10.1007/978-3-032-33486-2_1

2 Preliminaries

In this section, we give preliminaries on conditional logic (see [1] for more details).

2.1 Syntax

The language of conditional logic is defined as follows:

Definition 1 Fix a **finite** set Prop of propositional variables, we define the formulas of conditional logic (CL) as follows:

$$\varphi ::= p \mid \top \mid \bot \mid \neg\varphi \mid \varphi \vee \varphi \mid \varphi \wedge \varphi \mid \varphi \rightsquigarrow \psi$$

where $p \in \mathsf{Prop}$. The connectives $\rightarrow$, $\leftrightarrow$ are defined as usual.

Intuitively, $\varphi \rightsquigarrow \psi$ reads "φ is the case, conditional on ψ".

For CL-formulas, we define their conditional depth as the measure of complexity:

Definition 2 (Conditional Depth) The conditional depth $d(\varphi)$ of a CL-formula φ is defined as follows:

- $d(p) = d(\top) = d(\bot) = 0$.
- $d(\neg\varphi) = d(\varphi)$.
- $d(\varphi \wedge \psi) = d(\varphi \vee \psi) = max\{d(\varphi), d(\psi)\}$.
- $d(\varphi \rightsquigarrow \psi) = max\{d(\varphi), d(\psi)\} + 1$.

2.2 Semantics

We adopt the selection function semantics in the style of [6]. We use the definitions from [1]. The semantics of CL is given as follows:

Definition 3 (Conditional Frames, Conditional Models and Pointed Conditional Models)

- A (conditional) frame is a pair $\mathbb{F} = (W, f)$ where $W \neq \varnothing$ is the domain and $f : W \times \mathsf{P}(W) \to \mathsf{P}(W)$ is the selection function such that the following two conditions hold:
  - For all $w \in W$, we have $f(w, X) \subseteq X$;
  - If $X \subseteq Y$, then for all $w \in W$ we have that if $f(w, Y) \subseteq X$ then $f(w, Y) = f(w, X)$.
- Given a frame $\mathbb{F} = (W, f)$ and a valuation $V : \mathsf{Prop} \to \mathsf{P}(W)$, a (conditional) model is $\mathbb{M} = (\mathbb{F}, V)$. Typically, when we write $\mathbb{M}$ (resp. $\mathbb{M}'$), we denote its domain as W (resp. W'), selection function as f (resp. f'), and valuation as V (resp. V').
- Given a model $\mathbb{M} = (W, f, V)$ and a point $s \in W$, a pointed (conditional) model is a pair $(\mathbb{M}, s)$.

Definition 4 (Satisfaction Relation) The satisfaction relation $\mathbb{M}, s \Vdash \varphi$ is defined recursively. The atomic and Boolean cases are standard. We use $[\![\varphi]\!]^{\mathbb{M}} := \{s \in W \mid \mathbb{M}, s \Vdash \varphi\}$ to denote the truth set of φ in $\mathbb{M}$.

$$\mathbb{M}, s \Vdash \varphi \rightsquigarrow \psi \text{ iff } f(s, [\![\varphi]\!]^{\mathbb{M}}) \subseteq [\![\psi]\!]^{\mathbb{M}}.$$

Intuitively, the selection function $f : W \times \mathsf{P}(W) \to \mathsf{P}(W)$ selects the worlds $f(s, X)$ in X that are relevant at $s \in W$. Therefore, $\varphi \rightsquigarrow \psi$ is true at s iff all the worlds in $[\![\varphi]\!]^{\mathbb{M}}$ that are relevant at $s \in W$ according to f satisfy ψ (notice that $f(s, X) \subseteq X$).

The next proposition is useful in the proof of Proposition 2:

Proposition 1 When Prop is finite, there are finitely many CL-formulas of conditional depth $\leq n$ modulo semantic equivalence.

Proof We prove it by induction on n.

- When $n = 0$, it follows from the fact that Prop is finite.
- When $n = k + 1$, suppose that we have proved for the $n \leq k$ case, then each CL-formula θ with $d(\theta) \leq k+1$ can be written as a Boolean combination of propositional variables $p \in \mathsf{Prop}$ and formulas of the form $\varphi \rightsquigarrow \psi$ where $d(\varphi), d(\psi) \leq k$. Since there are finitely many possibilities of $p \in \mathsf{Prop}$ and $\varphi \rightsquigarrow \psi$ modulo semantic equivalence, we have that there are finitely many CL-formulas of conditional depth $\leq k + 1$ modulo semantic equivalence.

3 Bisimulation Concepts

In this section, we discuss various different bisimulation concepts relevant for conditional logic. First of all, we give an auxiliary definition:

Definition 5 Given pointed models $(\mathbb{M}, s)$ and $(\mathbb{M}', s')$, $Z \subseteq W \times W'$, $X \subseteq W$ and $X' \subseteq W'$,

- $Z[X] := \{x' \in W' \mid \text{ for some } x \in X, (x, x') \in Z\}$.
- $Z^{-1}[X'] := \{x \in W \mid \text{ for some } x' \in X', (x, x') \in Z\}$.

3.1 Definition by Baltag and Cinà

Now we look at [1, Definition 5], where a definition of bisimulation for conditional logic is given:

Definition 6 (Bisimulation, Definition 5 in [1]) Given two conditional models $\mathbb{M} = (W, f, V)$ and $\mathbb{M}' = (W', f', V')$, a conditional bisimulation is a non-empty relation $Z \subseteq W \times W'$ such that:

- If wZw' then $V(w) = V'(w')$.
- For all $w \in W$, $w' \in W'$ such that wZw' and for all $X \subseteq W$ and $X' \subseteq W'$ such that $Z[X] \subseteq X'$ and $Z^{-1}[X'] \subseteq X$ we have that:

- For every $x \in f(w, X)$ there is an $x' \in f'(w', X')$ such that $(x, x') \in Z$.
- For every $x' \in f'(w', X')$ there is an $x \in f(w, X)$ such that $(x, x') \in Z$.

As discussed on [1, page 6], one would want the sets X and X' in the definition to be definable by conditional formulas. However, to ensure that those sets are definable by conditional formulas one would have to quantify over the formulas in the language and it would violate the desideratum of having a structural bisimulation where no information about formulas should be in the definition except for the conditions for atomic formulas. The solution in [1] is aiming at giving a "closed enough" approximation of "definable by formulas". As a result, they can prove that their bisimulation concept implies semantic equivalence (i.e. bisimilar worlds satisfy the same CL-formulas; indeed, this direction does not require the "definability" requirements for X and X'), and in finite models, semantic equivalence implies bisimulation. However, the problem regarding the direction from semantic equivalence to bisimulation is an open question on infinite models.

3.2 *n*-Bisimulation

In what follows, we use the techniques in [4] to give a structural definition of n-bisimulation, which avoids using information about formulas except for the atomic case. We define n-bisimulation to characterize equivalence of conditional formulas up to depth n in the language CL. This definition (Definition 11) is inspired by [1, Definition 5], but it is slightly different.

In what follows, we give some auxiliary definitions:

Definition 7 Given any pointed model $(\mathbb{M}, s)$, $Z \subseteq W \times W$ and $X \subseteq W$, we say that X is Z-closed, if for any $s \in X$, $t \in W$, we have that sZt implies $t \in X$.

The next definition is already implicitly used in [1, Definition 5], which intends to characterize that X and X' are defined by the same formula:

Definition 8 (Coherence) Given two frames $\mathbb{F} = (W, f)$ and $\mathbb{F}' = (W', f')$ and $X \subseteq W$, $X' \subseteq W'$, $Z \subseteq W \times W'$, we say that (X, X') is Z-coherent, if $Z[X] \subseteq X'$ and $Z^{-1}[X'] \subseteq X$.

Definition 9 (Semantic Equivalence) Two pointed models $(\mathbb{M}, s)$ and $(\mathbb{M}', s')$ are semantically equivalent (notation: $(\mathbb{M}, s) \leftrightsquigarrow (\mathbb{M}', s')$), if $\mathbb{M}, s \Vdash \varphi \Leftrightarrow \mathbb{M}', s' \Vdash \varphi$ for all CL-formulas φ.

The next definition is a weak version of semantic equivalence:

Definition 10 (*n*-Equivalence). Two pointed models $(\mathbb{M}, s)$ and $(\mathbb{M}', s')$ are n-equivalent (notation: $(\mathbb{M}, s) \leftrightsquigarrow_n (\mathbb{M}', s')$), if $\mathbb{M}, s \Vdash \varphi \Leftrightarrow \mathbb{M}', s' \Vdash \varphi$ for all CL-formulas φ with $d(\varphi) \leq n$.

Now we are ready to define n-bisimulation, where a sequence of relations rather than a single relation is used, as in n-bisimulation of modal logic, see e.g. [2, Definition 2.30].

Definition 11 (***n*-Bisimulation**)**.** Given two pointed models $(\mathbb{M}, s)$ and $(\mathbb{M}', s')$, we say that $Z_n \subseteq Z_{n-1} \subseteq \ldots \subseteq Z_0 \subseteq W \times W'$ is an n-bisimulation between $(\mathbb{M}, s)$ and $(\mathbb{M}', s')$, if sZ_ns' and the following holds for all $0 \leq i \leq n-1$:

1. For any $v \in W, v' \in W'$, if vZ_0v' then v and v' satisfy the same propositional variables.
2. For any $X \subseteq W$ which is Z-closed under all i-bisimulations $Z \subseteq Z'_{i-1} \subseteq \ldots \subseteq Z'_0 \subseteq W \times W$, any $X' \subseteq W'$ which is Z'-closed under all i-bisimulations $Z' \subseteq Z''_{i-1} \subseteq \ldots \subseteq Z''_0 \subseteq W' \times W'$, any $t \in W, t' \in W'$, if $tZ_{i+1}t'$ and (X, X') is Z_i-coherent, then
   (a) For every $u \in f(t, X)$ there is a $u' \in f'(t', X')$ such that $(u, u') \in Z_i$.
   (b) For every $u' \in f'(t', X')$ there is a $u \in f(t, X)$ such that $(u, u') \in Z_i$.

We also say that Z_n is an n-bisimulation between $(\mathbb{M}, s)$ and $(\mathbb{M}', s')$ when we do not need to mention $Z_{n-1}, \ldots, Z_0$ explicitly. We say that $(\mathbb{M}, s)$ and $(\mathbb{M}', s')$ are n-bisimilar (notation: $(\mathbb{M}, s)\underline{\leftrightarrow}_n(\mathbb{M}', s')$), if there is an n-bisimulation between $(\mathbb{M}, s)$ and $(\mathbb{M}', s')$.

Remark 1 The most significant feature in Definition 11 is that we only consider subsets of W and W' which are closed under all i-bisimulations; indeed, this property is equivalent to definability by formulas of conditional depth $\leq i$. This is the main refinement from previous definitions in order to capture semantic equivalence. This is because we only want subsets on both models that are definable to have the properties involving $f(t, X)$ and $f'(t', X')$, since we want our definition to capture semantic equivalence, and definable subsets (i.e. the ones that are closed under all i-bisimulations for some $i \leq n-1$) are exactly the ones that we need for the induction step.

One might worry that the definition is circular. Indeed, it is not circular because when we define n-bisimulation, we use all i-bisimulations where $i \leq n-1$, so we define the concept of n-bisimulation by induction on n.

The next proposition shows the equivalence between the notion of n-bisimulation and the notion of n-equivalence:

Proposition 2 For any pointed models $(\mathbb{M}, s) = (W, f, V, s)$ and $(\mathbb{M}', s') = (W', f', V', s')$, it holds that $(\mathbb{M}, s)\underline{\leftrightarrow}_n(\mathbb{M}', s')$ iff $(\mathbb{M}, s)\leftrightsquigarrow\!\leftrightsquigarrow_n(\mathbb{M}', s')$.

Proof We follow the proof strategy in [4] and prove by induction on n. The case $n = 0$ is trivial. For the case $n = m + 1$,

$\Rightarrow$: Assume $(\mathbb{M}, s)\underline{\leftrightarrow}_{m+1}(\mathbb{M}', s')$, then there is an $m+1$-bisimulation $Z_{m+1} \subseteq Z_m \subseteq \ldots \subseteq Z_0 \subseteq W \times W'$ between $(\mathbb{M}, s)$ and $(\mathbb{M}', s')$. Suppose $\mathbb{M}, s \Vdash \varphi$ where $d(\varphi) \leq m+1$.

- If $d(\varphi) \leq m$, then $Z_m \subseteq \ldots \subseteq Z_0 \subseteq W \times W'$ is an m-bisimulation between $(\mathbb{M}, s)$ and $(\mathbb{M}', s')$, by the IH, $(\mathbb{M}, s)\leftrightsquigarrow\!\leftrightsquigarrow_m(\mathbb{M}', s')$. Therefore, $\mathbb{M}', s' \Vdash \varphi$.
- If $d(\varphi) = m + 1$, it suffices to consider the case where $\varphi = \psi \rightsquigarrow \theta$. Since $\mathbb{M}, s \Vdash \psi \rightsquigarrow \theta$, we have $f(s, [\![\psi]\!]^{\mathbb{M}}) \subseteq [\![\theta]\!]^{\mathbb{M}}$. We will show $f'(s', [\![\psi]\!]^{\mathbb{M}'}) \subseteq [\![\theta]\!]^{\mathbb{M}'}$.

  - We first show that $[\![\psi]\!]^{\mathbb{M}}$ is Z-closed under all m-bisimulations $Z \subseteq W \times W$: Suppose otherwise, there is an m-bisimulation $Z \subseteq W \times W$ such that $[\![\psi]\!]^{\mathbb{M}}$ is not Z-closed, i.e. there are $t, u \in W$ such that tZu, $t \in [\![\psi]\!]^{\mathbb{M}}$ and $u \notin [\![\psi]\!]^{\mathbb{M}}$, but by the IH and $(\mathbb{M}, t)\underline{\leftrightarrow}_m(\mathbb{M}, u)$ we have that $(\mathbb{M}, t)\leftrightsquigarrow\!\leftrightsquigarrow_m(\mathbb{M}, u)$, a contradiction to $t \in [\![\psi]\!]^{\mathbb{M}}$, $u \notin [\![\psi]\!]^{\mathbb{M}}$ and $d(\psi) \leq m$.

- Similarly, $[\![\psi]\!]^{\mathbb{M}'}$ is Z'-closed under all m-bisimulations $Z' \subseteq W' \times W'$.
- We can also show that $([\![\psi]\!]^{\mathbb{M}}, [\![\psi]\!]^{\mathbb{M}'})$ is Z_m-coherent. Suppose otherwise, there are $t \in W, t' \in W'$ with $tZ_m t'$ and "$t \in [\![\psi]\!]^{\mathbb{M}}$ iff $t' \in [\![\psi]\!]^{\mathbb{M}'}$" does not hold. Then by the IH, from $tZ_m t'$ we have $(\mathbb{M}, t) \leftrightsquigarrow\leftrightsquigarrow_m (\mathbb{M}', t')$, so "$t \in [\![\psi]\!]^{\mathbb{M}}$ iff $t' \in [\![\psi]\!]^{\mathbb{M}'}$" holds, a contradiction.

Therefore, for every $t' \in f'(s', [\![\psi]\!]^{\mathbb{M}'})$, there is a $t \in f(s, [\![\psi]\!]^{\mathbb{M}}) \subseteq [\![\theta]\!]^{\mathbb{M}}$ such that $(t, t') \in Z_m$, so by the IH, $(\mathbb{M}, t) \leftrightsquigarrow\leftrightsquigarrow_m (\mathbb{M}', t')$. Since $\mathbb{M}, t \Vdash \theta$ and $d(\theta) \leq m$, we have that $\mathbb{M}', t' \Vdash \theta$. Therefore, $f'(s', [\![\psi]\!]^{\mathbb{M}'}) \subseteq [\![\theta]\!]^{\mathbb{M}'}$, and thus $\mathbb{M}', s' \Vdash \psi \rightsquigarrow \theta$.

Therefore, $(\mathbb{M}, s) \underline{\leftrightarrow}_{m+1} (\mathbb{M}', s') \Rightarrow (\mathbb{M}, s) \leftrightsquigarrow\leftrightsquigarrow_{m+1} (\mathbb{M}', s')$.

$\Leftarrow$: Suppose $(\mathbb{M}, s) \leftrightsquigarrow\leftrightsquigarrow_n (\mathbb{M}', s')$, i.e. $(\mathbb{M}, s) \leftrightsquigarrow\leftrightsquigarrow_{m+1} (\mathbb{M}', s')$. Define $Z_i := \{(t, t') \mid (\mathbb{M}, t) \leftrightsquigarrow\leftrightsquigarrow_i (\mathbb{M}', t')\} \subseteq W \times W'$ for $0 \leq i \leq n$. We show that $Z_n \subseteq Z_{n-1} \subseteq \ldots \subseteq Z_0 \subseteq W \times W'$ satisfy the three conditions for n-bisimulation:

1. By the definition of Z_n, $(\mathbb{M}, s) \leftrightsquigarrow\leftrightsquigarrow_n (\mathbb{M}', s') \Rightarrow sZ_n s'$.
2. Since $tZ_0 t'$, we have that t and t' satisfy the same depth-0 formulas, therefore the same propositional variables.
3. Suppose $tZ_{i+1}t'$, $X \subseteq W$ is Z-closed under all i-bisimulations $Z \subseteq W \times W$, $X' \subseteq W'$ is Z'-closed under all i-bisimulations $Z' \subseteq W' \times W'$, and (X, X') is Z_i-coherent. We will show that conditions 3(a) and 3(b) hold.

   - We first show that X, X' are definable by CL-formulas φ_1, φ_2 respectively where $d(\varphi_1), d(\varphi_2) \leq i$: Consider $\Theta_u := \{\theta \mid \mathbb{M}, u \Vdash \theta \text{ and } d(\theta) \leq i\}$ where $u \in W$, then by Proposition 1, Θ_u contains finitely many non-equivalent representatives. Define θ_u to be the conjunction of these finitely many non-equivalent representatives, then θ_u is a CL-formula with $d(\theta_u) \leq i$. Now define $\Delta_X := \{\theta_u \mid u \in X\}$, then by Proposition 1, Δ_X contains finitely many non-equivalent representatives (since there are finitely many equivalence classes, we do not need to use the axiom of choice). Now define φ_1 to be the disjunction of these finitely many non-equivalent representatives, then we can show that $X = [\![\varphi_1]\!]^{\mathbb{M}}$: Since $\mathbb{M}, u \Vdash \theta_u$ for all $u \in W$, we have that $\mathbb{M}, u \Vdash \varphi_1$ for all $u \in X$, so $X \subseteq [\![\varphi_1]\!]^{\mathbb{M}}$. For the other direction, suppose that $\mathbb{M}, u \Vdash \varphi_1$, then $\mathbb{M}, u \Vdash \theta_v$ for some $v \in X$, so $(\mathbb{M}, u) \leftrightsquigarrow\leftrightsquigarrow_i (\mathbb{M}, v)$, by the IH, $(\mathbb{M}, u) \underline{\leftrightarrow}_i (\mathbb{M}, v)$. Since X is Z-closed under all i-bisimulations $Z \subseteq W \times W$ and $v \in X$, we have that $u \in X$. Therefore $[\![\varphi_1]\!]^{\mathbb{M}} \subseteq X$. Similarly, X' is definable by a CL-formula φ_2 where $d(\varphi_2) \leq i$.
   - Now we are going to show that $[\![\varphi_1]\!]^{\mathbb{M}'} \subseteq X'$ and $[\![\varphi_2]\!]^{\mathbb{M}} \subseteq X$. For the first condition, suppose $x' \in [\![\varphi_1]\!]^{\mathbb{M}'}$, then by the definition of φ_1, there is a $\theta_u \in \Delta_X$ such that $x' \in [\![\theta_u]\!]^{\mathbb{M}'}$. By the definition of θ_u, we have that $(\mathbb{M}', x') \leftrightsquigarrow\leftrightsquigarrow_i (\mathbb{M}, u)$, so $(\mathbb{M}', x') \underline{\leftrightarrow}_i (\mathbb{M}, u)$, i.e. $uZ_i x'$, so from $Z_i[X] \subseteq X'$ we get $x' \in X'$, therefore $[\![\varphi_1]\!]^{\mathbb{M}'} \subseteq X'$. Similarly, $[\![\varphi_2]\!]^{\mathbb{M}} \subseteq X$.
   - As a corollary, $[\![\varphi_1 \vee \varphi_2]\!]^{\mathbb{M}} = X$ and $[\![\varphi_1 \vee \varphi_2]\!]^{\mathbb{M}'} = X'$, so $f(t, [\![\varphi_1 \vee \varphi_2]\!]^{\mathbb{M}}) = f(t, X)$ and $f'(t', [\![\varphi_1 \vee \varphi_2]\!]^{\mathbb{M}'}) = f'(t', X')$.

– Now we are ready to prove that for every $u \in f(t, X)$ there is a $u' \in f'(t', X')$ such that $(u, u') \in Z_i$. Suppose otherwise, there is a $u \in f(t, X)$ such that for all $u' \in f'(t', X')$ we have that $(u, u') \notin Z_i$. Now we consider the set of formulas $\Gamma_{uf'(t',X')} := \{\theta_{u'} \wedge \neg\theta_u \mid u' \in f'(t', X')\}$, and take γ to be the disjunction of its finitely many non-equivalent representatives, then γ is false at u and true at all worlds in $f'(t', X')$, so $f'(t', [\![\varphi_1 \vee \varphi_2]\!]^{\mathbb{M}'}) = f'(t', X') \subseteq [\![\gamma]\!]^{\mathbb{M}'}$ and thus $t' \Vdash (\varphi_1 \vee \varphi_2) \rightsquigarrow \gamma$. However, $u \in f(t, X)$ but $u \nVdash \gamma$, so $f(t, [\![\varphi_1 \vee \varphi_2]\!]^{\mathbb{M}}) = f(t, X) \nsubseteq [\![\gamma]\!]^{\mathbb{M}}$, therefore $t \nVdash (\varphi_1 \vee \varphi_2) \rightsquigarrow \gamma$, a contradiction to $tZ_{i+1}t'$. So condition 3(a) holds. Condition 3(b) can be shown in a similar way.

Proposition 3 For any $n \in \mathbb{N}$ and any pointed models $(\mathbb{M}, s)$ and $(\mathbb{M}', s')$, if $(\mathbb{M}, s)\underline{\leftrightarrow}_n(\mathbb{M}', s')$, then there is a largest n-bisimulation $Z_n \subseteq Z_{n-1} \subseteq \ldots \subseteq Z_0 \subseteq W \times W'$ in the sense of set-theoretic inclusion, i.e. for any n-bisimulation $Z'_n \subseteq Z'_{n-1} \subseteq \ldots \subseteq Z'_0 \subseteq W \times W'$ between $(\mathbb{M}, s)$ and $(\mathbb{M}', s')$, we have $Z'_i \subseteq Z_i$ for $i = 0, \ldots, n$.

Proof Take $Z_m := \{(t, t') \mid (\mathbb{M}, t) \leftrightsquigarrow\leftrightsquigarrow_m (\mathbb{M}', t')\} \subseteq W \times W'$ for $0 \leq m \leq n$, then $Z_n \subseteq Z_{n-1} \subseteq \ldots \subseteq Z_0 \subseteq W \times W'$ is the largest n-bisimulation between $(\mathbb{M}, s)$ and $(\mathbb{M}', s')$.

3.3 More Discussions on Bisimulation Concepts

As discussed in [1], a good bisimulation concept should be closed under taking unions and relational composition. We will show that our notion of n-bisimulation satisfies the two requirements.

Proposition 4 (Closure under Union) For any $n \in \mathbb{N}$ and any pointed models $(\mathbb{M}, s) = (W, f, V, s)$ and $(\mathbb{M}', s') = (W', f', V', s')$, suppose for each $i \in I$, we have an n-bisimulation $Z^i_n \subseteq Z^i_{n-1} \subseteq \ldots \subseteq Z^i_0 \subseteq W \times W'$, then we have that $Z_n \subseteq Z_{n-1} \subseteq \ldots \subseteq Z_0$ is also an n-bisimulation, where $Z_k = \bigcup_{i \in I} Z^i_k$ for $k = 0, 1, \ldots, n$.

Proof

1. First of all, it is easy to see that $sZ^i_n s'$ for all $i \in I$, so $sZ_n s'$.
2. Secondly, for any $v \in W$, $v' \in W'$, if $vZ_0 v$ then $vZ^i_0 v'$ for some $i \in I$, so v and v' satisfy the same propositional variables.
3. Consider any $X \subseteq W$ that is Z-closed under all k-bisimulations $Z \subseteq Z'_{k-1} \subseteq \ldots \subseteq Z'_0 \subseteq W \times W$, any $X' \subseteq W'$ which is Z'-closed under all k-bisimulations $Z' \subseteq Z''_{k-1} \subseteq \ldots \subseteq Z''_0 \subseteq W' \times W'$, any $t \in W$, $t' \in W'$. Suppose $tZ_{k+1}t'$ and (X, X') is Z_k-coherent.

– From $tZ_{k+1}t'$ we know that $tZ^i_{k+1}t'$ for some $i \in I$.
– From the Z_k-coherence of (X, X'), we have that $Z_k[X] \subseteq X'$, so $Z^i_k[X] \subseteq Z_k[X] \subseteq X'$. Similarly we can get $(Z^i_k)^{-1}[X'] \subseteq X$.

Therefore, since $Z^i_n \subseteq Z^i_{n-1} \subseteq \ldots \subseteq Z^i_0 \subseteq W \times W'$ is an n-bisimulation, we have:

(a) For any $u \in f(t, X)$ there is a $u' \in f'(t', X')$ such that $(u, u') \in Z^i_k \subseteq Z_k$.
(b) For any $u' \in f'(t', X')$ there is a $u \in f(t, X)$ such that $(u, u') \in Z^i_k \subseteq Z_k$.
Therefore, $Z_n \subseteq Z_{n-1} \subseteq \ldots \subseteq Z_0$ is an n-bisimulation.

Proposition 5 (Closure under Relational Composition) For any $n \in \mathbb{N}$ and any pointed models $(\mathbb{M}, s) = (W, f, V, s)$, $(\mathbb{M}', s') = (W', f', V', s')$ and $(\mathbb{M}'', s'') = (W'', f'', V'', s'')$, suppose we have an n-bisimulation $Z^1_n \subseteq Z^1_{n-1} \subseteq \ldots \subseteq Z^1_0 \subseteq W \times W'$ between $(\mathbb{M}, s)$ and $(\mathbb{M}', s')$, and an n-bisimulation $Z^2_n \subseteq Z^2_{n-1} \subseteq \ldots \subseteq Z^2_0 \subseteq W' \times W''$ between $(\mathbb{M}', s')$ and $(\mathbb{M}'', s'')$, then $Z_n \subseteq Z_{n-1} \subseteq \ldots \subseteq Z_0 \subseteq W \times W''$ is an n-bisimulation between $(\mathbb{M}, s)$ and $(\mathbb{M}'', s'')$, where $Z_k := Z^1_k \circ Z^2_k$ for all $k = 0, 1, \ldots, n$.

Proof

1. It is easy to see that $sZ^1_n s'$ and $s'Z^2_n s''$, so $s(Z^1_n \circ Z^2_n)s''$.
2. Consider any $v \in W$ and $v'' \in W''$, suppose that $v(Z^1_0 \circ Z^2_0)v''$, then there is a $v' \in W'$ such that $vZ^1_0 v'$ and $v'Z^2_0 v''$. Therefore v, v' satisfy the same propositional variables and v', v'' satisfy the same propositional variables, so v, v'' satisfy the same propositional variables.
3. Consider any $X \subseteq W$ that is Z-closed under all k-bisimulations $Z \subseteq Z'_{k-1} \subseteq \ldots \subseteq Z'_0 \subseteq W \times W$, any $X'' \subseteq W''$ which is Z'-closed under all k-bisimulations $Z' \subseteq Z''_{k-1} \subseteq \ldots \subseteq Z''_0 \subseteq W'' \times W''$, any $t \in W$, $t'' \in W''$. Suppose $tZ_{k+1}t''$ and (X, X'') is Z_k-coherent.

   - Since $tZ_{k+1}t''$, we can find a $t' \in W'$ such that $tZ^1_{k+1}t'$ and $t'Z^2_{k+1}t''$.
   - By the proof of Proposition 2, there is a CL-formula $\varphi_1 \vee \varphi_2$ of conditional depth $d(\varphi_1 \vee \varphi_2) \leq k$ such that $X = [\![\varphi_1 \vee \varphi_2]\!]^{\mathbb{M}}$, $X'' = [\![\varphi_1 \vee \varphi_2]\!]^{\mathbb{M}''}$. Now define $X' := [\![\varphi_1 \vee \varphi_2]\!]^{\mathbb{M}'}$.

     - We will show that X' is closed under all k-bisimulations within $\mathbb{M}'$. It suffices to show that X' is closed under the largest k-bisimulation, namely the k-equivalence. Since X' is definable by a formula of depth $\leq k$, we have that for any $x \in X'$, $x' \in W'$ and $(\mathbb{M}', x) \leftrightsquigarrow\!\!\leftrightsquigarrow_k (\mathbb{M}', x')$, we have that $\mathbb{M}', x' \Vdash \varphi_1 \vee \varphi_2$, so $x' \in X'$. Therefore X' is closed under k-equivalence, so it is closed under all k-bisimulations in $\mathbb{M}'$.
     - We will show that (X, X') is Z^1_k-coherent. It suffices to show that $Z^1_k[X] \subseteq X'$ and $(Z^1_k)^{-1}[X'] \subseteq X$. Since worlds in X satisfy $\varphi_1 \vee \varphi_2$, and for any $x \in W$, $x' \in W'$, $xZ^1_k x'$ implies that x and x' satisfy the same formulas of conditional depth $\leq k$, we have that worlds in $Z^1_k[X]$ satisfy $\varphi_1 \vee \varphi_2$, therefore in X'. So $Z^1_k[X] \subseteq X'$. In a similar way, $(Z^1_k)^{-1}[X'] \subseteq X$. So (X, X') is Z^1_k-coherent.
     - Similarly, (X', X'') is Z^2_k-coherent.

   Since we have an n-bisimulation $Z^1_n \subseteq Z^1_{n-1} \subseteq \ldots \subseteq Z^1_0 \subseteq W \times W'$ between $(\mathbb{M}, s)$ and $(\mathbb{M}', s')$, and an n-bisimulation $Z^2_n \subseteq Z^2_{n-1} \subseteq \ldots \subseteq Z^2_0 \subseteq W' \times W''$ between $(\mathbb{M}', s')$ and $(\mathbb{M}'', s'')$, we get the following:
   (a) For any $u \in f(t, X)$ there is a $u' \in f'(t', X')$ such that $(u, u') \in Z^1_k$.
   (b) For any $u' \in f'(t', X')$ there is a $u \in f(t, X)$ such that $(u, u') \in Z^1_k$.

(c) For any $u' \in f'(t', X')$ there is a $u'' \in f''(t'', X'')$ such that $(u', u'') \in Z^2_k$.
(d) For any $u'' \in f''(t'', X'')$ there is a $u' \in f(t', X')$ such that $(u', u'') \in Z^2_k$.

Putting (a) and (c) together, we get that for every $u \in f(t, X)$ there is a $u'' \in f''(t'', X'')$ such that $(u, u'') \in (Z^1_k \circ Z^2_k)$. Similarly, putting (b) and (d) together, we get that for every $u'' \in f''(t'', X'')$ there is a $u \in f(t, X)$ such that $(u, u'') \in (Z^1_k \circ Z^2_k)$.

Therefore, $Z_n \subseteq Z_{n-1} \subseteq \ldots \subseteq Z_0 \subseteq W \times W''$ is an n-bisimulation between $(\mathbb{M}, s)$ and $(\mathbb{M}'', s'')$.

4 Model Comparison Game

We now introduce the n-round model comparison game. In what follows, we use A_1 and A_2 to denote the two players in the game. Given two pointed models $(\mathbb{M}, s)$, $(\mathbb{M}', s')$, player A_1 (resp. A_2) claims they are different (resp. similar) in terms of semantic equivalence and bisimulation. The game starts with $(A_1, (\mathbb{M}, s), (\mathbb{M}', s'), n)$, where the first component A_1 means that A_1 is the player trying to show that the two pointed models are different, and the opponent is trying to show that they are similar. The game is inspired from Definition 11.

Definition 12 (***n*-Round Model Comparison Game**)**.** The n-round model comparison game starts with $(A_1, (\mathbb{M}, s), (\mathbb{M}', s'), n)$ and proceeds as follows:

At $(A_1, (\mathbb{M}, s), (\mathbb{M}', s'), 0)$, if s, s' satisfy the same propositional variables, then A_2 wins.

During the game, at any position $(A_1, (\mathbb{M}, s), (\mathbb{M}', s'), m)$, if s, s' disagree on some propositional variables, then A_1 wins.

At any position $(A_1, (\mathbb{M}, s), (\mathbb{M}', s'), m)$ when $m > 0$ and s, s' agree on all propositional variables, player A_1 has the following choices:

1. A_1 chooses $X \subseteq W, X' \subseteq W'$ and $u \in f(s, X)$, and A_2 has the following choices:
   (a) A_2 picks $t_1 \in X$ and $t_2 \in W - X$ and the game continues at $(A_1, (\mathbb{M}, t_1), (\mathbb{M}, t_2), m - 1)$.
   (b) A_2 picks $t'_1 \in X'$ and $t'_2 \in W - X'$ and the game continues at $(A_1, (\mathbb{M}', t'_1), (\mathbb{M}', t'_2), m - 1)$.
   (c) A_2 picks $t \in X$ and $t' \notin X'$, and the game continues at $(A_1, (\mathbb{M}, t), (\mathbb{M}', t'), m - 1)$.
   (d) A_2 picks $t \notin X$ and $t' \in X'$, and the game continues at $(A_1, (\mathbb{M}, t), (\mathbb{M}', t'), m - 1)$.
   (e) A_2 picks $u' \in f'(s', X')$ and the game continues at $(A_1, (\mathbb{M}, u), (\mathbb{M}', u'), m - 1)$.
2. A_1 chooses $X \subseteq W, X' \subseteq W'$ and $u' \in f'(s', X')$, and A_2 has the following choices:
   (a) A_2 picks $t_1 \in X$ and $t_2 \in W - X$ and the game continues at $(A_1, (\mathbb{M}, t_1), (\mathbb{M}, t_2), m - 1)$.
   (b) A_2 picks $t'_1 \in X'$ and $t'_2 \in W - X'$ and the game continues at $(A_1, (\mathbb{M}', t'_1), (\mathbb{M}', t'_2), m - 1)$.
   (c) A_2 picks $t \in X$ and $t' \notin X'$, and the game continues at $(A_1, (\mathbb{M}, t), (\mathbb{M}', t'), m - 1)$.

(d) A_2 picks $t \notin X$ and $t' \in X'$, and the game continues at $(A_1, (\mathbb{M}, t), (\mathbb{M}', t'), m-1)$.

(e) A_2 picks $u \in f(s, X)$ and the game continues at $(A_1, (\mathbb{M}, u), (\mathbb{M}', u'), m-1)$.

Remark 2 The choices of A_2 essentially reflect the definition of n-bisimulation:

- For cases 1(a) and 2(a), they correspond to the attack of the m-bisimulation closure of X.
- For cases 1(b) and 2(b), they correspond to the attack of the m-bisimulation closure of X'.
- For cases 1(c)(d) and 2(c)(d), they correspond to the attack of the coherence condition.
- For cases 1(e) and 2(e), they correspond to the items 3(a)(b) of the definition of n-bisimulation.

By a winning strategy of player A_1, we mean that in any execution of the game, no matter how the opponent plays in the game, A_1 has a strategy to play in the game such that A_1 wins every game that she follows her strategy. The next lemma is obvious to see:

Lemma 1 If A_2 has a winning strategy at $(A_1, (\mathbb{M}, s), (\mathbb{M}', s'), n)$, then A_2 has a winning strategy at $(A_1, (\mathbb{M}, s), (\mathbb{M}', s'), m)$ for all $0 \leq m \leq n$.

The next theorem shows that the model comparison game characterizes n-bisimulation and n-equivalence:

Theorem 1 (Adequacy Theorem) The following are equivalent:

1. A_2 has a winning strategy at $(A_1, (\mathbb{M}, s), (\mathbb{M}', s'), n)$.
2. $(\mathbb{M}, s)\underline{\leftrightarrow}_n(\mathbb{M}', s')$.
3. $(\mathbb{M}, s)\leftrightsquigarrow_n(\mathbb{M}', s')$.

Proof 2 $\Leftrightarrow$ 3 is shown in Proposition 2. We prove 1 $\Leftrightarrow$ 2,3 by induction on n.

- For $n = 0$, trivial.
- For $n = k+1$, suppose 1 $\Leftrightarrow$ 2,3 for all $n \leq k$, and the largest n-bisimulation is $Z_n \subseteq Z_{n-1} \subseteq \ldots \subseteq Z_0 \subseteq W \times W'$ where $Z_i := \{(t, t') \mid (\mathbb{M}, t)\leftrightsquigarrow_i(\mathbb{M}', t')\} \subseteq W \times W'$ for $0 \leq i \leq n$. 2, 3 $\Rightarrow$ 1: We prove that 3 $\Rightarrow$ 1. Suppose $(\mathbb{M}, s)\leftrightsquigarrow_{k+1}(\mathbb{M}', s')$. We will show that A_2 has a winning strategy at $(A_1, (\mathbb{M}, s), (\mathbb{M}', s'), k+1)$. Consider the game $(A_1, (\mathbb{M}, s), (\mathbb{M}', s'), k+1)$:

  - If A_1 chooses $X \subseteq W, X' \subseteq W'$ and $u \in f(s, X)$, then there are the following possibilities:

    $*$ If X is not Z-closed under some k-bisimulation $Z \subseteq W \times W$, then there are $t_1 \in X$ and $t_2 \in W - X$ such that $(\mathbb{M}, t_1)\underline{\leftrightarrow}_k(\mathbb{M}, t_2)$. Therefore by the IH, A_2 has a winning strategy at $(A_1, (\mathbb{M}, t_1), (\mathbb{M}, t_2), k)$. Therefore, by picking $t_1 \in X$ and $t_2 \in W - X$, A_2 has a winning strategy at this response of A_1.
    $*$ If X' is not Z'-closed under some k-bisimulation $Z' \subseteq W' \times W'$, the situation is similar.
    If (X, X') is not Z_k-coherent, then either $Z_k[X] \nsubseteq X'$ or $Z_k^{-1}[X'] \nsubseteq X$.

$\cdot$ If $Z_k[X] \nsubseteq X'$, then there exist $t \in X, t' \notin X'$ such that tZ_kt' holds. Then let A_2 pick these $t \in X$ and $t' \notin X'$, then by the IH, A_2 has a winning strategy at the game $(A_1, (\mathbb{M}, t), (\mathbb{M}', t'), k)$. Therefore, A_2 has a winning strategy at this response of A_1.
If $Z_k^{-1}[X'] \nsubseteq X$, the situation is symmetric.

$*$ If X is Z-closed under all k-bisimulations $Z \subseteq W \times W$, X' is Z'-closed under all k-bisimulations $Z' \subseteq W' \times W'$ and (X, X') is Z_k-coherent, then there is a $u' \in f'(s', X')$ such that $(u, u') \in Z_k$. Then let A_2 pick this $u' \in f'(s', X')$, then at the game $(A_1, (\mathbb{M}, u), (\mathbb{M}', u'), k)$, A_2 has a winning strategy. Therefore, A_2 has a winning strategy at this response of A_1.

- If A_1 chooses $X \subseteq W, X' \subseteq W'$ and $u' \in f'(s', X')$, then the situation is similar.

To summarize, A_2 has a winning strategy at $(A_1, (\mathbb{M}, s), (\mathbb{M}', s'), k+1)$. $1 \Rightarrow 2, 3$: We prove that $1 \Rightarrow 2$. Suppose A_2 has a winning strategy at $(A_1, (\mathbb{M}, s), (\mathbb{M}', s'), k+1)$. We show $d(\varphi) \leq k+1 \ \Rightarrow\ (\mathbb{M}, s \Vdash \varphi \text{ iff } \mathbb{M}', s' \Vdash \varphi)$ by induction on φ.

- For atomic formulas, since A_2 has a winning strategy at $(A_1, (\mathbb{M}, s), (\mathbb{M}', s'), k+1)$, by Lemma 1, A_2 has a winning strategy at $(A_1, (\mathbb{M}, s), (\mathbb{M}', s'), 0)$. Therefore $\mathbb{M}, s \Vdash \varphi$ iff $\mathbb{M}', s' \Vdash \varphi$ for any $\varphi \in \mathsf{Prop}$.
- The Boolean cases are easy.
- For $\varphi = \psi \rightsquigarrow \theta$, if $d(\varphi) \leq k$, then since A_2 has a winning strategy at $(A_1, (\mathbb{M}, s), (\mathbb{M}', s'), k+1)$, by Lemma 1, A_2 has a winning strategy at $(A_1, (\mathbb{M}, s), (\mathbb{M}', s'), k)$. By the IH, $\mathbb{M}, s \Vdash \varphi$ iff $\mathbb{M}', s' \Vdash \varphi$. If $d(\varphi) = k+1$, suppose exactly one of $\mathbb{M}, s \Vdash \psi \rightsquigarrow \theta$ and $\mathbb{M}', s' \Vdash \psi \rightsquigarrow \theta$ holds (without loss of generality assume the former one holds), then $f(s, [\![\psi]\!]^{\mathbb{M}}) \subseteq [\![\theta]\!]^{\mathbb{M}}$ and $f'(s', [\![\psi]\!]^{\mathbb{M}'}) \nsubseteq [\![\theta]\!]^{\mathbb{M}'}$. Then, at the game $(A_1, (\mathbb{M}, s), (\mathbb{M}', s'), k+1)$, we let A_1 pick $[\![\psi]\!]^{\mathbb{M}} \subseteq W$, $[\![\psi]\!]^{\mathbb{M}'} \subseteq W'$ and $u' \in f'(s', [\![\psi]\!]^{\mathbb{M}'}) - [\![\theta]\!]^{\mathbb{M}'}$, then we consider the winning strategy of A_2:

  $*$ If A_2 picks $t_1 \in [\![\psi]\!]^{\mathbb{M}}$ and $t_2 \in W - [\![\psi]\!]^{\mathbb{M}}$ as the winning strategy and the game continues at $(A_1, (\mathbb{M}, t_1), (\mathbb{M}, t_2), k)$, then by the IH, $(\mathbb{M}, t_1) \leftrightsquigarrow_k (\mathbb{M}, t_2)$, a contradiction to $t_1 \in [\![\psi]\!]^{\mathbb{M}}$ and $t_2 \in W - [\![\psi]\!]^{\mathbb{M}}$.
  $*$ If A_2 picks $t_1' \in [\![\psi]\!]^{\mathbb{M}'}$ and $t_2' \in W' - [\![\psi]\!]^{\mathbb{M}'}$, the situation is similar.
  $*$ If A_2 picks $t \in [\![\psi]\!]^{\mathbb{M}}$ and $t' \notin [\![\psi]\!]^{\mathbb{M}'}$, then A_2 has a winning strategy at the game $(A_1, (\mathbb{M}, t), (\mathbb{M}', t'), k)$, which by the IH implies that $\mathbb{M}, t \Vdash \psi$ iff $\mathbb{M}', t' \Vdash \psi$, a contradiction.
  $*$ If A_2 picks $t \notin [\![\psi]\!]^{\mathbb{M}}$ and $t' \in [\![\psi]\!]^{\mathbb{M}'}$, the situation is similar.
  $*$ If A_2 picks $u \in f(s, [\![\psi]\!]^{\mathbb{M}})$, then from $f(s, [\![\psi]\!]^{\mathbb{M}}) \subseteq [\![\theta]\!]^{\mathbb{M}}$ we get $\mathbb{M}, u \Vdash \theta$, but $\mathbb{M}', u' \nVdash \theta$. Since A_2 has a winning strategy at the game $(A_1, (\mathbb{M}, u), (\mathbb{M}', u'), k)$, which by the IH implies that $\mathbb{M}, u \Vdash \theta$ iff $\mathbb{M}', u' \Vdash \theta$, a contradiction.

  Therefore, $\mathbb{M}, s \Vdash \psi \rightsquigarrow \theta$ iff $\mathbb{M}', s' \Vdash \psi \rightsquigarrow \theta$.

Therefore, if A_2 has a winning strategy at $(A_1, (\mathbb{M}, s), (\mathbb{M}', s'), k+1)$, then $(\mathbb{M}, s)\leftrightsquigarrow\leftrightsquigarrow_{k+1}(\mathbb{M}', s')$.

Corollary 1 The following are equivalent:

1. A_2 has a winning strategy at $(A_1, (\mathbb{M}, s), (\mathbb{M}', s'), n)$ for all $n \in \mathbb{N}$.
2. $(\mathbb{M}, s)\underline{\leftrightarrow}_n(\mathbb{M}', s')$ for all $n \in \mathbb{N}$.
3. $(\mathbb{M}, s)\leftrightsquigarrow\leftrightsquigarrow(\mathbb{M}', s')$.

5 Discussion

As we can see from [1, Definition 5] and Definition 11, apart from using n, the main difference is that we require X, X' to be closed under respective Z-type i-bisimulation relations. As can be seen from the proofs in the present paper, these closure conditions correspond to the definability of these subsets by formulas of depth $\leq i$. Therefore, the definability conditions are exactly what we need for the characterization of n-equivalence via n-bisimulation.

Similar situations can be observed in other settings such as basic neighbourhood logic, where the formulas are defined as follows:

$$\varphi ::= p \mid \top \mid \bot \mid \neg\varphi \mid \varphi \vee \varphi \mid \varphi \wedge \varphi \mid \Box\varphi$$

For the semantics, we have neighbourhood frames $\mathbb{F} = (W, N)$ where $W \neq \varnothing$ is the domain and $N : W \to \mathsf{P}(\mathsf{P}(W))$ is the neighbourhood function, neighbourhood models $\mathbb{M} = (\mathbb{F}, V)$ where $V : \mathsf{Prop} \to \mathsf{P}(W)$ is a valuation, pointed neighbourhood models $(\mathbb{M}, s)$ where $s \in W$. The satisfaction relation $\mathbb{M}, s \Vdash \varphi$ is defined in a recursive way where the atomic and Boolean cases are defined as usual, and $\mathbb{M}, s \Vdash \Box\varphi$ iff $[\![\varphi]\!]^{\mathbb{M}} \in N(s)$.

As we can see from the semantics, the modality in basic neighbourhood logic is not necessarily monotone in the sense that when $X \subseteq Y \subseteq W$ and $X \in N(s)$, we do not necessarily have $Y \in N(s)$.

In the definition of n-bisimulation for basic neighbourhood logic (see [4]), we have the following:

Definition 13 **(n-Bisimulation for Basic Neighbourhood Logic).** Given two pointed models $(\mathbb{M}, s)$ and $(\mathbb{M}', s')$, we say that $Z_n \subseteq Z_{n-1} \subseteq \ldots \subseteq Z_0 \subseteq W \times W'$ is an n-bisimulation between $(\mathbb{M}, s)$ and $(\mathbb{M}', s')$, if for all $0 \leq i \leq n-1$, the following holds:

1. sZ_ns'.
2. For any $v \in W$, $v' \in W'$, if vZ_0v' then v and v' agree on all propositional variables.
3. For any $X_1, X_2 \subseteq W$ which are Z-closed under all i-bisimulations $Z \subseteq Z'_{i-1} \subseteq \ldots \subseteq Z'_0 \subseteq W \times W$, any $t \in Z_{i+1}^{-1}[W']$, if $Z_i^{-1}[W'] \cap X_1 = Z_i^{-1}[W'] \cap X_2$, then $X_1 \in N(t)$ iff $X_2 \in N(t)$.
4. For any $X'_1, X'_2 \subseteq W'$ which are Z'-closed under all i-bisimulations $Z' \subseteq Z''_{i-1} \subseteq \ldots \subseteq Z''_0 \subseteq W' \times W'$, any $t' \in Z_{i+1}[W]$, if $Z_i[W] \cap X'_1 = Z_i[W] \cap X'_2$, then $X'_1 \in N'(t')$ iff $X'_2 \in N'(t')$.

5. For any $X \subseteq W$ which is Z-closed under all i-bisimulations $Z \subseteq Z'_{i-1} \subseteq \ldots \subseteq Z'_0 \subseteq W \times W$, any $X' \subseteq W'$ which is Z'-closed under all i-bisimulations $Z' \subseteq Z''_{i-1} \subseteq \ldots \subseteq Z''_0 \subseteq W' \times W'$, any $t \in W$, $t' \in W'$, if $tZ_{i+1}t'$ and (X, X') is Z_i-coherent, then $X \in N(t)$ iff $X' \in N'(t')$.

As we can see from the definition, we also have conditions about closure under Z-type i-bisimulation relations. This is the price one has to pay in order to deal with connectives which are not monotone. Here since we want to guarantee that our n-bisimulation captures exactly n-equivalence, we only focus on the subsets definable by formulas of depth $\leq n$, so not all subsets are what we care about. As discussed in [1], a good definition of bisimulation should be structural in the sense that no information about formulas should be involved in the definition except for the atomic formulas. Therefore, we use closure under i-equivalence to replace definability by formulas of depth $\leq i$. This makes the definition structural, but at the same time makes the definition complicated.

Acknowledgments. The research of Zhiguang Zhao is supported by Shandong Provincial Natural Science Foundation, China (project number: ZR2023QF021).

References

1. Baltag, A., Cinà, G.: Bisimulation for conditional modalities. Stud. Logica. **106**, 1–33 (2018)
2. Blackburn, P., de Rijke, M., Venema, Y.: Modal logic, volume 53 of Cambridge Tracts in Theoretical Computer Science. Cambridge University Press, Cambridge (2001)
3. Chellas, B.F.: Basic conditional logic. J. Philos. Log. **4**(2), 133–153 (1975)
4. Fu, X., Zhao, Z.: Modal equivalence, n-bisimulation and model comparison game for basic neighbourhood logic. In: Ågotnes, T., Doder, D. (eds.) Logic and Argumentation, pp. 53–65. Springer Nature Singapore, Singapore (2025). https://doi.org/10.1007/978-981-96-7956-0_4
5. Hodges, W.: Building models by games. London Mathematical Society Student Texts, Cambridge University Press, Cambridge (1985)
6. Lewis, D.K.: Counterfactuals. Mass, Blackwell, Malden (1973)
7. Segerberg, K.: Notes on conditional logic. Stud. Logica. **48**(2), 157–168 (1989)
8. Stalnaker, R.: A theory of conditionals. In: Rescher, N. (ed) Stud. Logical Theory, pp. 98–112. Blackwell (1968)
9. Väänänen, J.: Models and games. Cambridge Studies in Advanced Mathematics, Cambridge University Press (2011)
10. van Benthem, J.: Logic in games. MIT Press (2014)
11. Veltman, F.: Logic for Conditionals. University of Amsterdam (1985). PhD thesis

Knowledge and Common Knowledge of Strategies

Borja Sierra Miranda and Thomas Studer(✉)

University of Bern, Bern, Switzerland
borja.sierra@unibe.ch, thomas.studer@unibe.ch

Abstract. Most existing work on strategic reasoning simply adopts either an informed or an uninformed semantics. We propose a model in which knowledge of strategies can be specified at a fine-grained level. It is possible to distinguish first-order, higher-order, and common knowledge of strategies. We illustrate the effect of higher-order knowledge of strategies by studying the game Hanabi. Further, we show that common knowledge of strategies is necessary to solve the consensus problem. Finally, we study the decidability of the model checking problem.

Keywords: strategic reasoning · epistemic logic · consensus

1 Introduction

Strategic reasoning is a fundamental aspect of decision-making in multi-agent systems, game theory, and artificial intelligence. It involves the ability of agents to anticipate the actions of others, formulate plans, and achieve desired outcomes within competitive or cooperative settings. To formally analyze strategic interactions, researchers have developed logical frameworks such as Coalition Logic [21], Alternating-time Temporal Logic [1], and Strategy Logic [9,20]. Many of these systems have been extended to allow for epistemic reasoning [5,13,18].

Most works adopt one of two semantics regarding knowledge of strategies: in the uninformed semantics, agents do not know each other's strategies [13,18], while in the informed one, agents know everyone's strategies [23]. The uninformed semantics models situations where agents have neither a prior knowledge of other agents' strategies nor any means to communicate information about their strategies. In the informed semantics the agents' strategies are common knowledge, which makes it possible for the agents to infer additional information from observed actions.

A notable exception to the above-mentioned dichotomy is [5], which introduces a semantics for strategy logic where one can specify, for each agent a, the set of agents A_a whose strategy a is informed of. It captures the case of informed semantics, the case of uninformed semantics, and intermediate cases where, e.g., some agents may privately communicate their strategies to other agents.

The logical presentation of strategic games introduced in [2] also includes knowledge of strategies via formulas of the form $\mathsf{K}_a s^l_j$ stating *a knows that j has*

P. Johann and R. de Queiroz (Eds.): WoLLIC 2026, LNCS 16757, pp. 14–30, 2027.
https://doi.org/10.1007/978-3-032-33486-2_2

chosen her strategy l. Artemov uses this approach to study whether a game has a definitive solution under given epistemic/rationality conditions. However, since the paper does not introduce a concrete language or deductive system, questions of expressivity, decidability or complexity are not discussed.

Contribution. We introduce a novel approach where knowledge of strategies can be specified on a fine-grained level. In particular, our formulation makes it possible to distinguish first-order and various forms of higher-order knowledge of strategies.[1] Moreover, we can express that *everybody knows* someone's strategy but also that a strategy is *common knowledge* among a group of agents [11].

Our semantics is based on concurrent game structures. In order to specify (higher-order) knowledge of an agent about other agents' strategies, we introduce the notion of an *information perspective* that can be seen as a generalization of the sets A_a from [5] mentioned before. An information perspective is a set I containing sequences of agents. Such sequences are interpreted as follows: if, e.g., $abc \in \mathrm{I}$, then agent a knows that agent b knows agent c's strategy. The logical language we evaluate over these structures is the usual language of epistemic logic extended with a temporal *next*-operator. This is sufficient for our examples and to investigate the power and the effect of information perspectives.

We present two small examples showing the difference between having no knowledge and first-order knowledge of an agent's strategy. These examples will be useful to investigate basic epistemic properties such as positive and negative introspection and reflection. Moreover, these initial examples also show that the concurrent game structure is general background knowledge for all agents. The same phenomenon occurs in traditional epistemic logic where the Kripke structure is common knowledge among all agents [3].

Hanabi is a cooperative game with imperfect information. We investigate the role of higher-order knowledge of strategies in Hanabi. We show that if player b knows player a's strategy, then b can obtain new information from observing a's actions. Further, if a knows that b knows a's strategy, then a knows that b will obtain new information from observing a's action. In the situation that we study, this knowledge is a prerequisite for a to safely perform the given action. This illustrates how higher-order knowledge is necessary for successful gameplay.

Since an information perspective may be infinite, it is possible to express common knowledge of strategies. We show that if all strategies are common knowledge, then the individual knowledge operators satisfy the negative introspection property. Next, we turn to the binary consensus problem [7] and show that common knowledge of strategies is required to solve this task successfully.

Finally, we investigate the problem of model checking where we restrict ourselves to formulas that do not contain common knowledge operators. The key technical lemma shows that, in this case, only information perspectives of bounded size have to be considered. This yields the decidability of the corresponding model checking problem.

[1] First-order knowledge means factual knowledge, i.e. knowledge about the objective state of the world, whereas higher-oder knowledge denotes knowledge about knowledge, i.e. knowledge about the subjective epistemic state of some agent.

2 The Model

We start with a countable set of atomic propositions Prop and a finite set of agents Ag. $\mathcal{P}(X)$ denotes the power set of X and X^Y denotes the set of functions from Y to X.

A *concurrent game structure* is a tuple $(\mathsf{Ac}, \mathsf{V}, \mathsf{E}, \ell, \sim_a)$ where

1. Ac is a finite set of actions,
2. V is a finite set of positions,
3. $\mathsf{E} : \mathsf{V} \times \mathsf{Ac}^{\mathsf{Ag}} \to \mathsf{V}$ is a transition function,
4. $\ell : \mathsf{V} \to \mathcal{P}(\mathsf{Prop})$ a valuation function,
5. $\sim_a \subseteq (\mathsf{V} \times \mathsf{V}) \cup (\mathsf{Ac} \times \mathsf{Ac})$ is an equivalence relation for each agent $a \in \mathsf{Ag}$, called a's observation relation.

A *joint action* is a function $\alpha : \mathsf{Ag} \to \mathsf{Ac}$ mapping each agent to an action. A *history* is a finite sequence of positions and joint actions $\rho = v_0\alpha_1 v_1 \dots \alpha_n v_n$ such that $\mathsf{E}(v_i, \alpha_{i+1}) = v_{i+1}$. For a history $\rho = v_0\alpha_1 v_1 \dots \alpha_n v_n$ and $i \leq n$, we set $\rho_{\leq i} := v_0\alpha_1 v_1 \dots \alpha_i v_i$ and $\mathsf{last}(\rho) := v_n$. We let Hist be the set of all histories.

Two positions $v, v' \in \mathsf{V}$ are *indistinguishable* for an agent a if $v \sim_a v'$, and similarly for actions. Two joint actions α and β are indistinguishable for agent a, in symbols $\alpha \sim_a \beta$ if they are pointwise indistinguishable for a, i.e. for all $b \in \mathsf{Ag}$, we have that $\alpha(b) \sim_a \beta(b)$.

We assume synchronous perfect recall. That is, agents remember their observations of all past positions and actions. Hence, we extend the observation relations to histories as follows. Two histories $\rho = v_0\alpha_1 v_1 \dots \alpha_n v_n$ and $\rho' = v'_0\alpha'_1 v'_1 \dots \alpha'_m v_m$ are *indistinguishable* for agent a, in symbols $\rho \sim_a \rho'$, if $m = n$, $v_i \sim_a v'_i$ for all $0 \leq i \leq n$, and $\alpha_i \sim_a \alpha'_i$ for all $1 \leq i \leq n$.

A *strategy* is a function $\sigma : \mathsf{Hist} \to \mathsf{Ac}$. We let Str denote the set of all strategies.

An *assignment* $\chi : \mathsf{Ag} \to \mathsf{Str}$ is a mapping of agents to strategies. A history $\rho = v_0\alpha_1 v_1 \dots \alpha_n v_n$ is *consistent* with an assignment χ for a set of agents X if $\alpha_{i+1}(b) = \chi(b)(\rho_{\leq i})$ for all $i < n$ and agents $b \in X$.

Given a concurrent game structure $\mathcal{G}$, an assignment χ, and a history $\rho = v_0\alpha_1 v_1 \dots \alpha_n v_n$, we define the *one-step continuation of* ρ

$$\mathsf{X}^{\chi}_{\mathcal{G}}\rho := v_0\alpha_1 v_1 \dots \alpha_n v_n \alpha_{n+1} v_{n+1}$$

where the joint action α_{n+1} is given by $\alpha_{n+1}(b) := \chi(b)(\rho)$ for all agents b and $v_{n+1} := \mathsf{E}(v_n, \alpha_{n+1})$ is the next position.

Let X be a finite set. We use X^* to denote the set of all finite words with symbols from X without adjacent repetitions, that is if $x_n \cdots x_1 \in X^*$, then $x_i \neq x_{i+1}$ for all $1 \leq i < n$.

For a word $w = x_n \cdots x_1 \in X^*$ and an element $y \in X$, we write yw for the word $yx_n \cdots x_1$. The *length of a word* w, $\mathsf{len}(w)$, is the number of symbols of w. That is, for a word $w = x_n \cdots x_1 \in X^*$, we have $\mathsf{len}(w) = n$. Further, we set

$$X^{\geq n} := \{w \in X^* \mid \mathsf{len}(w) \geq n\},$$

that is $X^{\geq n}$ is the set of those words of X^* with a length of at least n.

An information perspective stores which agents are informed about the strategies of which other agents. Formally, an *information perspective* I is a subset of $\mathsf{Ag}^{\geq 2}$. Further, for an agent a, we set $\mathrm{I}_a := \{b \in \mathsf{Ag} \mid ab \in \mathrm{I}\} \cup \{a\}$ and

$$\mathrm{I}[a] := \{w \in \mathsf{Ag}^{\geq 2} \mid aw \in \mathrm{I}\} \cup \{w \in \mathrm{I} \mid w = aw' \text{ for some } w' \in \mathsf{Ag}^*\}.$$

Let $a, b, c \in \mathsf{Ag}$ be agents. We interpret $ab \in \mathrm{I}$ as *agent a knows (is informed about) agent b's strategy.* Hence, I_a is the set of all agents whose strategies agent a is informed about. We assume that each agent knows its own strategy. Therefore, we let $a \in \mathrm{I}_a$ by definition.

Further, $abc \in \mathrm{I}$ means that agent a knows that agent b knows agent c's strategy, and so on. The operation $\mathrm{I}[a]$ changes the information perspective to agent a's point of view. That is, $\mathrm{I}[a]$ contains the information that a knows. We assume positive introspection, that is, agents know about their own knowledge. This is reflected by the condition that for all w with $w = aw'$ for some w', we have $w \in \mathrm{I}$ implies $w \in \mathrm{I}[a]$.

An information perspective I is *truthful* if it is closed under suffixes, i.e. for any $a \in \mathsf{Ag}$ and any $w \in \mathsf{Ag}^{\geq 2}$ we have that

$$aw \in \mathrm{I} \text{ implies } w \in \mathrm{I}. \tag{1}$$

This means, for instance, if agent a knows that agent b knows agent c's strategy, then agent b must know agent c's strategy. Formally, (1) guarantees that $abc \in \mathrm{I}$ implies $bc \in \mathrm{I}$.

On a technical level, an important consequence of (1) is that for any truthful information perspective I and any agent a, we have

$$\mathrm{I}[a] \subseteq \mathrm{I}. \tag{2}$$

This will be essential when we establish a version of the knowledge axiom T.

An agent a cannot distinguish two assignments χ and χ' given an information perspective I if χ and χ' agree on the strategies of all agents that agent a is informed about according to I. As mentioned before, this includes the agent's own strategy. We say that two assignments χ and χ' are *indistinguishable* for agent a under the information perspective I, in symbols $\chi \sim_a^{\mathrm{I}} \chi'$, if we have $\chi(b) = \chi'(b)$ for all $b \in \mathrm{I}_a$.

A *state* in a concurrent game structure is a triple (χ, I, ρ) where

1. χ is an assignment,
2. I is an information perspective, and
3. ρ is a history.

Let a be an agent. We say that (χ, I, ρ) is *a-consistent* if ρ is consistent with χ under I_a. Further, we call a state $(\chi', \mathrm{I}', \rho')$ *accessible from* (χ, I, ρ) *for* a, in symbols $(\chi, \mathrm{I}, \rho) \trianglelefteq_a (\chi', \mathrm{I}', \rho')$, if

1. $\chi \sim_a^{\mathrm{I}} \chi'$,
2. $\mathrm{I}[a] \subseteq \mathrm{I}'$,
3. $\rho \sim_a \rho'$,
4. (χ, I, ρ) is a-consistent and
5. $(\chi', \mathrm{I}', \rho')$ is a-consistent.

In order to deal with common knowledge of a group of agents, we need the following definitions where $G \subseteq \mathsf{Ag}$:

$$Z \trianglelefteq_G Z' \text{ iff } Z \trianglelefteq_a Z' \text{ for some } a \in G,$$
$$Z \trianglelefteq_G^* Z' \text{ iff } Z \trianglelefteq_G Z_1 \trianglelefteq_G \cdots \trianglelefteq_G Z_n \trianglelefteq_G Z' \quad \text{for some states } Z_1, \ldots, Z_n.$$

Hence $Z \trianglelefteq_G^* Z'$ states that Z' is reachable from Z using agents from G. Its definition includes the case that $Z \trianglelefteq_G^* Z'$ if $Z \trianglelefteq_a Z'$ for some $a \in G$.

In the following, we study some basic properties of the accessibility relation. First, we observe that replacing the history in a state Z with a history that cannot be distinguished by agent a gives a state Z' that is accessible from Z for a (given that Z and Z' are a-consistent and the information perspective of Z is truthful). The following is an immediate consequence of $\chi \sim_a^{\mathrm{I}} \chi$ and (2).

Lemma 1. *Let* $\mathcal{G} = (\mathsf{Ac}, \mathsf{V}, \mathsf{E}, \ell, \sim_a)$ *be a concurrent game structure and let* a *be an agent. We let* (χ, I, ρ) *be an* a*-consistent state with a truthful information perspective* I. *For each history* ρ' *such that* $\rho \sim_a \rho'$ *and* ρ' *is consistent with* χ *under* I_a, *we have* $(\chi, \mathrm{I}, \rho) \trianglelefteq_a (\chi, \mathrm{I}, \rho')$.

The next lemma states that if $Z \trianglelefteq_a Z'$, then the history of the state Z' is consistent from the point of view of agent a in Z. This is related to the notation $\rho \sim_a^{\chi,\mathrm{I}} \rho'$ used in [5]. A proof of this lemma is given in Appendix A.

Lemma 2. *Let* $\mathcal{G} = (\mathsf{Ac}, \mathsf{V}, \mathsf{E}, \ell, \sim_a)$ *be a concurrent game structure and let* $Z = (\chi, \mathrm{I}, \rho)$ *and* $Z' = (\chi', \mathrm{I}', \rho')$ *be states with* $Z \trianglelefteq_a Z'$ *for some agent* a. *Then* ρ' *is consistent with* χ *under* I_a.

We now introduce our languages $\mathcal{L}$ and $\mathcal{L}^{\mathsf{C}}$, which includes formulas:

1. $\mathsf{K}_a\phi$ meaning *agent* a *knows that* ϕ;
2. $\mathsf{C}_G\phi$ meaning *it is common knowledge among* G *that* ϕ;
3. $\mathsf{X}\phi$ meaning *at the next point in time* ϕ *holds.*

Formulas of the language $\mathcal{L}$ are given by the following grammar

$$\phi ::= p \mid \bot \mid \phi \to \phi \mid \mathsf{K}_a\phi \mid \mathsf{X}\phi,$$

and formulas of the language $\mathcal{L}^{\mathsf{C}}$ are given by

$$\phi ::= p \mid \bot \mid \phi \to \phi \mid \mathsf{K}_a\phi \mid \mathsf{C}_G\phi \mid \mathsf{X}\phi,$$

where $p \in \mathsf{Prop}$, $a \in \mathsf{Ag}$, and $G \subseteq \mathsf{Ag}$. The remaining Boolean connectives are defined as usual.

The next-operator is the only temporal operator that we include in our language, as it is the only one needed for our examples. It is straightforward to include further temporal operators, see, e.g., [5] for the case of the until-operator.

Let $\mathcal{G} = (\mathsf{Ac}, \mathsf{V}, \mathsf{E}, \ell, \sim_a)$ be a concurrent game structure and $Z = (\chi, \mathrm{I}, \rho)$ be a state. *Truth* of a formula ϕ in $\mathcal{G}$ at state Z, in symbols $\mathcal{G}, Z \Vdash \phi$, is inductively defined as follows:

1. $\mathcal{G}, Z \Vdash p$ iff $p \in \ell(\mathsf{last}(\rho))$ where $p \in \mathsf{Prop}$,
2. $\mathcal{G}, Z \nVdash \bot$,
3. $\mathcal{G}, Z \Vdash \phi \to \psi$ iff $\mathcal{G}, Z \nVdash \phi$ or $\mathcal{G}, Z \Vdash \psi$,
4. $\mathcal{G}, Z \Vdash \mathsf{K}_a\phi$ iff $\mathcal{G}, Z' \Vdash \phi$ for all states Z' with $Z \trianglelefteq_a Z'$,
5. $\mathcal{G}, Z \Vdash \mathsf{C}_G\phi$ iff $\mathcal{G}, Z' \Vdash \phi$ for all states Z' with $Z \trianglelefteq_G^* Z'$,
6. $\mathcal{G}, Z \Vdash \mathsf{X}\phi$ iff $\mathcal{G}, Z' \Vdash \phi$ where $Z' = (\chi, \mathrm{I}, \mathsf{X}_{\mathcal{G}}^{\chi}\rho)$.

We say that a formula ϕ is *valid* if $\mathcal{G}, Z \Vdash \phi$ holds for all concurrent game structures $\mathcal{G}$ and states Z.

3 First Examples and Basic Properties

We give two basic examples to illustrate our truth definition. These examples will also be referred to in the proof of Lemma 5.

We consider a set Ag of two agents a and b and the concurrent game structure shown in Fig. 1. In position v_1, only agent a will perform an action. This can be either action α leading to position v_2 where p is true or action β leading to position v_3 where q is true. We assume that every agent can distinguish the different positions and also the two actions. Since the other agents' actions do not matter in these examples, we will not mention them and consider α and β also as joint actions. We also omit the loops on final positions.

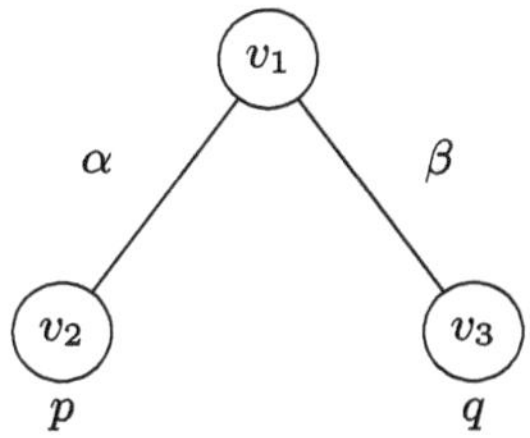

Fig. 1. The concurrent game structure $\mathcal{G}_1$.

Let the strategy σ_α be such that $\sigma_\alpha(v_1) = \alpha$ and let χ_α be an assignment with $\chi_\alpha(a) = \sigma_\alpha$. Similarly, let the strategy σ_β be such that $\sigma_\beta(v_1) = \beta$ and let χ_β be an assignment with $\chi(a) = \sigma_\beta$.

For the first example, we assume that agent b is informed about agent a's strategy.

Example 1. We set $\mathrm{I} := \{ba\}$ and consider the state $Z = (\chi_\alpha, \mathrm{I}, v_1)$. In this setting, we find that $\mathcal{G}_1, Z \Vdash \mathsf{K}_b\mathsf{X}p$ holds.

Indeed, let $Z' = (\chi', \mathrm{I}', v_1)$ be an arbitrary state with $Z \trianglelefteq_b Z'$. This implies $\chi_\alpha \sim_b^{\mathrm{I}} \chi'$, which by $a \in \mathrm{I}_b$ yields $\chi_\alpha(a) = \chi'(a)$. Therefore, we get $\mathsf{X}_{\mathcal{G}_1}^{\chi'} v_1 = v_1\alpha v_2$ and thus $\mathcal{G}_1, Z' \Vdash \mathsf{X}p$. Since Z' was arbitrary with $Z \trianglelefteq_b Z'$, we conclude $\mathcal{G}_1, Z \Vdash \mathsf{K}_b\mathsf{X}p$.

For the second example, we consider the case when b is not informed about a's strategy.

Example 2. We set $\mathrm{I} = \emptyset$, that is, in particular, $ba \notin \mathrm{I}$, and consider the state $Z = (\chi_\alpha, \mathrm{I}, v_1)$. We show that

$$\mathcal{G}_1, Z \not\Vdash \mathsf{K}_b \mathsf{X} p. \tag{3}$$

Indeed, we find $\chi_\alpha \sim_b^{\mathrm{I}} \chi_\beta$. Hence we obtain $Z \trianglelefteq_b Z'$ for $Z' = (\chi_\beta, \mathrm{I}, v_1)$. We get $\mathcal{G}_1, Z' \Vdash \mathsf{X}\neg p$ and thus conclude (3).

Similarly, we can also establish $\mathcal{G}_1, Z \not\Vdash \mathsf{K}_b \mathsf{X} q$. However, let us mention that, as usual, the concurrent game structure is general background knowledge. That means agent b knows that agent a will perform either action α or action β and thus reach a position where p holds or one where q holds. Formally, we have $\mathcal{G}_1, Z \Vdash \mathsf{K}_b(\mathsf{X} p \vee \mathsf{X} q)$.

Let us now examine basic properties of the individual knowledge operators. The proofs of the following three lemmas are ommited here for reasons of space; they can be found in the accompanying technical report [24]. We begin with positive introspection.

Lemma 3. *The formula* $\mathsf{K}_a \phi \to \mathsf{K}_a \mathsf{K}_a \phi$ *is valid.*

We defined truthful information perspectives to satisfy (1). This is a necessary condition for $Z \trianglelefteq_a Z$ to hold. However, it is not sufficient as the state Z may not be a-consistent.

We have the following lemma, which states that the Truth axiom for K_a holds at a-consistent states with truthful information perspectives. This is similar to the situation in simplicial semantics [8,12], which provides a model of epistemic logic for distributed systems, where the Truth axiom only holds for correct processes.

Lemma 4. *Let* $\mathcal{G}$ *be a concurrent game structure and* $Z = (\chi, \mathrm{I}, \rho)$ *be a state with a truthful information perspective. We have* $\mathcal{G}, Z \Vdash \neg K_a \bot \to (\mathsf{K}_a \phi \to \phi)$.

In general, agents cannot perform negative introspection.

Lemma 5. *The schema of negative introspection is not valid, i.e. there is a countermodel to* $\neg \mathsf{K}_b \phi \to \mathsf{K}_b \neg \mathsf{K}_b \phi$.

4 Hanabi

We illustrate the workings of our logic and the importance of higher-order knowledge of strategies by studying the game Hanabi. Hanabi is a cooperative game of imperfect information. Because of this particular combination, Hanabi has been proposed as a challenge for machine learning techniques in multi-agent settings [4]. Early work on Hanabi was mainly concerned with evaluating fixed strategies [10]. Later, Hanabi has been used to study, e.g., zero-shot coordination, that is, constructing agents that can coordinate with novel partners they have not seen before [14]. Most recently, Perrotin [22] provides an epistemic logic analysis of Hanabi that is based on (common) knowledge of game states. In contrast to our examples, knowledge of strategies is not relevant for that work.

The goal of the game is to play cards so as to form ordered stacks, one for each color, beginning with a card of rank 1 and ending with a card of rank 5. The game's twist is the imperfect information, which arises from each player being unable to see their own cards (but they can see the hands of the other players). Hence, players have to rely on receiving information from the other players.

Players take turns doing one of three actions: giving a hint, playing a card from their hand, or discarding a card. The number and types of hints that are allowed are very restricted. However, each action taken in a play is observed by all players and can, therefore, convey implicit information. This is possible, in particular, when players have pre-established conventions and tactics. In our example, we assume that the players use the following convention: if a player thinks that several of her cards are possible to play, she plays the leftmost of them.

We use Hanabi as a prime example of the role of higher-order knowledge when reasoning about strategies. In particular, we investigate a standard tactic of Hanabi, the so-called *finesse* move, see [4,26] for more details.

We consider a simplified situation, ignoring the color of the cards and the exact form of the hints. There are three players a, b, and c. It is player a's turn, then player b's, and then player c's. Player a sees that player b has a card of rank 1 on her leftmost position and player c has a card of rank 2. Player a could now

1. inform player b of her card of rank 1. Then player b will play that card.
2. inform player c of her card of rank 2 and assume that player b will infer that she must have a card 1. So player b will play her card 1, and then player c will play her card 2.

Of course, the second option is the better choice, as with one hint, two correct cards will be played. This is the essence of the *finesse*-move.

We model this situation with the concurrent game structure $\mathcal{G}_2$ given in Fig. 2.

Proposition p means that player b has a card 1. The positions v_1 and v_4 are two possible positions before a's move. At position v_1, player b does have a card 1, while she does not at v_4. The positions v_2, v_3, v_5, and v_6 represent the different possible results of a's action.

Action α means that player a gives player b the information that b has a card 1. Action β means that player a gives player c the information that she has a card 2. Action γ means that player a gives player b the information that b does not have a card 1. As in our previous examples, only the action of player a matters, and we consider α, β, and γ also as joint actions.

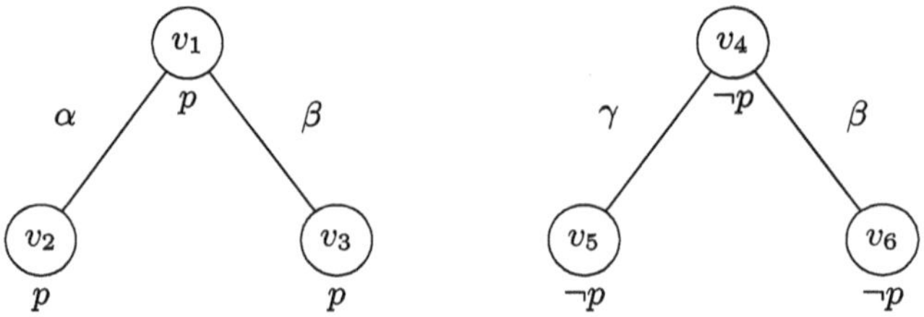

Fig. 2. The concurrent game structure $\mathcal{G}_2$.

All actions are public, and each agent can distinguish them. In particular, we have

$$\alpha \not\sim_b \beta \text{ and } \beta \not\sim_b \gamma \text{ and } \alpha \not\sim_b \gamma. \tag{4}$$

Player a can see player b's cards. Thus, a can distinguish the different states, i.e.

$$v_i \not\sim_a v_j \quad \text{for } i \neq j. \tag{5}$$

Player b does not know whether she has a card 1. Thus

$$v_1 \sim_b v_4. \tag{6}$$

If player a informs player b, then she knows whether she has a card 1. Thus $v_2 \not\sim_b v_5$. However, if player a gives information to player c, then b still does not know whether she has a card 1. Hence

$$v_3 \sim_b v_6. \tag{7}$$

Player a's strategy is as follows.

1. If player b does not have a card 1, then a gives b the information that b does not have a card 1, i.e. she performs action γ.
2. If player b has a card 1, then a informs c, i.e. she performs action β.

We denote this strategy by σ. That is $\sigma(v_1) := \beta$ and $\sigma(v_4) := \gamma$. Further, we let the assignment χ be such that $\chi(a) := \sigma$. We consider the history $\rho := v_1\beta v_3$, i.e. player b has a card 1 and player a gives information to c.

Assume that player b knows player a's strategy. We show that in this situation, b can infer from observing action β that she must have a card of rank 1.

Example 3. We consider an information perspective I with $ba \in \mathrm{I}$ and let Z be the state (χ, I, ρ). We find that in this situation, player b knows that she has a card 1, although player a informed player c. Formally, we have $\mathcal{G}_2, Z \Vdash \mathsf{K}_b p$. Indeed, let $Z' = (\chi', \mathrm{I}', \rho')$ be any state with $Z \trianglelefteq_b Z'$. This implies $\chi \sim_b^{\mathrm{I}} \chi'$, which by $a \in \mathrm{I}_b$ yields $\chi'(a) = \chi(a) = \sigma$.

Since ρ' must be consistent with χ' under I'_b, we get $\rho' = v_1\beta v_3$ or $\rho' = v_4\gamma v_5$. Since $\rho \sim_b \rho'$, we find by (4) that $\rho' = v_1\beta v_3$ or $\rho' = v_4\beta v_6$. Hence, we conclude $\rho' = v_1\beta v_3$. Therefore, $\mathcal{G}_2, Z' \Vdash p$ and $\mathcal{G}_2, Z \Vdash \mathsf{K}_b p$.

Now, we assume that player b does not know player a's strategy. In this situation, player b does not know that she has a card of rank 1 unless player a tells her so.

Example 4. Formally, we consider an information perspective I with $ba \notin \mathrm{I}$ and let Z be the state (χ, I, ρ). We will show $\mathcal{G}_2, Z \nVdash \mathsf{K}_b p$.

First, we observe that Z is b-consistent. Now let σ' be a strategy such that $\sigma'(v_1) = \beta$ and $\sigma'(v_4) = \beta$. Further let χ' be an assignment with $\chi'(a) = \sigma'$. Because of $ba \notin \mathrm{I}$ we find $a \notin \mathrm{I}_b$. Therefore $\chi \sim_b^{\mathrm{I}} \chi'$. We set $\rho' = v_4\beta v_6$ and observe by (6) and (7) that $\rho \sim_b \rho'$. Further we have that ρ' is consistent with χ' under I_b, which means that $(\chi', \mathrm{I}', \rho')$ is b-consistent. Therefore, we obtain $(\chi, \mathrm{I}, \rho) \trianglelefteq_b (\chi', \mathrm{I}', \rho')$. We have $(\chi', \mathrm{I}', \rho') \nVdash p$ and thus conclude $\mathcal{G}_2, Z \nVdash \mathsf{K}_b p$.

Let us again consider Example 3 where we established that

if b knows a's strategy, then b will infer from observing action β
that she must have a card of rank 1. (8)

However, note that this is not enough for player a to safely choose action β. What is required is that player a knows (8). Only then can a be sure that if she informs c, player b will play her card 1, and thus informing c about her card 2 is a good choice.

Hence, this is a situation where higher-order knowledge is relevant. Namely, we have that if player a knows that player b knows a's strategy, then player a knows that if she informs player c, then player b will know that she has a card 1. We can formalize this situation as follows.

Example 5. We let I be an information perspective with $aba \in \mathrm{I}$ and consider the state $Z = (\chi, \mathrm{I}, v_1)$. Let $Y = (\chi', \mathrm{I}', \rho')$ be an arbitrary state with $Z \trianglelefteq_a Y$. Thus $\rho \sim_a \rho'$. Therefore by (5), we get $\rho' = v_1$. Moreover, we have $\chi \sim_a^{\mathrm{I}} \chi'$. Because of $a \in \mathrm{I}_a$, we get $\chi'(a) = \chi(a) = \sigma$. Hence $\mathsf{X}_{\mathcal{G}_2}^{\chi'} \rho' = v_1\beta v_3$. So we let X be the state $(\chi', \mathrm{I}', v_1\beta v_3)$. We observe $ba \in \mathrm{I}[a] \subseteq \mathrm{I}'$. Therefore, we obtain $\mathcal{G}_2, X \Vdash \mathsf{K}_b p$ as in Example 3. Hence $\mathcal{G}_2, Y \Vdash \mathsf{X}\mathsf{K}_b p$. Since Y was arbitrary with $Z \trianglelefteq_a Y$, we conclude $\mathcal{G}_2, Z \Vdash \mathsf{K}_a\mathsf{X}\mathsf{K}_b p$.

The reasoning of the previous example is only possible if agent a knows that b is informed about a's strategy. Otherwise, a must take into account a situation where b is not informed about a's strategy, and thus a considers the situation of Example 4 possible. Hence, even though b will know that she has a card 1, player a will not know that b knows this.

Example 6. We let I be an information perspective with $ba \in \mathrm{I}$ but $aba \notin \mathrm{I}$ and consider an a-consistent state $Z = (\chi, \mathrm{I}, v_1)$. We set $Y = (\chi, \mathrm{I}[a], v_1)$ and find $Z \trianglelefteq_a Y$ and $ba \notin \mathrm{I}[a]$. Further, we have $\mathsf{X}_{\mathcal{G}_2}^{\chi} v_1 = v_1\beta v_3$ and let X be the state $(\chi, \mathrm{I}[a], v_1\beta v_3)$. As in Example 4, we find $\mathcal{G}_2, X \nVdash \mathsf{K}_b p$. Hence $\mathcal{G}_2, Y \nVdash \mathsf{X}\mathsf{K}_b p$ and finally $\mathcal{G}_2, Z \nVdash \mathsf{K}_a\mathsf{X}\mathsf{K}_b p$.

5 Common Knowledge

In this section, we investigate common knowledge of strategies. Agent a's strategy is common knowledge among a group of agents G if all agents in G are informed about it, all agents in G know that all agents in G are informed about it, all agents in G know that all agents in G know that all agents in G are informed about it, and so on. Hence, an information perspective I models that agent a's strategy is common knowledge among G if $wa \in \mathrm{I}$ for each $w \in G^{\geq 1}$.

We can recover negative introspection if all strategies are common knowledge. This is captured by the notion of a fully informed information perspective. Formally, we have the following definition.

Definition 1. *We say that the information perspective* I *is* fully informed *if* $\mathrm{I} = \mathsf{Ag}^{\geq 2}$.

A fully informed information perspective I satisfies the following important property for any agent a

$$\mathrm{I}[a] = \mathrm{I} = \mathsf{Ag}^{\geq 2}. \tag{9}$$

The following lemma states that Axiom B, which in modal logic is $\phi \to \Box\Diamond\phi$, and negative introspection hold for fully informed information perspectives. We omit the proof for reasons of space.

Lemma 6. *Let $\mathcal{G}$ be a concurrent game structure and $Z = (\chi, \mathrm{I}, \rho)$ be a state with a fully informed information perspective. We have $\mathcal{G}, Z \Vdash \phi \to \mathsf{K}_a\neg\mathsf{K}_a\neg\phi$. and $\mathcal{G}, Z \Vdash \neg\mathsf{K}_a\phi \to \mathsf{K}_a\neg\mathsf{K}_a\phi$.*

We illustrate the need for common knowledge of strategies with the problem of binary consensus. In this problem, we have two agents, each of whom has an input value that can be either 0 or 1, and they have to agree on a common value, which has to be one of their input values. In this context, agreeing on a value means that the value is common knowledge for the two agents.

We consider the following scenario. There are two agents, a and b, and the group G consists of these two agents. In the following, we will just say common knowledge when we mean common knowledge among G. One agent has 0 as the input value; the other agent has an input value of 1. They exchange their values using reliable communication. So, it is common knowledge that the agents have 0 and 1 as their respective input values. We represent this by the position v_1 in a concurrent game structure $\mathcal{G}_3$ that has the same form as the one given in Fig. 1.

Now, agent a has to choose its output value, and we only consider the question of whether her choice will be common knowledge. Action α means agent a uses the minimum function to choose its output value. Action β means agent a uses the maximum function. So p stands for a decided for 0, and q means that a decided for 1 as the output value.

We assume agent a uses the minimum function, i.e. her strategy is to perform action α. We let χ be such that $\chi(a)(v_1) = \alpha$ and χ' be such that $\chi'(a)(v_1) = \beta$. Agent a does not announce which output value she has chosen. That is in $\mathcal{G}_3$, we have $v_2 \sim_b v_3$ and $\alpha \sim_b \beta$. Let $\rho := v_1\alpha v_2$ and $\rho' := v_1\beta v_3$. We find that $\rho \sim_b \rho'$.

We observe that common knowledge of a's strategy is necessary for common knowledge of p. A proof of this theorem is given in Appendix B.

Theorem 1. *Let* I *be an information perspective such that a's strategy is not common knowledge. We have* $\mathcal{G}_3, (\chi, \mathrm{I}, \rho) \nVdash \mathsf{C}_G p$.

Further, if a's strategy is common knowledge, then p is common knowledge, see Appendix C for a proof.

Theorem 2. *Let* I *be such that a's strategy is common knowledge. We have* $\mathcal{G}_3, (\chi, \mathrm{I}, \rho) \Vdash \mathsf{C}_G p$.

6 Model Checking

Finally, we investigate the model checking problem. We will show that it is decidable for $\mathcal{L}$-formulas.

We begin with the following auxiliary notion. The K-depth of an $\mathcal{L}$-formula ϕ, in symbols $\mathsf{kd}(\phi)$, is inductively defined by:

$$\mathsf{kd}(p) := 0 \qquad \mathsf{kd}(\phi \to \psi) := \max(\mathsf{kd}(\phi), \mathsf{kd}(\phi))$$
$$\mathsf{kd}(\bot) := 0 \qquad \mathsf{kd}(\mathsf{K}_a\phi) := \mathsf{kd}(\phi) + 1$$
$$\mathsf{kd}(\mathsf{X}\phi) := \mathsf{kd}(\phi).$$

For $X \subseteq \mathsf{Ag}^*$ and a natural number n, we set $X\restriction_n := \{w \in X \mid \mathsf{len}(w) \leq n\}$. The following lemma is proved in Appendix D.

Lemma 7. *Let* $\mathcal{G}$ *be a concurrent game structure,* $Z = (\chi, \mathrm{I}, \rho)$ *be a state, and* ϕ *be an* $\mathcal{L}$*-formula. For any information perspective* I' *with* $\mathrm{I}\restriction_{\mathsf{kd}(\phi)+2} = \mathrm{I}'\restriction_{\mathsf{kd}(\phi)+2}$*, we have* $\mathcal{G}, (\chi, \mathrm{I}, \rho) \Vdash \phi$ *iff* $\mathcal{G}, (\chi, \mathrm{I}', \rho) \Vdash \phi$.

The *duration* of a history is the number of joint actions occurring in it, i.e. the duration of $v_0\alpha_1 v_1 \ldots \alpha_n v_n$ is n. The duration of a state (χ, I, ρ) is the duration of ρ. Let Z be a state with duration n. By the definition of truth, we find that

1. to evaluate a formula of the form $\mathsf{X}\phi$ at Z, we have to evaluate ϕ at a state with duration $n + 1$;
2. to evaluate a formula of the form $\mathsf{K}_a\phi$ at Z, we have to evaluate ϕ at states with duration n.

Let ϕ be an $\mathcal{L}$-formula with a maximal nesting depth of X-operators of m. We find that to evaluate ϕ at Z, we only have to consider states with a duration of at most $n + m$.

This, Lemma 7, and the fact that a concurrent game structure consists only of finitely many actions and finitely many positions together yield that to evaluate an $\mathcal{L}$-formula at a given state, we only have to consider finitely many other states. Therefore, we obtain the following corollary.

Corollary 1. *Model checking is decidable for* $\mathcal{L}$*-formulas.*

7 Conclusion

In this work, we introduced a model that can express first-order, higher-order, and common knowledge of strategies. We studied how higher-order knowledge of strategies affects agents' strategic abilities in the game Hanabi, and we showed that common knowledge of strategies is necessary to solve the consensus task. Finally, we established the decidability of the model checking problem for the language without common knowledge.

Three important topics are left for future work:

1. studying the model checking problem in the presence of common knowledge;
2. considering a language that includes more expressive temporal operators, in particular *until*;
3. extending our approach to proper strategy logic [9,20], i.e. to a language that treats strategies as explicit first-order objects.

With respect to the last topic, first steps towards to an extension to strategy logic are presented in [16]. The second topic, i.e. the combination of epistemic fixed points (common knowledge) and temporal fixed points (unti) [17], is also highly interesting form a proof-theoretic perspective. Cyclic and non-well founded systems [6,15,19,25] provide an promising approach to handle this.

Acknowledgments. We would like to thank the anonymous reviewers for their helpful comments.

Thomas Studer is supported by the Swiss National Science Foundation (SNSF) under grant number 10000440 (Epistemic Group Attitudes).

Disclosure of Interests. The authors have no competing interests to declare that are relevant to the content of this article.

A Proof of Lemma 2

We have

$$\alpha'_{i+1}(b) = \chi'(b)(\rho'_{\leq i}) \quad \text{for all } i < n \text{ and agents } b \in \mathrm{I}'_a.$$

By $\mathrm{I}[a] \subseteq \mathrm{I}'$ we get

$$\alpha'_{i+1}(b) = \chi'(b)(\rho'_{\leq i}) \quad \text{for all } i < n \text{ and agents } b \in \mathrm{I}_a.$$

Because of $\chi \sim^{\mathrm{I}}_a \chi'$, we conclude

$$\alpha'_{i+1}(b) = \chi(b)(\rho'_{\leq i}) \quad \text{for all } i < n \text{ and agents } b \in \mathrm{I}_a,$$

which means that ρ' is consistent with χ under I_a.

B Proof of Theorem 1

We define sequences $w_i \in \mathsf{Ag}^{\geq 2}$ for $i \geq 1$ as follows: $w_1 := ba$, $w_2 := aba$, $w_3 := baba$, and so on. For a sequence $w = x_n \cdots x_2 x_1 \in \mathsf{Ag}^{\geq 2}$, we let ϕ_w be the formula $\mathsf{K}_{x_n} \cdots \mathsf{K}_{x_2} p$. Further, we write ϕ_i for ϕ_{w_i}. For instance, we have $\phi_1 = \mathsf{K}_b p$ and $\phi_2 = \mathsf{K}_a \mathsf{K}_b p$.

We show

$$\text{for all information perspectives I,} \quad w_i \notin \mathrm{I} \text{ implies } \mathcal{G}_3, (\chi, \mathrm{I}, \rho) \not\Vdash \phi_i$$

by induction on i.

Case $i = 1$. Since $ba \notin \mathrm{I}$, we $a \notin \mathrm{I}_b$. Therefore, $\chi \sim_b^{\mathrm{I}} \chi'$. This yields $(\chi, \mathrm{I}, \rho) \trianglelefteq_b (\chi', \mathrm{I}[b], \rho')$. Because of $\mathcal{G}_3, (\chi', \mathrm{I}[b], \rho') \not\Vdash p$, we conclude

$$\mathcal{G}_3, (\chi, \mathrm{I}, \rho) \not\Vdash \mathsf{K}_b p.$$

Case $i = j + 1$. Let $x \in \mathsf{Ag}$ be such that $w_i = x w_j$. We have

$$(\chi, \mathrm{I}, \rho) \trianglelefteq_x (\chi, \mathrm{I}[x], \rho).$$

By the definition of $\mathrm{I}[x]$ and $w_i \notin \mathrm{I}$, we find $w_j \notin \mathrm{I}[x]$. Thus, by I.H., we obtain

$$\mathcal{G}_3, (\chi, \mathrm{I}[x], \rho) \not\Vdash \phi_j.$$

Therefore, $\mathcal{G}_3, (\chi, \mathrm{I}, \rho) \not\Vdash \mathsf{K}_x \phi_j$, which is

$$\mathcal{G}_3, (\chi, \mathrm{I}, \rho) \not\Vdash \phi_i.$$

If a's strategy is not common knowledge, there exists i with $w_i \notin \mathrm{I}$ and thus $\mathcal{G}_3, (\chi, \mathrm{I}, \rho) \not\Vdash \phi_i$. Since $\mathsf{C}_G p \to \phi_i$ is valid, we conclude $\mathcal{G}_3, (\chi, \mathrm{I}, \rho) \not\Vdash \mathsf{C}_G p$.

C Proof of Theorem 2

By induction on i we show that for all states $Z_0, \ldots, Z_i$ such that

$$(\chi, \mathrm{I}, \rho) =: Z_0 \trianglelefteq_{x_1} Z_1 \trianglelefteq_{x_2} \cdots \trianglelefteq_{x_i} Z_i,$$

we have

1. $\mathcal{G}_3, Z_i \Vdash p$ and
2. for $Z_i = (\sigma^i, \mathrm{I}^i, \rho^i)$, agent a's strategy is common knowledge in I^i.

Case $i = 0$. We have $\mathsf{last}(\rho) = v_2$ and hence $\mathcal{G}_3, (\chi, \mathrm{I}, \rho) \Vdash p$. By assumption, we also have that a's strategy is common knowledge in I.

Case $i = j + 1$. We let $Z_j = (\chi^j, \mathrm{I}^j, \rho^j)$. By I.H. we find $\mathcal{G}_3, Z_j \Vdash p$, which means that $\mathsf{last}(\rho^j) = v_2$, and

$$\text{agent } a\text{'s strategy is common knowledge in } \mathrm{I}^j. \tag{10}$$

Therefore, $a \in \mathrm{I}^j_{x_i}$. Since ρ^j is consistent with χ^j under $\mathrm{I}^j_{x_i}$, we find $\chi^j(a)(v_1) = \alpha$. We have $\chi^j \sim^{\mathrm{I}^j}_{x_i} \chi^i$. Therefore, $\chi^i(a)(v_1) = \chi^j(a)(v_1) = \alpha$. Since ρ^i is consistent with χ^i under $\mathrm{I}^i_{x_i}$, we get $\mathsf{last}(\rho^i) = v_2$. Hence, we conclude

$$\mathcal{G}_3, Z_i \Vdash p.$$

To show the second claim, we let $w = w_h \cdots w_1 \in \mathsf{Ag}^{\geq 1}$. If $w_h \neq x_i$, then by (10) we have $x_i wa \in \mathrm{I}^j$ and thus

$$wa \in \mathrm{I}[x_i] \subseteq \mathrm{I}^i.$$

If $w_h = x_i$, then by (10) we have $wa \in \mathrm{I}^j$ and again

$$wa \in \mathrm{I}[x_i] \subseteq \mathrm{I}^i.$$

Hence, a's strategy is common knowledge in I^i.

We have shown that for any state Z_i that is reachable from (χ, I, ρ), we have $\mathcal{G}_3, Z_i \Vdash p$. Therefore $\mathcal{G}_3, (\chi, \mathrm{I}, \rho) \Vdash \mathsf{C}_G p$ as desired.

D Proof of Lemma 7

We show by induction on n and subinduction on ϕ: if $\mathrm{I} \restriction_{n+2} = \mathrm{I}' \restriction_{n+2}$, then for any $\mathcal{L}$-formula ϕ with $\mathsf{kd}(\phi) \leq n$, we have

$$\mathcal{G}, (\chi, \mathrm{I}, \rho) \Vdash \phi \quad \text{iff} \quad \mathcal{G}, (\chi, \mathrm{I}', \rho) \Vdash \phi. \tag{11}$$

Case $n = 0$. The formula ϕ does not contain any K-modality, and (11) trivially holds.

Case $n = k + 1$. For the subinduction, we only show the case $\phi = \mathsf{K}_a \psi$. We show the direction from left to right by contraposition. The other direction is analogous. Assume

$$\mathcal{G}, (\chi, \mathrm{I}', \rho) \nVdash \mathsf{K}_a \psi.$$

Thus, there exists an information perspective I'_0 such that

$$\mathcal{G}, (\chi, \mathrm{I}'_0, \rho) \nVdash \psi \tag{12}$$

and

$$(\chi, \mathrm{I}', \rho) \trianglelefteq_a (\chi, \mathrm{I}'_0, \rho). \tag{13}$$

Hence

$$\mathrm{I}'[a] \subseteq \mathrm{I}'_0. \tag{14}$$

Now we set

$$\mathrm{I}_0 := \mathrm{I}[a] \cup \mathrm{I}'_0. \tag{15}$$

We trivially have

$$\mathrm{I}[a] \subseteq \mathrm{I}_0. \tag{16}$$

Further we have

$$\mathrm{I}_0 \restriction_{n+1} = \mathrm{I}'_0 \restriction_{n+1} . \tag{17}$$

Indeed, $\supseteq$ holds by definition (15). For $\subseteq$, we assume $w \in \mathrm{I}_0 \restriction_{n+1}$ and distinguish the cases according to (15): If $w \in \mathrm{I}'_0$, then $w \in \mathrm{I}'_0 \restriction_{n+1}$ and we are done. If $w \in \mathrm{I}[a]$, then we distinguish:

1. $aw \in \mathrm{I}$. We have $aw \in \mathrm{I}\restriction_{n+2} = \mathrm{I}'\restriction_{n+2}$. Thus $w \in \mathrm{I}'[a]$ and by (14), we get $w \in \mathrm{I}'_0$. Hence $w \in \mathrm{I}'_0\restriction_{n+1}$.
2. $w \in \mathrm{I}$ and $w = aw'$ for some w'. Similar to the previous case.

From (17) and (12), we get by I.H. that $\mathcal{G}, (\chi, \mathrm{I}_0, \rho) \not\Vdash \psi$. Further we have $\mathrm{I}\restriction_2 = \mathrm{I}'\restriction_2$ by assumption and $\mathrm{I}_0\restriction_2 = \mathrm{I}'_0\restriction_2$ by (17). We obtain $\mathrm{I}_a = \mathrm{I}'_a$ and $(\mathrm{I}_0)_a = (\mathrm{I}'_0)_a$, respectively. Hence, using (13), we find that (χ, I, ρ) and $(\chi, \mathrm{I}_0, \rho)$ are a-consistent. Together with (16), this yields

$$(\chi, \mathrm{I}, \rho) \trianglelefteq_a (\chi, \mathrm{I}_0, \rho).$$

We finally conclude $\mathcal{G}, (\chi, \mathrm{I}, \rho) \not\Vdash \mathsf{K}_a\psi$.

References

1. Alur, R., Henzinger, T.A., Kupferman, O.: Alternating-time temporal logic. J. ACM **49**(5), 672–713 (2002). https://doi.org/10.1145/585265.585270
2. Artemov, S.: On definitive solutions of strategic games. In: Baltag, A., Smets, S. (eds.) Johan van Benthem on Logic and Information Dynamics, pp. 487–507. Springer International Publishing (2014). https://doi.org/10.1007/978-3-319-06025-5_17
3. Artemov, S.: Beyond knowledge of the model. In: Weiss, Y., Birman, R. (eds.) Saul Kripke on Modal Logic, pp. 23–41. Springer International Publishing (2024). https://doi.org/10.1007/978-3-031-57635-5_3
4. Bard, N., et al.: The Hanabi challenge: a new frontier for AI research. Artif. Intell. **280**, 103216 (2020). https://doi.org/10.1016/j.artint.2019.103216
5. Belardinelli, F., Knight, S., Lomuscio, A., Maubert, B., Murano, A., Rubin, S.: Reasoning about agents that may know other agents' strategies. In: Zhou, Z.H. (ed.) Proceedings of the Thirtieth International Joint Conference on Artificial Intelligence, IJCAI-21, pp. 1787–1793. International Joint Conferences on Artificial Intelligence Organization (2021).https://doi.org/10.24963/ijcai.2021/246, https://doi.org/10.24963/ijcai.2021/246
6. Bucheli, S., Kuznets, R., Studer, T.: Two ways to common knowledge. Electron. Notes Theor. Comput. Sci. **262**, 83–98 (2010). https://doi.org/10.1016/j.entcs.2010.04.007, Proceedings of the 6th Workshop on Methods for Modalities (M4M-6 2009)
7. Cachin, C., Guerraoui, R., Rodrigues, L.: Introduction to reliable and secure distributed programming. Springer, Berlin, Heidelberg (2011). https://doi.org/10.1007/978-3-642-15260-3
8. Cachin, C., Lehnherr, D., Studer, T.: Synergistic knowledge. Theoret. Comput. Sci. **1023**, 114902 (2025). https://doi.org/10.1016/j.tcs.2024.114902
9. Chatterjee, K., Henzinger, T.A., Piterman, N.: Strategy logic. Inf. Comput. **208**(6), 677–693 (2010). https://doi.org/10.1016/j.ic.2009.07.004
10. Cox, C., De Silva, J., Deorsey, P., Kenter, F.H.J., Retter, T., Tobin, J.: How to make the perfect fireworks display: two strategies for Hanabi. Math. Mag. **88**(5), 323–336 (2015). https://doi.org/10.4169/math.mag.88.5.323
11. Fagin, R., Halpern, J.Y., Moses, Y., Vardi, M.Y.: Reasoning about Knowledge. MIT Press (1995)

12. Goubault, É., Kniazev, R., Ledent, J., Rajsbaum, S.: Simplicial models for the epistemic logic of faulty agents. Boletín de la Sociedad Matemática Mexicana **30**(3) (2024).https://doi.org/10.1007/s40590-024-00656-x
13. van der Hoek, W., Wooldridge, M.J.: Cooperation, knowledge, and time: alternating-time temporal epistemic logic and its applications. Stud. Logica. **75**(1), 125–157 (2003). https://doi.org/10.1023/A:1026185103185
14. Hu, H., Lerer, A., Peysakhovich, A., Foerster, J.: Other-play for zero-shot coordination. In: Proceedings of the 37th International Conference on Machine Learning. JMLR.org (2020)
15. Kokkinis, I., Studer, T.: Cyclic proofs for linear temporal logic. In: Probst, D., Schuster, P. (eds.) Concepts of Proof in Mathematics, Philosophy, and Computer Science, pp. 171–192. De Gruyter, Berlin, Boston (2016). https://doi.org/10.1515/9781501502620-011
16. Luo, J., Studer, T.: Strategic knowledge in multi-agent systems (2026)
17. Marinković, B., Glavan, P., Ognjanović, Z., Studer, T.: A temporal epistemic logic with a non-rigid set of agents for analyzing the blockchain protocol. J. Log. Comput. **29**(5), 803–830 (2019)
18. Maubert, B., Murano, A.: Reasoning about knowledge and strategies under hierarchical information. In: Thielscher, M., Toni, F., Wolter, F. (eds.) Principles of Knowledge Representation and Reasoning 2018, pp. 530–540. AAAI Press (2018)
19. Menéndez Turata, G.: Cyclic proof systems for modal fixpoint logics, Universiteit van Amsterdam (2024). Ph.D. thesis
20. Mogavero, F., Murano, A., Perelli, G., Vardi, M.Y.: Reasoning about strategies: on the model-checking problem. ACM Trans. Comput. Logic **15**(4), 1–47 (2014). https://doi.org/10.1145/2631917
21. Pauly, M.: A modal logic for coalitional power in games. J. Log. Comput. **12**(1), 149–166 (2002). https://doi.org/10.1093/logcom/12.1.149
22. Perrotin, E.: A logical analysis of Hanabi. In: Proceedings of the 39th AAAI Conference on Artificial Intelligence (2025)
23. Saffidine, A., Schwarzentruber, F., Zanuttini, B.: Knowledge-based policies for qualitative decentralized POMDPs. In: Proceedings of the AAAI Conference on Artificial Intelligence, vol. 32, issue (1) (2018). https://doi.org/10.1609/aaai.v32i1.12085, https://ojs.aaai.org/index.php/AAAI/article/view/12085
24. Sierra Miranda, B., Studer, T.: Knowledge and common knowledge of strategies (2025). https://arxiv.org/abs/2510.19298
25. Miranda, S., Studer, B., Zenger, T., L.: Coalgebraic proof translations for non-well founded proofs. In: Ciabattoni, A., Gabelaia, D., Sedlár, I. (eds.) Advances in Modal Logic 2024, pp. 527–548 (2024)
26. Volrath, Z.: H-group conventions (2026). https://hanabi.github.io. Accessed 19 Jan 2026

Axiomatizing Eventual Common Knowledge

Roman Kuznets[1], Rojo Randrianomentsoa[2(✉)], and Thomas Studer[2]

[1] Institute of Computer Science of the Czech Academy of Sciences, Prague, Czech Republic
kuznets@cs.cas.cz
[2] Institute of Computer Science, University of Bern, Bern, Switzerland
{rojo.randrianomentsoa,thomas.studer}@unibe.ch

Abstract. Common knowledge plays a central role in modeling coordination in multi-agent systems, yet classical results show that even arbitrarily small temporal uncertainty prevents it from ever being attained in practical systems. This has motivated a range of approximations to common knowledge, including ε-common knowledge and eventual common knowledge, which relax the requirement that all levels of mutual knowledge hold simultaneously. These notions aim to retain the logical structure of common knowledge while making it compatible with temporal imprecision. In this paper, we investigate the logic of eventual common knowledge and provide a sound and complete Hilbert-style axiomatization.

Keywords: Eventual common knowledge · Fixed point · Axiomatization

1 Introduction

Beyond its foundational logical interest, common knowledge plays a central role in modeling coordination and agreement in multi-agent systems [5,8,13]. In their seminal paper [8], Halpern and Moses showed that common knowledge is a necessary condition for certain forms of coordinated action in distributed environments. A key insight of their analysis is that common knowledge is extremely fragile: even arbitrarily small uncertainty about message delivery times or clock synchronization suffices to prevent agents from ever attaining common knowledge. As a result, in practical systems with temporal imprecision, facts that intuitively ought to become "publicly known" never formally become common knowledge. This phenomenon—often referred to as the Halpern–Moses paradox [7,15]—highlights that the standard notion of common knowledge implicitly relies on idealized assumptions about simultaneity and timing.

In many settings, coordination requirements are inherently approximate, and small temporal discrepancies in agents' higher-order knowledge are inconsequential for successful joint action. Relaxing the simultaneity requirement therefore

P. Johann and R. de Queiroz (Eds.): WoLLIC 2026, LNCS 16757, pp. 31–49, 2027.
https://doi.org/10.1007/978-3-032-33486-2_3

yields epistemic notions that are both attainable under temporal uncertainty and sufficient for the forms of coordination that arise in practice. This has motivated a line of work on *approximations* to common knowledge that weaken the classical definition accordingly. Examples include *eventual common knowledge*, which is studied in this paper, as well as ε-common knowledge [5,8], *probabilistic common knowledge* [2,10], and *concurrent common knowledge* [18].

Notions of this kind are employed in particular for modelling applications in distributed computing. The Firing Rebels with Relay problem [6], which is a simplified version of the consistent broadcasting primitive introduced by Srikanth and Toueg in [19], is closely related to eventual common hope, an epistemic attitude that lies in a certain sense between belief and knoweldge. Distributed ledger protocols, such as Bitcoin, have been analyzed using Δ-$\Box$-common knowledge [9] and probabilistic common knowledge [11]. Related epistemic analyses of blockchain protocols are, *e.g.*, [3,12,16,17], where the standard notion of common knowledge is used.

Just as common knowledge is defined as a fixed point of the mutual knowledge operator [4], eventual common knowledge is defined as a fixed point of the *eventual mutual knowledge* operator. A group G of agents has eventual mutual knowledge of a fact φ, and we say that $E^{\Diamond}_{G}\varphi$ holds, if for each agent i there exists some time at which i knows φ. In contrast to standard mutual knowledge, no simultaneity requirement is imposed: the agents' knowledge of φ need not hold at the same point in time. While common knowledge and eventual common knowledge are defined analogously as fixed points, it turns out that they behave differently when viewed as infinite conjunctions. In particular, our result shows that eventual common knowledge is strictly stronger than the infinite conjunction of iterated eventual mutual knowledge operators.

Since our main goal here is to provide a Hilbert-style axiomatization of eventual common knowledge, we work in a simplified framework compared to the runs-and-systems setting in which the operator was originally introduced [5,8]. In particular, in order to apply the standard completeness proof via canonical model construction, we use Kripke models with an epistemic accessibility relation for each agent and a temporal relation, rather than interpreted systems. This simplification is primarily technical and preserves the essential behavior of the original operator. A somewhat surprising feature of our framework is that we model time as an equivalence relation. This choice is motivated by the semantics of eventual mutual knowledge in the runs-and-systems framework. There, a system is represented as a non-empty set of runs, where each run r is a function mapping each point m in time to a global state of the system, and formulas are evaluated at points (r, m). Eventual mutual knowledge is interpreted as follows:

$$\mathcal{I}, r, m \vDash E^{\Diamond}_{G}\varphi \text{ iff } \forall i \in G, \exists m_i \text{ such that } \mathcal{I}, r, m_i \vDash K_i\varphi.$$

In this definition, the quantification ranges over points within a single run, regardless of their temporal order. Therefore, modeling time as an equivalence relation preserves the distinctions that are relevant to eventual common knowledge. An ill-founded proof system for eventual common knowledge that works with interpreted systems and treats the eventual-modality as a proper fixed point is presented in [14].

Paper organization: In Sect. 2.1, we introduce the formal languages as well as the relevant class of Kripke models. We then present the semantics in Sect. 2.2 and investigate a few expected validities in Sect. 2.3. In Sect. 2.4, we study approximations of eventual common knowledge. We present a sound and complete axiomatization in Sect. 3 and conclude with further discussions in Sect. 4.

2 Preliminaries

2.1 Languages and Models

Throughout this paper, we consider a set $\mathcal{A} = \{1, \dots, n\}$ of agents and a non-empty countable set Prop of atomic propositions. We define two languages, $\mathcal{L}_C$ and $\mathcal{L}_C^x$, to separate the object language from the fixed-point machinery needed for the analysis of eventual common knowledge. The language $\mathcal{L}_C$ is a temporal epistemic language in which the eventual common knowledge operator $C_G^\diamond$ is treated as a primitive modality. The language $\mathcal{L}_C^x$ extends $\mathcal{L}_C$ with a single variable x, providing just enough expressive power to characterize $C_G^\diamond$ as the greatest fixed point of eventual mutual knowledge $E_G^\diamond$, while avoiding the additional syntactic overhead of a full fixed point language.

Definition 1 (Languages). *We define the language $\mathcal{L}_C$ by the grammar*

$$\varphi ::= p \mid \neg\varphi \mid (\varphi \wedge \varphi) \mid K_a\varphi \mid \Box\varphi \mid C_G^\diamond\varphi$$

where $a \in \mathcal{A}$, $\varnothing \neq G \subseteq \mathcal{A}$, and $p \in \mathsf{Prop}$. Considering a single variable x, we also define the language $\mathcal{L}_C^x$ by the grammar

$$\psi ::= \varphi \mid x \mid \neg\psi \mid (\psi \wedge \psi) \mid K_a\psi \mid \Box\psi$$

where $a \in \mathcal{A}$ and $\varphi \in \mathcal{L}_C$. In addition to the logical constants and propositional connectives expressed via standard notational abbreviations, we also use $\Diamond\psi := \neg\Box\neg\psi$, $E_G^\diamond\psi := \bigwedge_{a\in G} \Diamond K_a\psi$, $(E_G^\diamond)^0\psi := \psi$, and $(E_G^\diamond)^{k+1}\psi := E_G^\diamond\left((E_G^\diamond)^k\psi\right)$ for any $\varnothing \neq G \subseteq \mathcal{A}$ and $k \geq 0$.

In the completeness proof in Sect. 3.2, we construct a canonical model for each formula $\varphi \in \mathcal{L}_C$ based on its closure $cl(\varphi)$, defined in Definition 3. Lemma 4 establishes that $cl(\varphi)$ is finite and closed under subformulas and negation.

Definition 2 (Subformula) *The set $\mathsf{Sub}(\varphi)$ of subformulas of $\varphi \in \mathcal{L}_C$ is defined by induction on the construction of φ:*

$$\begin{aligned}
\mathsf{Sub}(p) &:= \{p\};\\
\mathsf{Sub}(\neg\varphi) &:= \{\neg\varphi\} \cup \mathsf{Sub}(\varphi);\\
\mathsf{Sub}(\varphi_1 \wedge \varphi_2) &:= \{\varphi_1 \wedge \varphi_2\} \cup \mathsf{Sub}(\varphi_1) \cup \mathsf{Sub}(\varphi_2);\\
\mathsf{Sub}(K_a\varphi) &:= \{K_a\varphi\} \cup \mathsf{Sub}(\varphi);\\
\mathsf{Sub}(\Box\varphi) &:= \{\Box\varphi\} \cup \mathsf{Sub}(\varphi);\\
\mathsf{Sub}(C_G^\diamond\varphi) &:= \{C_G^\diamond\varphi\} \cup \mathsf{Sub}(\varphi).
\end{aligned}$$

Definition 3. *For a formula $\varphi \in \mathcal{L}_C$, we define the following sets.*

- $cl_0(\varphi)$ *is the smallest set closed under the following conditions:*
  1. $\{\varphi\} \cup \{K_a \top \mid a \in \mathcal{A}\} \subset cl_0(\varphi)$;
  2. *if* $\chi \in cl_0(\varphi)$, *then* $\mathsf{Sub}(\chi) \subseteq cl_0(\varphi)$;
  3. *if* $C_G^\diamond \chi \in cl_0(\varphi)$, *then* $E_G^\diamond(\chi \wedge C_G^\diamond \chi) \in cl_0(\varphi)$.
- $K_a^\varphi := \{K_a\chi \mid K_a\chi \in cl_0(\varphi)\}$.
- $cl_1(\varphi) := cl_0(\varphi) \cup \{\neg\chi \mid \chi \in cl_0(\varphi)\}$.
- $cl_2(\varphi)$ *is the smallest set closed under the following conditions:*
  1. $cl_1(\varphi) \subseteq cl_2(\varphi)$;
  2. *if* $\chi \in cl_2(\varphi)$, *then* $\mathsf{Sub}(\chi) \subseteq cl_2(\varphi)$;
  3. *if* $\varnothing \neq \Delta \subseteq K_a^\varphi$, *then* $\{\Box(\bigwedge_{K_a\chi\in\Delta} K_a\chi), \Box\neg(\bigwedge_{K_a\chi\in\Delta} K_a\chi)\} \subset cl_2(\varphi)$.
- $cl_3(\varphi) := cl_2(\varphi) \cup \{\neg\chi \mid \chi \in cl_2(\varphi)\}$.
- $cl_4(\varphi) := cl_3(\varphi) \cup \{\Box\Box\chi \mid \Box\chi \in cl_3(\varphi)\} \cup \{\Box\neg\Box\chi \mid \neg\Box\chi \in cl_3(\varphi)\}$.
- $cl(\varphi) := cl_4(\varphi) \cup \{\neg\chi \mid \chi \in cl_4(\varphi)\}$.

We have $cl_0(\varphi) \subset cl_1(\varphi) \subseteq cl_2(\varphi) \subset cl_3(\varphi) \subset cl_4(\varphi) \subset cl(\varphi)$.

Lemma 4. *For any formula $\varphi \in \mathcal{L}_C$, the set $cl(\varphi)$ is finite. If $\chi \in cl(\varphi)$, then* $\mathsf{Sub}(\chi) \subseteq cl(\varphi)$. *Moreover, if $\chi \in cl(\varphi)$ is not a negation, then $\neg\chi \in cl(\varphi)$.*

As mentioned in Sect. 1, we consider Kripke models with an epistemic accessibility relation for each agent and a temporal relation. While we require an equivalence relation for time, we allow arbitrary relations for knowledge.

Definition 5 (Kripke models). *A* Kripke model $\mathcal{M} = (W, \pi, \mathcal{K}_1, \dots, \mathcal{K}_n, \sim)$ *consists of*

- *a non-empty set W of* possible worlds, *also referred to as the domain $\mathcal{D}(\mathcal{M})$ of $\mathcal{M}$,*
- *a* valuation function $\pi\colon \mathsf{Prop} \to 2^W$,
- *and binary relations $\mathcal{K}_1, \dots, \mathcal{K}_n$, and $\sim$ on W.*

Definition 6 (Class). *The class $\mathcal{C}_{eck}$ consists of all models of the form $\mathcal{M} = (W, \pi, \mathcal{K}_1, \dots, \mathcal{K}_n, \sim)$, where the relation $\sim$ is an equivalence relation.*

2.2 Semantics

In this section, we define the semantics of eventual common knowledge.

Definition 7. *Given a Kripke model $\mathcal{M} = (W, \pi, \mathcal{K}_1, \dots, \mathcal{K}_n, \sim)$, we define $f_\psi\colon 2^W \to 2^W$ for each $\psi \in \mathcal{L}_C^x$ by induction on a suitable size measure for $\mathcal{L}_C^x$-formulas.*

1. $f_p(A) := \pi(p)$ *for* $p \in \mathsf{Prop}$,
2. $f_x(A) := A$,
3. $f_{\neg\psi}(A) := W \setminus f_\psi(A)$,
4. $f_{\psi\wedge\psi'}(A) := f_\psi(A) \cap f_{\psi'}(A)$,

5. $f_{K_a\psi}(A) := \{w \mid w' \in f_\psi(A) \text{ for all } w' \text{ s.t. } w\mathcal{K}_a w'\}$,
6. $f_{\Box\psi}(A) := \{w \mid w' \in f_\psi(A) \text{ for all } w' \text{ s.t. } w \sim w'\}$,
7. $f_{C^\diamond_G\varphi}(A) := \bigcup\{B \subseteq W \mid B \subseteq f_{E^\diamond_G(\varphi\wedge x)}(B)\}$ *for* $\varphi \in \mathcal{L}_C$.

Lemma 8 and Lemma 9 establish that Item 7 of Definition 7 is correct and that $C^\diamond_G$ is indeed the greatest fixed point corresponding to $E^\diamond_G$.

Lemma 8. *Let a Kripke model* $\mathcal{M} = (W, \pi, \mathcal{K}_1, \ldots, \mathcal{K}_n, \sim)$ *be given. For any formula* $\varphi \in \mathcal{L}_C$ *and any group* $\varnothing \neq G \subseteq \mathcal{A}$ *of agents, the function* $f_{E^\diamond_G(\varphi\wedge x)}$ *is monotone increasing.*

Proof. For any set $A \subseteq W$, we have

$$
\begin{aligned}
f_{E^\diamond_G(\varphi\wedge x)}(A) &= \bigcap_{a\in G} f_{\diamond K_a(\varphi\wedge x)}(A),\\
f_{\diamond K_a(\varphi\wedge x)}(A) &= W \setminus f_{\Box\neg K_a(\varphi\wedge x)}(A),\\
f_{\Box\neg K_a(\varphi\wedge x)}(A) &= \{w \mid w' \in f_{\neg K_a(\varphi\wedge x)}(A) \text{ for all } w' \text{ s.t. } w \sim w'\},\\
f_{\neg K_a(\varphi\wedge x)}(A) &= W \setminus f_{K_a(\varphi\wedge x)}(A),\\
f_{K_a(\varphi\wedge x)}(A) &= \{w'' \mid w''' \in f_{\varphi\wedge x}(A) \text{ for all } w''' \text{ s.t. } w''\mathcal{K}_a w'''\}\\
&= \{w'' \mid w''' \in f_\varphi(A) \cap A \text{ for all } w''' \text{ s.t. } w''\mathcal{K}_a w'''\}.
\end{aligned}
$$

Consider sets $A \subseteq B \subseteq W$. It is not difficult to see that if $f_\varphi(A) \subseteq f_\varphi(B)$, then we have

$$
\begin{aligned}
f_\varphi(A) \cap A &\subseteq f_\varphi(B) \cap B,\\
f_{K_a(\varphi\wedge x)}(A) &\subseteq f_{K_a(\varphi\wedge x)}(B),\\
f_{\neg K_a(\varphi\wedge x)}(A) &\supseteq f_{\neg K_a(\varphi\wedge x)}(B),\\
f_{\Box\neg K_a(\varphi\wedge x)}(A) &\supseteq f_{\Box\neg K_a(\varphi\wedge x)}(B),\\
f_{\diamond K_a(\varphi\wedge x)}(A) &\subseteq f_{\diamond K_a(\varphi\wedge x)}(B),\\
f_{E^\diamond_G(\varphi\wedge x)}(A) &\subseteq f_{E^\diamond_G(\varphi\wedge x)}(B).
\end{aligned}
$$

Therefore, it is enough to show that $f_\varphi(A) \subseteq f_\varphi(B)$ holds. However, we are going to show that in fact $f_\varphi(A) = f_\varphi(B)$ by induction on the structure of $\varphi \in \mathcal{L}_C$.

For $\varphi = p \in \mathsf{Prop}$: We have $f_\varphi(A) = \pi(p) = f_\varphi(B)$.
For $\varphi = \neg\chi$: We have $f_\varphi(A) = W \setminus f_\chi(A) =_{\text{IH}} W \setminus f_\chi(B) = f_\varphi(B)$.
For $\varphi = \chi_1 \wedge \chi_2$: We have $f_\varphi(A) = f_{\chi_1}(A) \cap f_{\chi_2}(A) =_{\text{IH}} f_{\chi_1}(B) \cap f_{\chi_2}(B) = f_\varphi(B)$.
For $\varphi = K_a\chi$: We have

$$
\begin{aligned}
f_\varphi(A) &= \{w \mid w' \in f_\chi(A) \text{ for all } w' \text{ s.t. } w\mathcal{K}_a w'\}\\
&=_{\text{IH}} \{w \mid w' \in f_\chi(B) \text{ for all } w' \text{ s.t. } w\mathcal{K}_a w'\}\\
&= f_\varphi(B).
\end{aligned}
$$

For $\varphi = \Box\chi$: We have

$$\begin{aligned} f_\varphi(A) &= \{w \mid w' \in f_\chi(A) \text{ for all } w' \text{ s.t. } w \sim w'\} \\ &=_{\text{IH}} \{w \mid w' \in f_\chi(B) \text{ for all } w' \text{ s.t. } w \sim w'\} \\ &= f_\varphi(B). \end{aligned}$$

For $\varphi = C^{\diamond}_G\chi$: We have $f_\varphi(A) = \bigcup\{C \subseteq W \mid C \subseteq f_{E^{\diamond}_G(\chi\wedge x)}(C)\} = f_\varphi(B)$. □

In the proof of Lemma 8, we showed that $f_\varphi(A)$ does not depend on $A \subseteq W$ for any formula $\varphi \in \mathcal{L}_C$. Therefore, we omit the argument and simply write $f_\varphi(\star)$ for $\varphi \in \mathcal{L}_C$.

Lemma 9. *For any Kripke model $\mathcal{M} = (W, \pi, \mathcal{K}_1, \ldots, \mathcal{K}_n, \sim)$ and any formula $\varphi \in \mathcal{L}_C$,*

$$f_{E^{\diamond}_G(\varphi\wedge x)}\big(f_{C^{\diamond}_G\varphi}(\star)\big) = f_{C^{\diamond}_G\varphi}(\star).$$

Proof. The proof can be found in Appendix A.

Lemma 10 shows that semantic interpretation commutes with syntactic substitution.

Lemma 10. *For any Kripke model $\mathcal{M} = (W, \pi, \mathcal{K}_1, \ldots, \mathcal{K}_n, \sim)$ and any formulas $\psi \in \mathcal{L}^x_C$ and $\varphi \in \mathcal{L}_C$,*

$$f_\psi\big(f_\varphi(\star)\big) = f_{\psi[x/\varphi]}(\star).$$

Proof. The proof can be found in Appendix A.

Definition 11 (Truth and validity). *A formula $\varphi \in \mathcal{L}_C$ is* true *in a world w of a given model $\mathcal{M} = (W, \pi, \mathcal{K}_1, \ldots, \mathcal{K}_n, \sim)$ and we write $\mathcal{M}, w \vDash \varphi$ iff $w \in f_\varphi(\star)$. If $\mathcal{M}, w \vDash \varphi$ for all $w \in \mathcal{D}(\mathcal{M})$, we write $\mathcal{M} \vDash \varphi$ and say that φ is* valid *in $\mathcal{M}$. If $\mathcal{M} \vDash \varphi$ for any model $\mathcal{M} \in \mathcal{C}_{eck}$, then we write $\mathcal{C}_{eck} \vDash \varphi$ and say that φ is* valid.

Remark 12. It is not difficult to check that Definition 11 coincides with the standard semantics for the atomic propositions p, the connectives $\neg$ and $\wedge$, and the modal operators K_a and $\Box$.

2.3 Some Validities and Counterexamples

We now investigate a few expected principles and their validity with respect to the semantics introduced in Sect. 2.2. First, Lemma 13 shows that the Fixed Point Axiom is valid.

Lemma 13. *For any formula $\varphi \in \mathcal{L}_C$, we have $\mathcal{C}_{eck} \vDash C^{\diamond}_G\varphi \leftrightarrow E^{\diamond}_G(\varphi \wedge C^{\diamond}_G\varphi)$.*

Proof. For an arbitrary $\mathcal{M} = (W, \pi, \mathcal{K}_1, \ldots, \mathcal{K}_n, \sim) \in \mathcal{C}_{eck}$, we have

$$f_{C^{\diamond}_G\varphi}(\star) =_{\text{Lem.9}} f_{E^{\diamond}_G(\varphi\wedge x)}\big(f_{C^{\diamond}_G\varphi}(\star)\big) =_{\text{Lem.10}} f_{E^{\diamond}_G(\varphi\wedge C^{\diamond}_G\varphi)}(\star).$$

Therefore, $\mathcal{C}_{eck} \vDash C^{\diamond}_G\varphi \leftrightarrow E^{\diamond}_G(\varphi \wedge C^{\diamond}_G\varphi)$. □

Lemma 14. *For any formulas $\varphi, \psi \in \mathcal{L}_C$ and any group $\varnothing \neq G \subseteq \mathcal{A}$:*

$$\mathcal{C}_{eck} \vDash E_G^{\diamond}(\varphi \wedge \psi) \rightarrow (E_G^{\diamond}\varphi \wedge E_G^{\diamond}\psi).$$

Proof. Let $\mathcal{M} = (W, \pi, \mathcal{K}_1, \ldots, \mathcal{K}_n, \sim) \in \mathcal{C}_{eck}$ and $w \in W$ be such that $\mathcal{M}, w \vDash E_G^{\diamond}(\varphi \wedge \psi)$. Then $\mathcal{M}, w \vDash \bigwedge_{a \in G} \diamond K_a(\varphi \wedge \psi)$. Fix an arbitrary $a \in G$. We have $\mathcal{M}, w \vDash \diamond K_a(\varphi \wedge \psi)$, that is $\mathcal{M}, w_a \vDash K_a(\varphi \wedge \psi)$ for some w_a with $w \sim w_a$. It follows that $\mathcal{M}, w' \vDash \varphi \wedge \psi$ for any w' with $w_a \mathcal{K}_a w'$. Therefore, $\mathcal{M}, w' \vDash \varphi$ and $\mathcal{M}, w' \vDash \psi$ for any w' with $w_a \mathcal{K}_a w'$. Hence, we obtain $\mathcal{M}, w_a \vDash K_a\varphi$ and $\mathcal{M}, w_a \vDash K_a\psi$, which imply that $\mathcal{M}, w \vDash \diamond K_a\varphi$ and $\mathcal{M}, w \vDash \diamond K_a\psi$. Since $a \in G$ is arbitrary, it follows that $\mathcal{M}, w \vDash \bigwedge_{a \in G} \diamond K_a\varphi$ and $\mathcal{M}, w \vDash \bigwedge_{a \in G} \diamond K_a\psi$. Thus $\mathcal{M}, w \vDash E_G^{\diamond}\varphi \wedge E_G^{\diamond}\psi$. □

Proposition 15 states that even if the epistemic relations $\mathcal{K}_a$ are equivalence relations, eventual common knowledge is not factive: a group can have eventual common knowledge of φ at a world where φ is false.

Proposition 15. *There exists a model $\mathcal{M} = (W, \pi, \mathcal{K}_1, \ldots, \mathcal{K}_n, \sim) \in \mathcal{C}_{eck}$, a world $w \in W$, and a formula $\varphi \in \mathcal{L}_C$ such that $\mathcal{K}_1, \ldots, \mathcal{K}_n$ are equivalence relations and $\mathcal{M}, w \nvDash C_G^{\diamond}\varphi \rightarrow \varphi$ for any group $\varnothing \neq G \subseteq \mathcal{A}$.*

Proof. Consider a proposition $\varphi = p \in$ Prop and a model $\mathcal{M}$ consisting of two worlds w_1 and w_2, where $\mathcal{K}_a := \{(w_1, w_1), (w_2, w_2)\}$ for all $a \in \mathcal{A}$, $\sim := \{(w_1, w_2), (w_2, w_1), (w_1, w_1), (w_2, w_2)\}$, and $\pi(p) := \{w_2\}$. Then, for any $\varnothing \neq G \subseteq \mathcal{A}$ we have $\mathcal{M}, w_1 \vDash C_G^{\diamond}p$, but $\mathcal{M}, w_1 \nvDash p$. □

Similarly, Proposition 16 shows that eventual common knowledge fails the normality axiom: a group may have eventual common knowledge of both φ and $\varphi \rightarrow \psi$ without having eventual common knowledge of ψ.

Proposition 16. *There exists a model $\mathcal{M} = (W, \pi, \mathcal{K}_1, \ldots, \mathcal{K}_n, \sim) \in \mathcal{C}_{eck}$, a world $w \in W$, and formulas $\varphi, \psi \in \mathcal{L}_C$ such that $\mathcal{K}_1, \ldots, \mathcal{K}_n$ are equivalence relations and for any group $\varnothing \neq G \subseteq \mathcal{A}$ we have $\mathcal{M}, w \nvDash C_G^{\diamond}(\varphi \rightarrow \psi) \wedge C_G^{\diamond}\varphi \rightarrow C_G^{\diamond}\psi$.*

Proof. Consider two distinct propositions p and q and a model $\mathcal{M}$ consisting of two worlds w_1 and w_2, where $\mathcal{K}_a := \{(w_1, w_1), (w_2, w_2)\}$ for all $a \in \mathcal{A}$, $\sim := \{(w_1, w_2), (w_2, w_1), (w_1, w_1), (w_2, w_2)\}$, $\pi(p) := \{w_2\}$, and $\pi(q) := \varnothing$. Then $\mathcal{M}, w_1 \vDash C_G^{\diamond}p$ and $\mathcal{M}, w_1 \vDash C_G^{\diamond}(p \rightarrow q)$, but $\mathcal{M}, w_1 \nvDash C_G^{\diamond}q$. □

2.4 Fixed Point Approximations

Eventual common knowledge, defined as a fixed point, is not equivalent to an infinite conjunction. Halpern and Moses established this result in [8] via an analysis of the coordinated attack problem, where assumptions about unreliable communication and other features of distributed systems play an essential role. By contrast, we provide a Kripke model as a counterexample, establishing the result at a purely logical level.

Theorem 17. *1. For any formula $\varphi \in \mathcal{L}_C$ and any group $\varnothing \neq G \subseteq \mathcal{A}$:*

$$\mathcal{C}_{eck} \vDash C_G^{\diamond}\varphi \to (E_G^{\diamond})^k\varphi, \text{ for all } k > 0.$$

2. There exist a model $\mathcal{M} = (W, \pi, \mathcal{K}_1, \dots, \mathcal{K}_n, \sim) \in \mathcal{C}_{eck}$, a world $w \in W$, and a formula $\varphi \in \mathcal{L}_C$ such that for any group $\varnothing \neq G \subseteq \mathcal{A}$

$$\mathcal{M}, w \vDash (E_G^{\diamond})^k\varphi \text{ for all } k \geq 0, \text{ but } \mathcal{M}, w \nvDash C_G^{\diamond}\varphi.$$

Proof. 1. Let $k > 0$ and consider a model $\mathcal{M} = (W, \pi, \mathcal{K}_1, \dots, \mathcal{K}_n, \sim) \in \mathcal{C}_{eck}$ and a world $w \in W$ such that $\mathcal{M}, w \vDash C_G^{\diamond}\varphi$. Then we have $\mathcal{M}, w \vDash E_G^{\diamond}(\varphi \wedge C_G^{\diamond}\varphi)$ by Lemma 13. Using the same valid equivalence, we substitute $E_G^{\diamond}(\varphi \wedge C_G^{\diamond}\varphi)$ for $C_G^{\diamond}\varphi$ additional $k-1$ times and obtain

$$\mathcal{M}, w \vDash E_G^{\diamond}\Big(\varphi \wedge E_G^{\diamond}(\varphi \wedge \cdots E_G^{\diamond}(\varphi \wedge C_G^{\diamond}\varphi)\cdots)\Big)$$

where $E_G^{\diamond}$ occurs k times. It follows from Lemma 14 that

$$\mathcal{M}, w \vDash E_G^{\diamond}\varphi \wedge (E_G^{\diamond})^2\varphi \wedge \cdots \wedge (E_G^{\diamond})^k\varphi \wedge (E_G^{\diamond})^k C_G^{\diamond}\varphi.$$

Consequently, $\mathcal{M}, w \vDash (E_G^{\diamond})^k\varphi$ and we proved that $\mathcal{M}, w \vDash C_G^{\diamond}\varphi \to (E_G^{\diamond})^k\varphi$.

2. Consider the model $\mathcal{M} = (W, \pi, \mathcal{K}_1, \dots, \mathcal{K}_n, \sim)$ depicted in Fig. 1, where
- $W := \{w_{m,n} \mid m \geq 1 \text{ and } 1 \leq n \leq m+2\}$,
- $\mathcal{K}_a := \{(w_{m,n}, w_{m,n+1}) \mid m \geq 1 \text{ and } 1 \leq n \leq m+1\}$ for all $a \in \mathcal{A}$,
- $\sim$ is the equivalence relation generated by $\{(w_{m,1}, w_{m+1,1}) \mid m \geq 1\}$,
- $\pi(p) := W \setminus \{w_{m,m+2} \mid m \geq 1\}$.

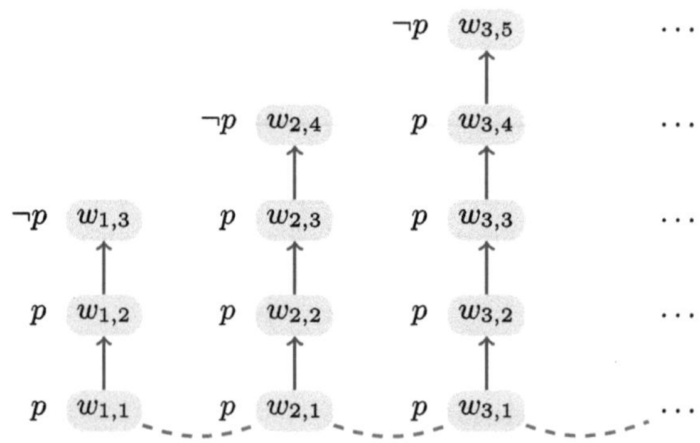

Fig. 1. The red dashed edges depict the (bidirectional) temporal relation and the blue arrows represent the epistemic relation. The reflexive loops are omitted for both relations; additionally, red dashed transitive edges are omitted. (Color figure online)

By the definition of $\sim$, it is clear that $\mathcal{M} \in \mathcal{C}_{eck}$. We observe that $\mathcal{M}, w_{m,m} \vDash K_a p$ and $\mathcal{M}, w_{m,m+1} \nvDash K_a p$ for any $m \geq 1$ and any $a \in A$. This implies that $\mathcal{M}, w_{m,m} \models E^{\diamond}_{G}p$ for any $m \geq 1$ and any group $\varnothing \neq G \subseteq \mathcal{A}$. It also follows that $\mathcal{M}, w_{m,m-l} \models (E^{\diamond}_{G})^{l+1}p$ for any $0 \leq l \leq m-1$. Consequently, $\mathcal{M}, w_{1,1} \models (E^{\diamond}_{G})^{k}p$ for any $k \geq 0$.

Next we prove that $\mathcal{M}, w_{1,1} \not\models C^{\diamond}_{G}p$.
Assume towards a contradiction that $\mathcal{M}, w_{1,1} \models C^{\diamond}_{G}p$. Then we have $\mathcal{M}, w_{1,1} \models E^{\diamond}_{G}(p \wedge C^{\diamond}_{G}p)$ by Lemma 13, and $\mathcal{M}, w_{1,1} \models E^{\diamond}_{G}p \wedge E^{\diamond}_{G}C^{\diamond}_{G}p$ by Lemma 14. It follows that $\mathcal{M}, w_{1,1} \models E^{\diamond}_{G}C^{\diamond}_{G}p$, that is $\mathcal{M}, w_{1,1} \models \bigwedge_{a \in G} \diamond K_a C^{\diamond}_{G}p$. Fix an arbitrary $a \in G$. Then we have $\mathcal{M}, w_{1,1} \models \diamond K_a C^{\diamond}_{G}p$, which implies that $\mathcal{M}, w_{m_a,1} \models K_a C^{\diamond}_{G}p$ for some $m_a \geq 1$. By construction, we then obtain $\mathcal{M}, w_{m_a,2} \models C^{\diamond}_{G}p$. As with $w_{1,1}$, we can infer that $\mathcal{M}, w_{m_a,2} \models \diamond K_a C^{\diamond}_{G}p$. But because $w_{m_a,2}$ is the only $\sim$-accessible world from $w_{m_a,2}$, it follows that $\mathcal{M}, w_{m_a,2} \models K_a C^{\diamond}_{G}p$. Again by construction, we obtain $\mathcal{M}, w_{m_a,3} \models C^{\diamond}_{G}p$. Iterating the same reasoning, we establish that $\mathcal{M}, w_{m_a,m_a+1} \models C^{\diamond}_{G}p$, which implies that $\mathcal{M}, w_{m_a,m_a+1} \models E^{\diamond}_{G}p$. Therefore, we have $\mathcal{M}, w_{m_a,m_a+1} \models \diamond K_a p$. However, because w_{m_a,m_a+1} is the only $\sim$-accessible world from w_{m_a,m_a+1}, we obtain $\mathcal{M}, w_{m_a,m_a+1} \models K_a p$ and we arrive at a contradiction. □

Lemma 19 presents a standard result (see, *e.g.*, [1]) that is useful for the completeness proof.

Definition 18. *For any formula* $\varphi \in \mathcal{L}_C$*, we define* $\varepsilon^{0}_{\varphi,G} := E^{\diamond}_{G}\varphi$ *and* $\varepsilon^{k+1}_{\varphi,G} := E^{\diamond}_{G}(\varphi \wedge \varepsilon^{k}_{\varphi,G})$ *for any* $k \geq 0$.

Lemma 19. *Consider any formula* $\varphi \in \mathcal{L}_C$*, any group* $\varnothing \neq G \subseteq \mathcal{A}$*, and any Kripke model* $\mathcal{M} = (W, \pi, \mathcal{K}_1, \ldots, \mathcal{K}_n, \sim)$*. For any ordinal* α*, we define subsets* $J^{\alpha}_{\varphi,G}$ *of* W *by*

$$J^{\alpha}_{\varphi,G} := f_{E^{\diamond}_{G}(\varphi \wedge x)}\left(\bigcap_{\beta<\alpha} J^{\beta}_{\varphi,G}\right).$$

Then we have

$$f_{C^{\diamond}_{G}\varphi}(\star) = \bigcap_{\alpha} J^{\alpha}_{\varphi,G}. \tag{1}$$

If W *is finite, then there exists some natural number* $l \leq \mathsf{card}(W)$ *such that*

$$f_{C^{\diamond}_{G}\varphi}(\star) = \bigcap_{k<l} J^{k}_{\varphi,G}. \tag{2}$$

Moreover, for any world $w \in W$ *and any natural number* $k \geq 0$*, we have*

$$w \in J^{k}_{\varphi,G} \text{ if and only if } \mathcal{M}, w \models \varepsilon^{k}_{\varphi,G}. \tag{3}$$

Proof. For equivalence (3), we have $J^{0}_{\varphi,G} = f_{E^{\diamond}_{G}(\varphi \wedge x)}(W) = f_{E^{\diamond}_{G}\varphi}(\star) = f_{\varepsilon^{0}_{\varphi,G}}(\star)$ and can prove by induction on k that $J^{k+1}_{\varphi,G} \subseteq J^{k}_{\varphi,G}$ and $J^{k}_{\varphi,G} = f_{\varepsilon^{k}_{\varphi,G}}(\star)$. □

3 Axiomatization

In this section, we present a sound and complete Hilbert-style axiomatization, called ECK, for the logic of eventual common knowledge. ECK is obtained by combining K for the epistemic modalities and S5 for the temporal modality with the Mix Axiom and the Induction Rule for $C^{\Diamond}_{G}$.

3.1 The System

We formally present the axiomatic system ECK in Definition 20 and prove in Theorem 22 that it is strongly sound with respect to the class $\mathcal{C}_{eck}$ defined in Definition 6.

Definition 20 (Axiomatic system). *The axiomatic system* ECK *consists of the following axioms and rules.*

Taut	*all propositional tautologies*
$\mathbf{K^K}$	$K_a(\varphi \to \psi) \wedge K_a\varphi \to K_a\psi$
$\mathbf{K^\Box}$	$\Box(\varphi \to \psi) \wedge \Box\varphi \to \Box\psi$
$\mathbf{T^\Box}$	$\Box\varphi \to \varphi$
$\mathbf{4^\Box}$	$\Box\varphi \to \Box\Box\varphi$
$\mathbf{5^\Box}$	$\neg\Box\varphi \to \Box\neg\Box\varphi$
Mix	$C^{\Diamond}_{G}\varphi \to E^{\Diamond}_{G}(\varphi \wedge C^{\Diamond}_{G}\varphi)$
MP	*from* φ *and* $\varphi \to \psi$, *infer* ψ
$\mathbf{Nec^K}$	*from* φ, *infer* $K_a\varphi$
$\mathbf{Nec^\Box}$	*from* φ, *infer* $\Box\varphi$
Ind	*from* $\psi \to E^{\Diamond}_{G}(\varphi \wedge \psi)$, *infer* $\psi \to C^{\Diamond}_{G}\varphi$

Definition 21 (Derivability). *A formula* φ *is* derivable *in* ECK, *written* $\vdash \varphi$, *iff there is a finite sequence* $\psi_1, \dots, \psi_k$ *of formulas such that* $\psi_k = \varphi$ *and each formula in the sequence is either an instance of one of the axioms of* ECK *or follows from earlier formulas in the sequence by one of the rules of* ECK. *A formula* φ *is derivable in* ECK *from a set* Γ *of formulas, written* $\Gamma \vdash \varphi$, *iff* $\vdash \bigwedge \Gamma_0 \to \varphi$ *for some finite* $\Gamma_0 \subseteq \Gamma$.

Theorem 22 (Soundness). *The axiomatic system* ECK *is strongly sound with respect to* $\mathcal{C}_{eck}$.

Proof. The proof is standard: one shows that all axioms are valid and all rules preserve validity.

Ind: Let $\mathcal{M} = (W, \pi, \mathcal{K}_1, \dots, \mathcal{K}_n, \sim) \in \mathcal{C}_{eck}$ be such that $\mathcal{M} \vDash \psi \to E^{\Diamond}_{G}(\varphi \wedge \psi)$. Then

$$f_\psi(\star) \subseteq f_{E^{\Diamond}_{G}(\varphi\wedge\psi)}(\star) =_{\text{Lem.10}} f_{E^{\Diamond}_{G}(\varphi\wedge x)}(f_\psi(\star)),$$

that is $f_\psi(\star) \in \{B \subseteq W \mid B \subseteq f_{E^{\Diamond}_{G}(\varphi\wedge x)}(B)\}$. Consequently, we have $f_\psi(\star) \subseteq f_{C^{\Diamond}_{G}\varphi}(\star)$ and $\mathcal{M} \vDash \psi \to C^{\Diamond}_{G}\varphi$.

The case of **Mix** follows from Lemma 13 and the remaining cases are standard. $\Box$

3.2 Completeness

The completeness proof follows the standard approach for common knowledge. For any formula $\varphi \in \mathcal{L}_C$, we construct a canonical φ-model from the maximal consistent subsets of $cl(\varphi)$. Then we prove that whenever $\nvdash \varphi$, φ is false at some world of the canonical φ-model. For this proof, we require two key lemmas. The first is Lemma 24, the *Lindenbaum Lemma*, which states that every φ-consistent set can be extended to a maximal φ-consistent set. The second is Lemma 30, the *Truth Lemma*, which states that every formula $\chi \in cl(\varphi)$ is true at a world Γ of the canonical φ-model if and only if $\chi \in \Gamma$.

Definition 23 (Maximal consistent). *Let $\varphi \in \mathcal{L}_C$ be given. A set Γ of formulas is* φ-consistent *iff $\Gamma \subseteq cl(\varphi)$ and $\Gamma \nvdash \bot$. Moreover, if no Γ' with $\Gamma \subsetneq \Gamma'$ is φ-consistent, we say that Γ is* maximal φ-consistent. *We define $Con(\varphi)$ to consist of all maximal φ-consistent sets.*

The proof of Lemma 24 is standard (see, *e.g.*, Sect. 7.3 of [20]) and is therefore omitted.

Lemma 24 (Lindenbaum). *Let $\varphi \in \mathcal{L}_C$ be given. Every φ-consistent set of formulas is a subset of a maximal φ-consistent set of formulas.*

To establish Lemma 30, we first derive several properties of maximal φ-consistent sets. A particularly unusual and crucial one is Item 6 of Lemma 25. This property is closely related to the semantic fact that $\Diamond K_a\chi$ either holds at all points in time or at none. It is precisely here that the choice of equivalence relation for the temporal modality proves essential.

Lemma 25. *Let $\varphi \in \mathcal{L}_C$ be given. For any set $\Gamma \in Con(\varphi)$ and any formulas $\chi, \chi' \in cl(\varphi)$:*

1. *If $\Gamma \vdash \chi$, then $\chi \in \Gamma$.*
2. *If $\chi \in \Gamma$ and $\chi \to \chi' \in \Gamma$, then $\chi' \in \Gamma$.*
3. *If $\chi \in \Gamma$, then $\neg\chi \notin \Gamma$. Additionally, if $\neg\chi \in cl(\varphi) \setminus \Gamma$, then $\chi \in \Gamma$.*
4. *If $\chi \wedge \chi' \in \Gamma$, then $\chi \in \Gamma$ and $\chi' \in \Gamma$. Additionally, if $\chi \in \Gamma$ and $\chi' \in \Gamma$ and $\chi \wedge \chi' \in cl(\varphi)$, then $\chi \wedge \chi' \in \Gamma$.*
5. *$\{K_a\top \mid a \in \mathcal{A}\} \subset \Gamma$.*
6. *For $a \in \mathcal{A}$, we have $\{K_a\chi \mid K_a\chi \in \Gamma\} \neq \varnothing$, $\Diamond(\bigwedge_{K_a\chi\in\Gamma} K_a\chi) \in \Gamma$, and $\Box\Diamond(\bigwedge_{K_a\chi\in\Gamma} K_a\chi) \in \Gamma$.*

Proof. Proofs of Items 1–5 are standard.

Item 6 **:** It follows from Item 5 that $\{K_a\chi \mid K_a\chi \in \Gamma\} \neq \varnothing$. Moreover by Definition 3, we have $\{K_a\chi \mid K_a\chi \in \Gamma\} \subseteq K_a^{\varphi}$, $\Diamond(\bigwedge_{K_a\chi\in\Gamma} K_a\chi) \in cl(\varphi)$, and $\Box\Diamond(\bigwedge_{K_a\chi\in\Gamma} K_a\chi) \in cl(\varphi)$. Since $\vdash \bigwedge_{K_a\chi\in\Gamma} K_a\chi \to \Diamond(\bigwedge_{K_a\chi\in\Gamma} K_a\chi)$ by $\mathbf{T}^{\Box}$, it follows from Item 1 that $\Diamond(\bigwedge_{K_a\chi\in\Gamma} K_a\chi) \in \Gamma$. Finally, given that by $\mathbf{5}^{\Box}$ we have $\vdash \Diamond(\bigwedge_{K_a\chi\in\Gamma} K_a\chi) \to \Box\Diamond(\bigwedge_{K_a\chi\in\Gamma} K_a\chi)$, it follows from Item 1 that $\Box\Diamond(\bigwedge_{K_a\chi\in\Gamma} K_a\chi) \in \Gamma$. □

For any finite set Δ of formulas, we denote $\underline{\Delta} := \bigwedge_{\chi \in \Delta} \chi$.

Lemma 26. *For any formula $\varphi \in \mathcal{L}_C$,*

1. $\vdash \bigvee_{\Gamma \in Con(\varphi)} \underline{\Gamma}$,
2. $\vdash \neg\underline{\Gamma} \vee \neg\underline{\Delta}$ *for any distinct* $\Gamma, \Delta \in Con(\varphi)$,
3. $\vdash \bigvee_{\Gamma \in S} \underline{\Gamma} \leftrightarrow \bigwedge_{\Delta \in Con(\varphi) \setminus S} \neg\underline{\Delta}$ *for any* $S \subseteq Con(\varphi)$.

We now formally define the canonical φ-model and prove that it is indeed of the correct kind.

Definition 27 (Canonical model). *Let a formula $\varphi \in \mathcal{L}_C$ be given. The* canonical φ-model $\mathcal{M}^\varphi = (W^\varphi, \pi^\varphi, \mathcal{K}_1^\varphi, \ldots, \mathcal{K}_n^\varphi, \sim^\varphi)$ *is defined as follows*

- $W^\varphi := Con(\varphi)$
- $\pi^\varphi(p) := \{\Gamma \in W^\varphi \mid p \in \Gamma\}$
- $\mathcal{K}_a^\varphi := \{(\Gamma, \Delta) \mid \forall K_a\chi \in \Gamma, \chi \in \Delta\}$ *for all* $a \in \mathcal{A}$
- $\sim^\varphi := \{(\Gamma, \Delta) \mid \forall \Box\chi \in \Gamma, \chi \in \Delta\}$

Lemma 28. *For any formula $\varphi \in \mathcal{L}_C$, the canonical φ-model $\mathcal{M}^\varphi$ from Definition 27 is in the class C_{eck}. Moreover, W^φ is finite and non-empty.*

Proof. The proof can be found in Appendix A.

Lemma 29 establishes a property of the canonical φ-model, namely that any world containing an eventual common knowledge formula has a $\sim^\varphi$-reachable world.

Lemma 29. *Let $\varphi \in \mathcal{L}_C$ and $\Delta \in Con(\varphi)$ be given. Assume that $C_G^\diamond\theta \in \Delta$ for some formula θ. Then the set*

$$S_\Delta^a := \{\Sigma \in Con(\varphi) \mid \Delta \sim^\varphi \Sigma \text{ and } K_a(\theta \wedge C_G^\diamond\theta) \in \Sigma\}$$

is non-empty for any $a \in \mathcal{A}$.

Proof. The proof can be found in Appendix A.

We are now ready to prove Lemma 30 and, subsequently, Theorem 31.

Lemma 30 (Truth). *For any formulas $\varphi \in \mathcal{L}_C$ and $\chi \in cl(\varphi)$, for any set $\Gamma \in Con(\varphi)$:*

$$\chi \in \Gamma \text{ iff } \mathcal{M}^\varphi, \Gamma \vDash \chi.$$

Proof. The cases of $p, \neg\theta, \theta_1 \wedge \theta_2, K_a\theta, \Box\theta$ are standard. We proceed for $C_G^\diamond\theta$ with the induction hypothesis:

θ**IH :** $\theta \in \Gamma$ iff $\mathcal{M}^\varphi, \Gamma \vDash \theta$.

($\Rightarrow$) Assume that $C_G^\diamond\theta \in \Gamma$. Because $Con(\varphi)$ is finite, we can prove that $\mathcal{M}^\varphi, \Gamma \vDash C_G^\diamond\theta$ by showing that for any natural number k and any $\Delta \in Con(\varphi)$, $C_G^\diamond\theta \in \Delta$ implies that $\Delta \in J_{\theta,G}^k$ where $J_{\theta,G}^k$ is as defined in Lemma 19.

For $k = 0$: Assume that $C^{\diamond}_G\theta \in \Delta$ and let $a \in G$. Then by Lemma 29, there is some $\Sigma^{\diamond} \in Con(\varphi)$ such that $\Delta \sim^{\varphi} \Sigma^{\diamond}$ and $K_a(\theta \wedge C^{\diamond}_G\theta) \in \Sigma^{\diamond}$. Consider any arbitrary $\Sigma^a \in Con(\varphi)$ such that $\Sigma^{\diamond}\mathcal{K}^{\varphi}_a\Sigma^a$. Then we have $\theta \wedge C^{\diamond}_G\theta \in \Sigma^a$ which implies that $\theta \in \Sigma^a$ and $C^{\diamond}_G\theta \in \Sigma^a$. Consequently $\mathcal{M}^{\varphi}, \Sigma^a \models \theta$ by θIH. Because Σ^a is arbitrary, we obtain $\mathcal{M}^{\varphi}, \Sigma^{\diamond} \models K_a\theta$ and $\mathcal{M}^{\varphi}, \Delta \models \diamond K_a\theta$. Again because $a \in G$ is arbitrary, we have $\mathcal{M}^{\varphi}, \Delta \models E^{\diamond}_G\theta$ and $E^{\diamond}_G\theta = \varepsilon^0_{\theta,G}$ so we can conclude by Lemma 19 that $\Delta \in J^0_{\theta,G}$.

kIH: For any $k \leq l$ and any $\Delta \in Con(\varphi)$, $C^{\diamond}_G\theta \in \Delta$ implies that $\Delta \in J^k_{\theta,G}$.

For $k = l+1$: Assume that $C^{\diamond}_G\theta \in \Delta$ and consider any $a \in G$. Then by Lemma 29, there is some $\Sigma^{\diamond} \in Con(\varphi)$ such that $\Delta \sim^{\varphi} \Sigma^{\diamond}$ and $K_a(\theta \wedge C^{\diamond}_G\theta) \in \Sigma^{\diamond}$. Consider any arbitrary $\Sigma^a \in Con(\varphi)$ such that $\Sigma^{\diamond}\mathcal{K}^{\varphi}_a\Sigma^a$. Then we have $\theta \wedge C^{\diamond}_G\theta \in \Sigma^a$ which implies that $\theta \in \Sigma^a$ and $C^{\diamond}_G\theta \in \Sigma^a$. Consequently $\mathcal{M}^{\varphi}, \Sigma^a \models \theta$ by θIH and $\Sigma^a \in J^l_{\theta,G}$ by kIH. It follows from Lemma 19 that $\mathcal{M}^{\varphi}, \Sigma^a \models \varepsilon^l_{\theta,G}$. Therefore, $\mathcal{M}^{\varphi}, \Sigma^a \models \theta \wedge \varepsilon^l_{\theta,G}$. Because Σ^a is arbitrary, we obtain $\mathcal{M}^{\varphi}, \Sigma^{\diamond} \models K_a(\theta \wedge \varepsilon^l_{\theta,G})$ and hence $\mathcal{M}^{\varphi}, \Delta \models \diamond K_a(\theta \wedge \varepsilon^l_{\theta,G})$. Again because $a \in G$ is arbitrary, we have $\mathcal{M}^{\varphi}, \Delta \models E^{\diamond}_G(\theta \wedge \varepsilon^l_{\theta,G})$. But because $E^{\diamond}_G(\theta \wedge \varepsilon^l_{\theta,G}) = \varepsilon^{l+1}_{\theta,G}$, we can conclude by Lemma 19 that $\Delta \in J^{l+1}_{\theta,G}$.

($\Leftarrow$) Assume that $\mathcal{M}^{\varphi}, \Gamma \models C^{\diamond}_G\theta$. Let $C_\theta := \{\Delta \in Con(\varphi) \mid \mathcal{M}^{\varphi}, \Delta \models C^{\diamond}_G\theta\}$ and $C^{\not\models}_\theta := Con(\varphi) \setminus C_\theta$. We first prove that for any $\Delta \in C_\theta$ we have $\vdash \underline{\Delta} \to E^{\diamond}_G\left(\theta \wedge \bigwedge_{\Sigma \in C^{\not\models}_\theta} \neg\underline{\Sigma}\right)$.

Consider any arbitrary $\Delta \in C_\theta$. We have $\mathcal{M}^{\varphi}, \Delta \models E^{\diamond}_G(\theta \wedge C^{\diamond}_G\theta)$; that is $\mathcal{M}^{\varphi}, \Delta \models \diamond K_a(\theta \wedge C^{\diamond}_G\theta)$ for each $a \in G$. Fix $a \in G$. We have $\mathcal{M}^{\varphi}, \Delta_a \models K_a(\theta \wedge C^{\diamond}_G\theta)$ for some $\Delta_a \in Con(\varphi)$ with $\Delta \sim^{\varphi} \Delta_a$. Fix such Δ_a. Then we have $\mathcal{M}^{\varphi}, \Lambda \models \theta$ and $\mathcal{M}^{\varphi}, \Lambda \models C^{\diamond}_G\theta$ for any $\Lambda \in Con(\varphi)$ such that $\Delta_a\mathcal{K}^{\varphi}_a\Lambda$.
On the one hand, it follows that $\{\chi \mid K_a\chi \in \Delta_a\} \cup \{\neg\theta\}$ is not φ-consistent; otherwise it can be extended to some $\Lambda \in Con(\varphi)$ by Lemma 24, but by construction we have $\neg\theta \in \Lambda$ and $\Delta_a\mathcal{K}^{\varphi}_a\Lambda$, the latter implying $\theta \in \Lambda$ by θIH. Thus we obtain $\vdash \bigwedge_{K_a\chi \in \Delta_a} \chi \to \theta$ and

$$\vdash \bigwedge_{K_a\chi \in \Delta_a} K_a\chi \to K_a\theta. \tag{4}$$

On the other hand, if $\Sigma \in C^{\not\models}_\theta$, then we do not have $\Delta_a\mathcal{K}^{\varphi}_a\Sigma$. Therefore, we obtain some $\chi_\Sigma \in \mathcal{L}_C$ such that $K_a\chi_\Sigma \in \Delta_a$ but $\chi_\Sigma \notin \Sigma$ for each $\Sigma \in C^{\not\models}_\theta$. For such a set Σ, we have $\neg\chi_\Sigma \in \Sigma$ and

$$\vdash \underline{\Sigma} \to \neg\chi_\Sigma,$$
$$\vdash \chi_\Sigma \to \neg\underline{\Sigma},$$
$$\vdash K_a\chi_\Sigma \to K_a\neg\underline{\Sigma},$$

$$\vdash \bigwedge_{K_a\chi \in \Delta_a} K_a\chi \to K_a\neg\underline{\Sigma}. \tag{5}$$

It follows from (4) and (5) that $\vdash \bigwedge_{K_a\chi\in\Delta_a} K_a\chi \to K_a\left(\theta \wedge \bigwedge_{\Sigma\in C_\theta^{\not\models}} \neg\underline{\Sigma}\right)$ and

$$\vdash \Diamond \bigwedge_{K_a\chi\in\Delta_a} K_a\chi \to \Diamond K_a\left(\theta \wedge \bigwedge_{\Sigma\in C_\theta^{\not\models}} \neg\underline{\Sigma}\right). \tag{6}$$

By Item 6 of Lemma 25, we have $\Box\Diamond \bigwedge_{K_a\chi\in\Delta_a} K_a\chi \in \Delta_a$. Because $\Delta \sim^{\varphi} \Delta_a$ and $\sim^{\varphi}$ is an equivalence relation, it follows that $\Diamond \bigwedge_{K_a\chi\in\Delta_a} K_a\chi \in \Delta$. Therefore,

$$\vdash \underline{\Delta} \to \Diamond K_a\left(\theta \wedge \bigwedge_{\Sigma\in C_\theta^{\not\models}} \neg\underline{\Sigma}\right). \tag{7}$$

Because $a \in G$ is arbitrary, we then obtain

$$\vdash \underline{\Delta} \to E_G^{\Diamond}\left(\theta \wedge \bigwedge_{\Sigma\in C_\theta^{\not\models}} \neg\underline{\Sigma}\right). \tag{8}$$

Using Item 3 of Lemma 26 and the fact that $\Delta \in C_\theta$ is arbitrary, we obtain

$$\vdash \bigvee_{\Delta\in C_\theta} \underline{\Delta} \to E_G^{\Diamond}\left(\theta \wedge \bigvee_{\Delta\in C_\theta} \underline{\Delta}\right). \tag{9}$$

By **Ind**, we have $\vdash \bigvee_{\Delta\in C_\theta} \underline{\Delta} \to C_G^{\Diamond}\theta$. Consequently, we have $\vdash \underline{\Gamma} \to C_G^{\Diamond}\theta$ and we can conclude following Item 1 of Lemma 25 that $C_G^{\Diamond}\theta \in \Gamma$. □

Theorem 31 (Completeness). *The axiomatic system* ECK *is complete w.r.t. the class* $\mathcal{C}_{eck}$.

Proof. Let $\varphi \in \mathcal{L}_C$ be such that $\nvdash \varphi$. Then $\{\neg\varphi\}$ is φ-consistent. By Lemma 24, $\neg\varphi \in \Gamma$ for some $\Gamma \in Con(\varphi)$. It follows from Lemma 30 that $\mathcal{M}^{\varphi}, \Gamma \models \neg\varphi$. Thus $\not\models \varphi$. □

3.3 Decidability

As shown in Sect. 3.2, the canonical φ-model $\mathcal{M}^{\varphi}$ provides a finite countermodel for any $\varphi \in \mathcal{L}_C$ with $\nvdash \varphi$. Therefore, we can immediately conclude the following standard results.

Proposition 32. *The logic* ECK *has the finite model property.*

Proposition 33. *The logic* ECK *is decidable.*

4 Conclusion

In this paper we investigated the logic of eventual common knowledge and provided a sound and complete Hilbert-style axiomatization. The completeness proof relies on a canonical model construction based on an appropriate closure condition on formulas. As shown, this construction yields finite countermodels, which in turn implies the finite model property and decidability of the logic.

We also established that eventual common knowledge differs substantially from standard common knowledge: it is not equivalent to an infinite conjunction of iterated operators, is not factive, and fails the normality axiom. Finally, although the framework developed here allows arbitrary accessibility relations for individual knowledge operators, the completeness proof can be straightforwardly adapted to more restricted frame classes.

Acknowledgments. The authors thank the anonymous reviewers for their constructive feedback and comments. Rojo Randrianomentsoa and Thomas Studer were supported by the Swiss National Science Foundation (SNSF) under grant number 10000440 (Epistemic Group Attitudes). Roman Kuznets was supported by ERDF-Project Knowledge in the Age of Distrust, No. CZ.02.01.01/00/23_025/0008711.

Disclosure of Interests. The authors declare no competing interests.

A Appendix

Lemma 9. *For any Kripke model* $\mathcal{M} = (W, \pi, \mathcal{K}_1, \ldots, \mathcal{K}_n, \sim)$ *and any formula* $\varphi \in \mathcal{L}_C$,

$$f_{E^{\diamond}_G(\varphi \wedge x)}\big(f_{C^{\diamond}_G\varphi}(\star)\big) = f_{C^{\diamond}_G\varphi}(\star).$$

Proof. $\supseteq$: For an arbitrary $C \in \{B \subseteq W \mid B \subseteq f_{E^{\diamond}_G(\varphi\wedge x)}(B)\}$, we have $C \subseteq f_{C^{\diamond}_G\varphi}(\star)$ by definition. Therefore, $f_{E^{\diamond}_G(\varphi\wedge x)}(C) \subseteq f_{E^{\diamond}_G(\varphi\wedge x)}\big(f_{C^{\diamond}_G\varphi}(\star)\big)$ because $f_{E^{\diamond}_G(\varphi\wedge x)}$ is monotone increasing by Lemma 8. It follows that $C \subseteq f_{E^{\diamond}_G(\varphi\wedge x)}\big(f_{C^{\diamond}_G\varphi}(\star)\big)$. Since C is arbitrary, we conclude that $f_{C^{\diamond}_G\varphi}(\star) \subseteq f_{E^{\diamond}_G(\varphi\wedge x)}\big(f_{C^{\diamond}_G\varphi}(\star)\big)$.

$\subseteq$: From the previous item and the fact that $f_{E^{\diamond}_G(\varphi\wedge x)}$ is monotone increasing, it follows that $f_{E^{\diamond}_G(\varphi\wedge x)}\big(f_{C^{\diamond}_G\varphi}(\star)\big) \in \{B \subseteq W \mid B \subseteq f_{E^{\diamond}_G(\varphi\wedge x)}(B)\}$. This entails the other inclusion. □

Lemma 10. *For any Kripke model* $\mathcal{M} = (W, \pi, \mathcal{K}_1, \ldots, \mathcal{K}_n, \sim)$ *and any formulas* $\psi \in \mathcal{L}^x_C$ *and* $\varphi \in \mathcal{L}_C$,

$$f_\psi\big(f_\varphi(\star)\big) = f_{\psi[x/\varphi]}(\star).$$

Proof. We proceed by induction on the structure of $\psi \in \mathcal{L}^x_C$.

For $\psi \in \mathcal{L}_C$**:** In this case, there is no occurrence of x in ψ. Therefore, we have $\psi[x/\varphi] = \psi$ and $f_\psi\big(f_\varphi(\star)\big) = f_\psi(\star) = f_{\psi[x/\varphi]}(\star)$.

For $\psi = x$**:** We have $\psi[x/\varphi] = \varphi$ and $f_\psi\big(f_\varphi(\star)\big) = f_\varphi(\star) = f_{\psi[x/\varphi]}(\star)$.

For $\psi = \neg\chi$: We have $f_\psi(f_\varphi(\star)) = W \setminus f_\chi(f_\varphi(\star)) =_{\text{IH}} W \setminus f_{\chi[x/\varphi]}(\star) = f_{\psi[x/\varphi]}(\star)$.

For $\psi = \chi_1 \wedge \chi_2$: We have

$$\begin{aligned} f_\psi(f_\varphi(\star)) &= f_{\chi_1\wedge\chi_2}(f_\varphi(\star)) \\ &= f_{\chi_1}(f_\varphi(\star)) \cap f_{\chi_2}(f_\varphi(\star)) \\ &=_{\text{IH}} f_{\chi_1[x/\varphi]}(\star) \cap f_{\chi_2[x/\varphi]}(\star) \\ &= f_{\chi_1[x/\varphi]\wedge\chi_2[x/\varphi]}(\star) \\ &= f_{(\chi_1\wedge\chi_2)[x/\varphi]}(\star) \\ &= f_{\psi[x/\varphi]}(\star). \end{aligned}$$

For $\psi = K_a\chi$: We have

$$\begin{aligned} f_\psi(f_\varphi(\star)) &= f_{K_a\chi}(f_\varphi(\star)) \\ &= \{w \mid w' \in f_\chi(f_\varphi(\star)) \text{ for all } w' \text{ s.t. } w\mathcal{K}_a w'\} \\ &=_{\text{IH}} \{w \mid w' \in f_{\chi[x/\varphi]}(\star) \text{ for all } w' \text{ s.t. } w\mathcal{K}_a w'\} \\ &= f_{K_a(\chi[x/\varphi])}(\star) \\ &= f_{(K_a\chi)[x/\varphi]}(\star) \\ &= f_{\psi[x/\varphi]}(\star). \end{aligned}$$

For $\psi = \Box\chi$: We have

$$\begin{aligned} f_\psi(f_\varphi(\star)) &= f_{\Box\chi}(f_\varphi(\star)) \\ &= \{w \mid w' \in f_\chi(f_\varphi(\star)) \text{ for all } w' \text{ s.t. } w \sim w'\} \\ &=_{\text{IH}} \{w \mid w' \in f_{\chi[x/\varphi]}(\star) \text{ for all } w' \text{ s.t. } w \sim w'\} \\ &= f_{\Box(\chi[x/\varphi])}(\star) \\ &= f_{(\Box\chi)[x/\varphi]}(\star) \\ &= f_{\psi[x/\varphi]}(\star). \end{aligned}$$

□

Lemma 28. *For any formula $\varphi \in \mathcal{L}_C$, the canonical φ-model $\mathcal{M}^\varphi$ from Definition 27 is in the class $\mathcal{C}_{eck}$. Moreover, W^φ is finite* and non-empty.

Proof. $W^\varphi \neq \varnothing$ follows from the fact that, for any world w of any model $\mathcal{M} \in \mathcal{C}_{eck}$, we have $cl(\varphi) \cap \{\chi \mid \mathcal{M}, w \vDash \chi\} \in Con(\varphi)$ by Theorem 22. It remains to prove that $\sim^\varphi$ is an equivalence relation.

Reflexivity: By $\mathbf{T}^\Box$ and Item 1 of Lemma 25, $\chi \in \Gamma$ whenever $\Box\chi \in \Gamma$. Hence, $\Gamma \sim^\varphi \Gamma$.

Transitivity: Assume that $\Gamma_1 \sim^\varphi \Gamma_2$ and $\Gamma_2 \sim^\varphi \Gamma_3$. Let $\Box\chi \in \Gamma_1$.

- Assume that $\Box\chi \in cl_3(\varphi) \subset cl(\varphi)$. By Definition 3, we have $\Box\Box\chi \in cl(\varphi)$. By $\mathbf{4}^\Box$ and Item 1 of Lemma 25, it follows that $\Box\Box\chi \in \Gamma_1$. Therefore, we obtain $\Box\chi \in \Gamma_2$ and $\chi \in \Gamma_3$.

- Assume that $\Box\chi \in cl(\varphi) \setminus cl_3(\varphi)$. Then we have two cases:
  - Case $\chi = \Box\theta$ for some $\Box\theta \in cl_3(\varphi)$. Because $\Box\Box\theta \in \Gamma_1$, we have $\Box\theta \in \Gamma_2$. By $\mathbf{4}^{\Box}$ and Item 1 of Lemma 25, we obtain $\Box\Box\theta \in \Gamma_2$. It follows that $\chi = \Box\theta \in \Gamma_3$.
  - Case $\chi = \neg\Box\theta$ for some $\neg\Box\theta \in cl_3(\varphi)$. Because $\Box\neg\Box\theta \in \Gamma_1$, we have $\neg\Box\theta \in \Gamma_2$. By $\mathbf{5}^{\Box}$ and Item 1 of Lemma 25, we obtain $\Box\neg\Box\theta \in \Gamma_2$. It follows that $\chi = \neg\Box\theta \in \Gamma_3$.

Euclideanity: Assume that $\Gamma_1 \sim^{\varphi} \Gamma_2$ and $\Gamma_1 \sim^{\varphi} \Gamma_3$. Let $\Box\chi \in \Gamma_2$. By Lemma 4, $\neg\Box\chi \in cl(\varphi)$. To show that $\chi \in \Gamma_3$, it suffices to show that $\Box\chi \in \Gamma_1$.

- Assume that $\neg\Box\chi \in cl_3(\varphi) \subset cl(\varphi)$. By Definition 3, we have $\Box\neg\Box\chi \in cl(\varphi)$. Because $\Box\chi \in \Gamma_2$ and $\Gamma_1 \sim^{\varphi} \Gamma_2$, it follows that $\neg\Box\chi \notin \Gamma_2$ and $\Box\neg\Box\chi \notin \Gamma_1$. If $\neg\Box\chi \in \Gamma_1$, we would have $\Box\neg\Box\chi \in \Gamma_1$ by $\mathbf{5}^{\Box}$ and Item 1 of Lemma 25. Consequently, $\neg\Box\chi \notin \Gamma_1$ and $\Box\chi \in \Gamma_1$.
- Assume that $\neg\Box\chi \in cl(\varphi) \setminus cl_3(\varphi)$. Then we have two cases:
  - Case $\chi = \Box\theta$ for some $\Box\theta \in cl_3(\varphi)$. By Definition 3, $\Box\neg\Box\theta \in cl(\varphi)$. By $\mathbf{T}^{\Box}$ and Item 1 of Lemma 25, $\Box\theta \in \Gamma_2$. Consequently $\neg\Box\theta \notin \Gamma_2$ and hence $\Box\neg\Box\theta \notin \Gamma_1$. If $\neg\Box\theta \in \Gamma_1$, we would have $\Box\neg\Box\theta \in \Gamma_1$ by $\mathbf{5}^{\Box}$ and Item 1 of Lemma 25. Therefore, $\neg\Box\theta \notin \Gamma_1$ and $\Box\theta \in \Gamma_1$. It follows from $\mathbf{4}^{\Box}$ and Item 1 of Lemma 25 that $\Box\chi = \Box\Box\theta \in \Gamma_1$.
  - Case $\chi = \neg\Box\theta$ for some $\neg\Box\theta \in cl_3(\varphi)$. By Definition 3, $\Box\Box\theta \in cl(\varphi)$. By $\mathbf{T}^{\Box}$ and Item 1 of Lemma 25, we have $\neg\Box\theta \in \Gamma_2$. Consequently $\Box\theta \notin \Gamma_2$ and hence $\Box\Box\theta \notin \Gamma_1$. If $\Box\theta \in \Gamma_1$, we would have $\Box\Box\theta \in \Gamma_1$ by $\mathbf{4}^{\Box}$ and Item 1 of Lemma 25. Therefore, $\Box\theta \notin \Gamma_1$ and $\neg\Box\theta \in \Gamma_1$. It follows from $\mathbf{5}^{\Box}$ and Item 1 of Lemma 25 that $\Box\chi = \Box\neg\Box\theta \in \Gamma_1$.

□

Lemma 29. *Let $\varphi \in \mathcal{L}_C$ and $\Delta \in Con(\varphi)$ be given. Assume that $C_G^{\Diamond}\theta \in \Delta$ for some formula θ. Then the set*

$$S_{\Delta}^{a} := \{\Sigma \in Con(\varphi) \mid \Delta \sim^{\varphi} \Sigma \text{ and } K_a(\theta \wedge C_G^{\Diamond}\theta) \in \Sigma\}$$

is non-empty for any $a \in \mathcal{A}$.

Proof. Consider any $a \in \mathcal{A}$. By assumption, we have $C_G^{\Diamond}\theta \in cl(\varphi)$. It follows by Definition 3 that $E_G^{\Diamond}(\theta \wedge C_G^{\Diamond}\theta) \in cl(\varphi)$, $\neg\Box\neg K_a(\theta \wedge C_G^{\Diamond}\theta) \in cl(\varphi)$, and $K_a(\theta \wedge C_G^{\Diamond}\theta) \in cl(\varphi)$. Then because $\{K_a(\theta \wedge C_G^{\Diamond}\theta)\}$ is φ-consistent, it can be extended to a maximal φ-consistent set by Lemma 24. Consequently, the set $S_{\theta}^{a} := \{\Sigma \in Con(\varphi) \mid K_a(\theta \wedge C_G^{\Diamond}\theta) \in \Sigma\}$ is non-empty.
Assume towards a contradiction that for any $\Sigma \in S_{\theta}^{a}$ we do not have $\Delta \sim^{\varphi} \Sigma$. Then for each $\Sigma \in S_{\theta}^{a}$, there is some formula $\chi_{\Sigma} \in cl(\varphi)$ such that $\Box\chi_{\Sigma} \in \Delta$ but $\chi_{\Sigma} \notin \Sigma$. It follows that the set $\{\chi_{\Sigma} \mid \Sigma \in S_{\theta}^{a}\} \cup \{K_a(\theta \wedge C_G^{\Diamond}\theta)\}$ is not φ-consistent, otherwise it would be a subset of some element of S_{θ}^{a} and that would lead to a contradiction. Therefore,

$$\vdash \bigwedge_{\Sigma \in S_{\theta}^{a}} \chi_{\Sigma} \to \neg K_a(\theta \wedge C_G^{\Diamond}\theta).$$

Consequently,

$$\vdash \bigwedge_{\Sigma \in S_\theta^a} \Box \chi_\Sigma \to \Box \neg K_a(\theta \wedge C_G^\Diamond \theta),$$

and by Lemma 25 we obtain $\Box \neg K_a(\theta \wedge C_G^\Diamond \theta) \in \Delta$. However, this leads to a contradiction because $C_G^\Diamond \theta \in \Delta$ and $\vdash C_G^\Diamond \theta \to \neg \Box \neg K_a(\theta \wedge C_G^\Diamond \theta)$. □

References

1. Barwise, J.: Admissible Sets and Structures, vol. 7. Perspectives in Logic. Cambridge University Press (2017). https://doi.org/10.1017/9781316717196
2. Brandenburger, A., Dekel, E.: Common knowledge with probability 1. J. Math. Econ. **16**(3), 237–245 (1987). https://doi.org/10.1016/0304-4068(87)90010-3
3. Brünnler, K., Flumini, D., Studer, T.: A logic of blockchain updates. J. Log. Comput. **30**(8), 1469–1485 (2020). https://doi.org/10.1093/logcom/exaa045
4. Bucheli, S., Kuznets, R., Studer, T.: Two ways to common knowledge. Electronic Notes Theor. Comput. Sci. **26**(2), 83–98 (2010). In: Proceedings of the 6th Workshop on Methods for Modalities (M4M-6 2009). https://doi.org/10.1016/j.entcs.2010.04.007
5. Fagin, R., Halpern, J.Y., Moses, Y., Vardi, M.Y.: Reasoning About Knowledge. MIT Press (1995). https://doi.org/10.7551/mitpress/5803.001.0001
6. Fruzsa, K., Kuznets, R., Schmid, U.: Fire! In: Halpern, J., Perea, A. (eds.) Proceedings of the Eighteenth Conference on Theoretical Aspects of Rationality and Knowledge, Beijing, China, June 25–27, 2021, vol. 335. Electronic Proceedings in Theoretical Computer Science, pp. 139–153. Open Publishing Association (2021). https://doi.org/10.4204/EPTCS.335.13
7. Gonczarowski, Y.A., Moses, Y.: Common knowledge, regained. In: EC 2024: Proceedings of the 25th Conference on Economics and Computation, p. 208. Association for Computing Machinery (2024). https://doi.org/10.1145/3670865.3673442
8. Halpern, J.Y., Moses, Y.: Knowledge and common knowledge in a distributed environment. J. ACM **37**(3), 549–587 (1990). https://doi.org/10.1145/79147.79161
9. Halpern, J.Y., Pass, R.: A knowledge-based analysis of the blockchain protocol. In: Lang, J. (ed.) Proceedings of the Sixteenth Conference on Theoretical Aspects of Rationality and Knowledge, Liverpool, UK, 24–26 July 2017, number 251 in Electronic Proceedings in Theoretical Computer Science, pp. 324–335 (2017). https://doi.org/10.4204/EPTCS.251.22
10. Halpern, J.Y., Tuttle, M.R.: Knowledge, probability, and adversaries. J. ACM **40**(4), 917–960 (1993). https://doi.org/10.1145/153724.153770
11. Marinković, B., Glavan, P., Ognjanović, Z., Doder, D., Studer, T.: Probabilistic consensus of the blockchain protocol. In: Kern-Isberner, G., Ognjanović, Z. (eds.) Symbolic and Quantitative Approaches to Reasoning with Uncertainty: 15th European Conference, ECSQARU 2019, Belgrade, Serbia, September 18–20, 2019, Proceedings, vol. 11726. Lecture Notes in Artificial Intelligence, pp. 469–480. Springer (2019). https://doi.org/10.1007/978-3-030-29765-7_39
12. Marinković, B., Glavan, P., Ognjanović, Z., Studer, T.: A temporal epistemic logic with a non-rigid set of agents for analyzing the blockchain protocol. J. Log. Comput. **29**(5), 803–830 (2019). https://doi.org/10.1093/logcom/exz007

13. Ch Meyer, J.-J., van der Hoek, W.: Epistemic Logic for AI and Computer Science, vol. 41. Cambridge Tracts in Theoretical Computer Science. Cambridge University Press (1995). https://doi.org/10.1017/CBO9780511569852
14. Turata, G.M.: An ill-founded proof system for eventual common knowledge logic with finite-past modalities. in preparation
15. Morris, S.: Coordination, timing and common knowledge. Res. Econ. **68**(4), 306–314 (2014). https://doi.org/10.1016/j.rie.2014.04.004
16. Ognjanović, Z., Stepić, A.I., Perović, A.: A probabilistic temporal epistemic logic: strong completeness. Logic J. IGPL **32**(1), 94–138 (2024). https://doi.org/10.1093/jigpal/jzac072
17. Ognjanović, Z., Stepić, A.I., Perović, A.: A probabilistic temporal epistemic logic: decidability. Logic J. IGPL **32**(5), 827–879 (2024). https://doi.org/10.1093/jigpal/jzac080
18. Panangaden, P., Taylor, K.: Concurrent common knowledge: defining agreement for asynchronous systems. Distrib. Comput. **6**(2), 73–93 (1992). https://doi.org/10.1007/BF02252679
19. Srikanth, T.K., Toueg, S.: Optimal clock synchronization. J. ACM **34**(3), 626–645 (1987). https://doi.org/10.1145/28869.28876
20. van Ditmarsch, H., van der Hoek, W., Kooi, B.: Dynamic Epistemic Logic, vol. 337. Synthese Library. Springer (2007). https://doi.org/10.1007/978-1-4020-5839-4

Possible and Impossible Conditionals for Team Logics

Fausto Barbero[1(✉)] and Fan Yang[2]

[1] Department of Philosophy, History and Art Studies, University of Helsinki, Helsinki, Finland
fausto.barbero@helsinki.fi

[2] Department of Philosophy and Religious Studies, Utrecht University, Utrecht, Netherlands

Abstract. We study whether a logic based on team semantics can be enriched with a conditional satisfying minimal requirements, such as preservation of the closure property of the logic, Modus Ponens, and the Deduction Theorem. We show that such well-behaved conditionals exist for downward or upward closed logics, but do not typically exist for union closed, convex or intersection closed logics. We also briefly investigate conditionals satisfying weaker requirements.

Keywords: Team semantics · Conditionals · Deduction theorem · Modus Ponens

In this paper, we study the possibility of having well-behaved conditionals in logics based on teams semantics. Team semantics is a generalization of Tarskian semantics in which formulas are evaluated on *teams*, which are *sets* of evaluation points (such as propositional valuations), rather than on single evaluation points. It was introduced by Hodges [11] to characterise dependencies between first-order variables, in the context of independence-friendly logic ([10], see also [15]). The framework has been developed further by Väänänen in dependence logic [17], and inquisitive logic [5] essentially uses the same semantics. Many more team-based logics have then been introduced, including propositional [23] and modal [18] dependence logic. These logics are extensions of classical logic, and thus inherit the classical implication $\alpha \to \beta := \neg\alpha \vee \beta$ over classical formulas. The earliest versions of these logics (such as independence-friendly logic and dependence logic), however, do not have a conditional in their syntax for arbitrary formulas. In [1], an adequate conditional $\to$ (known as *intuitionistic implication*) was introduced for dependence logic, a language which has the *downward closure property*. The conditional was also used in inquisitive logic. While adding $\to$ to first-order dependence logic increases its expressive power significantly [20], the conditional is generally well behaved in downward closed logics, in the sense that it preserves downward closure, and satisfies both Modus Ponens and the Deduction Theorem.

In recent years, many variants of dependence logic with different closure properties have received increasing attention, particularly *union closed* and *convex* logics. None of the union closed languages in the literature has a conditional (applied to arbitrary formulas) in their syntax, and the intuitionistic implication $\to$ clearly does not preserve union closure. While some of the convex logics do have $\to$ in their language (as $\to$ preserves convexity), the Deduction Theorem clearly fails in this context.

P. Johann and R. de Queiroz (Eds.): WoLLIC 2026, LNCS 16757, pp. 50–66, 2027.
https://doi.org/10.1007/978-3-032-33486-2_4

In this paper, we raise the question whether a team logic with a certain closure property can have a conditional > that is well-behaved in the sense that (1) > preserves the closure property, (2) Modus Ponens and (3) Deduction Theorem hold for > over the logic; namely, for any set $\{\varphi, \psi\} \cup \Gamma$ of formulas in the logic, the following hold:

(Preservation) If φ and ψ have the closure property, so does $\varphi > \psi$.
(Modus Ponens) $\varphi, \varphi > \psi \models \psi$.
(Deduction Theorem) If $\Gamma, \varphi \models \psi$, then $\Gamma \models \varphi > \psi$.

Modus Ponens and the Deduction Theorem are of clear importance to ensure that a logic admits good axiomatic systems, so much so that e.g. the logicality of quantum logic was at times put in doubt (see e.g. [12]) by noting its lack of a conditional satisfying these constraints. In team semantics, we find it natural to add the requirement of Preservation, since the loss of a closure property has heavy repercussions on the validity of inference rules. We here address our question in the context of propositional languages, but many of our insights apply as well to first-order or modal team logics.

The material implication $\multimap$ in team semantics satisfies both Modus Ponens and the Deduction Theorem, and, as we shall prove, it is the unique such conditional for languages that meet certain expressivity requirements. Then, the fact that $\multimap$ does not preserve e.g. union closure or convexity can be used to show that well-behaved conditionals do not exist for expressively complete languages with these closure properties. This impossibility result naturally leads us to consider weaker constraints, such as:

(Feeble Modus Ponens) $\alpha, \alpha > \psi \models \psi$ for flat formulas α.
(Feeble Deduction Theorem) If $\Delta, \varphi \models \psi$, then $\Delta \models \varphi > \psi$ for sets Δ of flat formulas.

We shall see that, in union closed and convex languages, impossibility results are obtained also when assuming some of the weaker constraints.

In Sect. 2, we prove that in downward closed languages, the intuitionistic implication $\rightarrow$ is the unique well-behaved conditional that satisfies all the requirements, and we also identify a unique well-behaved conditional for upward closed languages.

We open Sect. 3 by showing a similar characterization of the uniquenss of material implication $\multimap$ and its weaker variant, from which our impossibility results for several non-downward closed, expressively complete languages follow. We then proceed to show that this result can be sharpened to cover less expressive union closed languages and by weakening the requirement of the Deduction Theorem to its Feeble variant. This argument is essentially Hardegree's proof of the impossibility of well-behaved conditionals for quantum logic [8] recast in our setting. The main idea is to construct formulas for which the distributivity law $\varphi \wedge (\psi \vee \chi) \models (\varphi \wedge \psi) \vee (\varphi \wedge \chi)$ fails, and to derive a contradiction from the existence of such a well-behaved conditional.

In Sect. 4, we adapt the argument to prove that for convex logics and intersection closed logics well-behaved conditional cannot in general exist either; in the convex case, it suffices to assume Modus Ponens to be in its Feeble variant. Our argument for convex logics uses the failure of a different type of distributivity law $\varphi \wedge (\psi \mathbin{\bar{\mathbb{V}}} \chi) \models (\varphi \wedge \psi) \mathbin{\bar{\mathbb{V}}} (\varphi \wedge \chi)$, or in fact, the failure of a strengthened version of it, where $\bar{\mathbb{V}}$ is a variant of the global (or inquisitive) disjunction $\mathbb{V}$ as introduced in [3]. For intersection closed logics, which currently lack a (complete) syntax in the literature, we work on an abstract level, and use the failure of the distributivity of conjunction over tensor conjunction $\triangle$ from [9].

In Sect. 5, we consider some weak conditionals that can still be obtained, along the lines, e.g., suggested by van Fraassen [19] in the context of quantum logic. We use some of these conditionals to show that the impossibility results are, in a sense, optimal.

We end the paper in Sect. 6 with some concluding remarks.

1 Classical and Non-classical Languages

Let us start by defining the classical language in the team semantics setting. Let *Prop* be a set of propositional variables; for simplicity, we assume that *Prop* is finite[1]. The language L_c of classical propositional logic is defined by the grammar

$$\alpha ::= p \in Prop \mid \bot \mid \neg\alpha \mid \alpha \wedge \alpha \mid \alpha \vee \alpha \mid \alpha \to \alpha$$

We shall use the first Greek letters $\alpha, \beta, \ldots$ to denote classical formulas. Generic formulas in the extensions of L_c to be discussed are denoted by $\varphi, \psi, \chi, \theta$, etc.

A *valuation* (over *Prop*) is a function $v : Prop \to \{0, 1\}$. A *team* T is a set of valuations. The team semantics for L_c is defined inductively as:

- $T \models p$ iff for all $v \in T$, $v(p) = 1$.
- $T \models \bot$ iff $T = \emptyset$.
- $T \models \neg\alpha$ iff for all $v \in T$, $\{v\} \not\models \alpha$.
- $T \models \alpha \wedge \beta$ iff $T \models \alpha$ and $T \models \beta$.
- $T \models \alpha \vee \beta$ iff there are T_1, T_2 with $T = T_1 \cup T_2$, $T_1 \models \alpha$ and $T_2 \models \beta$.
- $T \models \alpha \to \beta$ iff for all $S \subseteq T$, $S \models \alpha$ implies $S \models \beta$.

We assert that $\Gamma \models \varphi$, if for all teams T, $T \models \Gamma$ implies $T \models \varphi$.

It can be easily verified that classical formulas have the empty team property, are downward and union closed, convex, and flat; these concepts are defined as:

- φ has the *empty team property* or is *empty team closed* if $\emptyset \models \varphi$.
- φ is *downward closed* if, whenever $T \models \varphi$ and $S \subseteq T$, we have $S \models \varphi$
- φ is *convex* if, whenever $S, T \models \varphi$ and $S \subseteq R \subseteq T$, we have $R \models \varphi$.
- φ is *union closed* if, whenever $T \models \varphi$ and $S \models \varphi$, we have $S \cup T \models \varphi$
- φ is *flat* in case $T \models \varphi$ iff for all $v \in T$, $\{v\} \models \varphi$.

Clearly, downward closure implies convexity; moreover, a formula is flat if and only if it is union closed, downward closed and empty team closed.

By using flatness, one can easily show that all classical tautologies are valid in team semantics as well. In particular, we have that $\neg\alpha \equiv \alpha \to \bot$ and $\alpha \to \beta \equiv \neg\alpha \vee \beta$. This conditional $\to$ satisfies both Modus Ponens and the Deduction Theorem over the classical language. Moreover, $\alpha \wedge (\beta \vee \gamma) \models (\alpha \wedge \beta) \vee (\alpha \wedge \gamma)$ (distributivity) holds.

[1] Propositional team logics are more commonly defined using a countably infinite set of propositional variables. Since all of the languages considered in the paper enjoy the *locality* property (i.e., whether a formula is satisfied only depends on the variables that actually occur in the formula), this restriction is not substantial.

We also consider closure properties on their own, independently of any specific syntax, in the following sense: A *team proposition* $\mathbb{P}$ (over *Prop*) is a set of teams (over *Prop*). We say that $\mathbb{P}$ is *empty team closed* if $\emptyset \in \mathbb{P}$; $\mathbb{P}$ is downward closed if, $T \in \mathbb{P}$ and $S \subseteq T$ imply $S \in \mathbb{P}$; and similarly for other closure properties. A classical formula α defines a team proposition

$$[\![\alpha]\!] := \{T \subseteq \{0,1\}^{Prop} : T \models \alpha\},$$

and it is clearly empty team closed, downward closed, union closed, convex and flat.

The classical language L_c is *expressively complete* for flat team propositions, in the sense that

(1) for every formula $\alpha \in L_c$, the team proposition $[\![\alpha]\!]$ defined by α is flat, and
(2) every flat team proposition $\mathbb{P}$ can be defined by a formula $\alpha \in L_c$, i.e., $\mathbb{P} = [\![\alpha]\!]$.

To see why item (2) above holds, observe first that for a flat team proposition $\mathbb{P}$, we have $\mathbb{P} = \mathcal{P}(\bigcup \mathbb{P})$. Put $T = \bigcup \mathbb{P}$. Let $Prop = \{p_1, \ldots, p_n\}$, and let

$$\alpha_T = \bigvee_{v \in T} (p_1^{v(p_1)} \wedge \cdots \wedge p_n^{v(p_n)}), \tag{1}$$

where $p_i^1 := p_i$ and $p_i^0 = \neg p_i$. It can be easily verified that $S \models \alpha_T$ iff $S \subseteq T$ iff $S \in \mathcal{P}(T) = \mathbb{P}$. Thus, $\mathbb{P} = [\![\alpha_T]\!]$.

In this paper, we also consider the dual properties of downward and union closure, namely upward closure and intersection closure: a team proposition $\mathbb{P}$ is said to be

- *upward closed* if $T \in \mathbb{P}$ and $T \subseteq S$ imply $S \in \mathbb{P}$.
- *closed under intersection* if $S, T \in \mathbb{P}$ implies $S \cap T \in \mathbb{P}$.

These two closure properties arise naturally in our context, although they are less well studied in the team semantics literature. Upward closure clearly implies union closure, and downward closure implies intersection closure. The classical language is therefore closed under intersection, but it is clearly not upward closed (as, e.g., any propositional variable p is not upward closed). For (non-trivial) examples of the two new closure properties, consider two arbitrary distinct non-empty teams $T, S \subseteq \{0,1\}^{Prop}$ such that $S \nsubseteq T$, $T \nsubseteq S$ and $S \cap T \neq \emptyset$. The team proposition

$$\mathbb{P}_1 = \{R \subseteq \{0,1\}^{Prop} : R \supseteq T \text{ or } R \supseteq S\}$$

is upward closed (but not intersection closed), and $\mathbb{P}_2 = \{T, S, T \cap S\}$ is intersection closed (but neither upward closed nor downward closed).

In the following, we will consider languages (or "logics") $[\circ_1, \ldots, \circ_n]$ generated by connectives $\circ_1, \ldots, \circ_n$, or extensions $L[\circ_1, \ldots, \circ_n]$ of a language L with the listed connectives. This list may include some connectives of L_c and other ones, such as those we will introduce in later sections. If the formulas of $[\circ_1, \ldots, \circ_n]$ are not all flat, we will say that this language is *non-classical*.

As with the usual (single-valuation based) classical language, the sets of connectives $\{\neg, \wedge\}$, $\{\neg, \wedge, \vee\}$ and $\{\bot, \wedge, \to\}$ are *functionally complete* for the classical language L_c, in the sense that all the other connectives can be defined in terms of those from each of these sets. In particular, the formula (1) can also be written in these languages; thus, each of the languages $[\neg, \wedge]$, $[\neg, \wedge, \vee]$ and $[\bot, \wedge, \rightarrow]$ is expressively complete for flat properties. When building a non-classical language, on the other hand, the choice of a classical basis matters: while all the connectives of L_c preserve downward closure, it is not hard to see that union closure is preserved only by $\neg, \wedge, \vee$, convexity only by $\neg, \wedge, \rightarrow$, and intersection closure only by $\neg, \wedge$.

2 Well-Behaved Conditionals for Downward and Upward Closed Logics

We first consider downward and upward closed languages L, where conditionals that preserve the corresponding closure property and satisfy Modus Ponens and the Deduction Theorem can be found, and they are also unique if L is sufficiently expressive.

We start with downward closed languages, which are well studied in the literature. One such example is the extension of the classical language $[\neg, \wedge, \vee]$ with the global disjunction $\vee\!\!\!\vee$, whose semantic is defined as

- $T \models \varphi \vee\!\!\!\vee \psi$ iff $T \models \varphi$ or $T \models \psi$.

More explicitly, formulas of the language $[\neg, \wedge, \vee, \vee\!\!\!\vee]$ are formed by:

$$\varphi ::= p \mid \neg\varphi \mid \varphi \wedge \varphi \mid \varphi \vee \varphi \mid \varphi \vee\!\!\!\vee \varphi$$

It was shown in [23] that this language is expressively complete for empty team closed and downward closed team propositions ([23] restricts negation to propositional variables only, which is not a substantial restriction for our purpose; cf. [22]).

In downward closed languages, the conditional $\rightarrow$ (*intuitionistic implication*) already defined in the previous section is well-known to preserve downward closure, and satisfies Modus Ponens and the Deduction Theorem in downward closed languages. If, in addition, L can express all flat team propositions (i.e., team propositions of the form $\mathcal{P}(T) = \{S : S \subseteq T\}$), $\rightarrow$ is the unique such conditional, as shown in the next theorem, whose proof is included in Appendix A.

Theorem 2.1. *Let L be a downward closed language that can express all flat team propositions, and $>$ a binary operator. Then $L[>]$ is downward closed and satisfies both Modus Ponens and the Deduction Theorem for $>$ iff $>$ is equivalent to $\rightarrow$ over $L[>]$, meaning that $\varphi > \psi \equiv \varphi \rightarrow \psi$ for all formulas φ, ψ in $L[>]$.*

Next, we turn to logics with the upward closure property, the dual of downward closure. In contrast to downward closure, upward closed languages are not yet well understood in the literature. To the best of our knowledge, the only systematic treatment to date appears in very recent work by Häggblom [7], where she introduced the following language that is expressively complete for upward closed team propositions:

$$\varphi ::= \top \mid p \mid \neg p \mid \varphi \wedge \varphi \mid \varphi \vee\!\!\!\vee \varphi \mid \triangledown\varphi$$

where the propositional variables adopt the so-called existential semantics (rather than the usual one, which clearly violates upward closure) and the operator $\triangledown$ defined as:

- $T \models p$ iff there is an $v \in T$ such that $v(p) = 1$
- $T \models \triangledown\varphi$ iff there exists $v \in T$ such that $\{v\} \models \varphi$.

In the upward closed context, let us introduce a new conditional $\prec$, the dual of intuitionistic implication, which has the following semantics:

- $T \models \varphi \prec \psi$ iff for all $S \supseteq T$, $S \models \varphi$ implies $S \models \psi$.

This conditional $\prec$ clearly preserves upward closure, and respects Modus Ponens and the Deduction Theorem relative to upward closed languages L. In addition, if L can express all co-flat team propositions, i.e., all team propositions of the form $Up(T) = \{S : S \supseteq T\}$, then $\prec$ is the unique such conditional; i.e., an analogue of Theorem 2.1 holds for $\prec$ over upward closed languages that can express all co-flat team propositions.

3 Impossibility of Well-Behaved Conditionals for Union Closed Logics

Having seen two types of logics with well-behaved conditionals, in the rest of the paper we prove that such conditionals do not exist for non-classical logics with the other closure properties we consider. In this section, we first provide an argument that covers all languages that are *expressively complete* for these closure properties. Since many known logics in the literature are expressively complete, this suggests that the requirements we imposed on well-behaved conditionals may need to be weakened. Yet, we shall show that the impossibility results persist for these languages even under weaker requirements. We prove this sharper impossibility result for union closed languages in this section; languages with other closure properties are treated in the next section.

Let us first observe that if we drop the Preservation requirement, there is a conditional in the literature that satisfies both Modus Ponens and the Deduction Theorem, namely the material implication $\multimap$:

- $T \models \varphi \multimap \psi$ iff $T \models \varphi$ implies $T \models \psi$. (material implication)

Material implication, however, does not preserve any of the closure properties we consider (see Appendix B for counterexamples). Among these, preservation of the empty team closure is easily recovered by considering a variant of the material implication:

- $T \models \varphi \twoheadrightarrow \psi$ iff $T = \emptyset$ or $T \models \varphi$ implies $T \models \psi$. (weak material implication)

We now give a characterization of these two versions of material implication that is similar to Theorem 2.1. We show that the (strong) material implication $\multimap$ is actually the unique conditional that satisfies the Modus Ponens and the Deduction Theorem, if the underlying language is sufficiently expressive[2], and similarly, its weaker version $\twoheadrightarrow$ is the unique such for sufficiently expressive languages that are empty team closed.

[2] We are very grateful to an anonymous referee for suggesting this characterization and sketching the proof, which constitutes the crucial part of Theorem 3.2.

Theorem 3.2. *Let L be a language that can express all team propositions of the form $\{T\}$ for arbitrary T. Then L[>] satisfies both Modus Ponens and the Deduction Theorem for > iff > is equivalent to the material implication* $\rightarrow$ *over L[>].*

Similarly, let L be an empty team closed language that can express all team propositions of the form $\{\emptyset, T\}$ for arbitrary T. Then L[>] is empty team closed and satisfies both Modus Ponens and the Deduction Theorem for > iff > is equivalent to the weak material implication $\twoheadrightarrow$ *over L[>].*

Proof. We give the detailed proof of the characterization for the weak material implication $\twoheadrightarrow$; the proof for the strong one $\rightarrow$ is similar. We prove the nontrivial left to right direction. Suppose $L[>]$ is empty team closed and satisfies both Modus Ponens and the Deduction Theorem. We prove that $\varphi > \psi \equiv \varphi \twoheadrightarrow \psi$ for any formulas φ, ψ in $L[>]$.

Clearly, $\emptyset \models \varphi \twoheadrightarrow \psi$ by definition, and $\emptyset \models \varphi > \psi$ as $L[>]$ is empty team closed. Now, take $T \neq \emptyset$. Suppose $T \models \varphi > \psi$ and $T \models \varphi$. By Modus Ponens for $>$, $T \models \psi$, giving $T \models \varphi \twoheadrightarrow \psi$. Conversely, suppose $T \models \varphi \twoheadrightarrow \psi$. Let χ_T be an L-formula such that $[\![\chi_T]\!] = \{\emptyset, T\}$. It suffices to show that $\chi_T, \varphi \models \psi$, as then we would obtain $\chi_T \models \varphi > \psi$ by the Deduction Theorem for $>$, from which $T \models \varphi > \psi$ would follow as $T \models \chi_T$.

Now, to show $\chi_T, \varphi \models \psi$, suppose $S \models \chi_T$ and $S \models \varphi$. Then either $S = \emptyset$ or $S = T$. If $S = \emptyset$, since $L[>]$ is empty team closed, we have $S \models \psi$. Otherwise, if $S = T$, since $S \models \varphi$ and $S \models \varphi \twoheadrightarrow \psi$ we obtain $S \models \psi$ by Modus Ponens, as required. □

Our impossibility result follows now as a corollary, since the weak and strong material implication clearly do not preserve union closure, convexity, intersection closure, and some of their combinations (see Appendix B for the proof).

Corollary 3.3. *If L is expressively complete for union and empty team closed team propositions, then there is no binary operator > such that L[>] is closed under empty team and unions, and satisfies both Modus Ponens and the Deduction theorem for >.*

Similarly for languages expressively complete for any of the following classes of team propositions: union closed, convex, intersection closed, convex and union closed, intersection and empty team closed, and convex and intersection closed.

Proof. Suppose such a binary operator $>$ exists for a language L that is expressively complete for empty team and union closed team propositions. Observe that each team proposition of the form $\{\emptyset, T\}$ is closed under empty team and unions, and L can thus express all such team propositions. It then follows from Theorem 3.2 that $>$ is equivalent to $\twoheadrightarrow$, which leads to a contradiction as $\twoheadrightarrow$ does not preserve union closure.

The other cases follows similarly, by observing that each team proposition $\{T\}$ is convex and closed under unions and intersections, and additionally $\emptyset \in \{\emptyset, T\}$. □

The above result applies to a number of known expressively complete logics in the literature, such as the extension of the classical language $[\neg, \wedge, \vee]$ with inclusion atoms $\vec{a} \subseteq \vec{b}$ with each $a_i, b_i \in Prop \cup \{\bot, \top\}$ (known as *propositional inclusion logic*), which is expressively complete for empty team and union closed team propositions [21], where

- $T \models \vec{a} \subseteq \vec{b}$ iff for each $v \in T$, there exists $u \in T$ such that $v(\vec{a}) = u(\vec{b})$.

However, Corollary 3.3 or Theorem 3.2 does not apply, for example, to a weaker version of propositional inclusion logic with inclusion atoms restricted to the form $\vec{p} \subseteq \vec{q}$ (i.e., without occurrences of $\bot, \top$), as this weaker language is known ([21]) not to be expressively complete, and even flat in the one-variable case $Prop = \{p\}$. It cannot then express all propositions of the form $\{\emptyset, T\}$, because e.g. the proposition $\{\emptyset, T\}$, where T is the full team in one variable with valuations $u(p) = 0$ and $v(p) = 1$, is not flat.

In addition to considering weaker logics, a natural alternative for avoiding Corollary 3.3 or Theorem 3.2 while still obtaining relatively well-behaved conditionals is to impose restrictions on the kinds of formulas allowed in Modus Ponens and Deduction Theorem schemes. Plausible as this approach may seem, we show in the rest of the paper that several impossibility results are still obtained when replacing either Modus Ponens or the Deduction Theorem with their Feeble counterparts.

One crucial fact on which our argument relies is the failure of distributivity of conjunction $\wedge$ over disjunction $\vee$ in non-downward closed languages. We begin by proving a general characterisation of the distributive law.

Proposition 3.4. *Let L be a language that can express all flat team propositions, and φ a formula of L. Then φ is downward closed iff $\varphi \wedge (\psi \vee \chi) \models (\varphi \wedge \psi) \vee (\varphi \wedge \chi)$ holds for all formulas ψ, χ of L.*

Proof. The left to right direction is easy to verify. For the other direction, suppose φ is not downward closed. Then there are teams S, T such that $S \subseteq T$, $T \models \varphi$ and $S \not\models \varphi$. Consider the team propositions $\mathbb{P}_S = \mathcal{P}(S)$ and $\mathbb{P}_{T\setminus S} = \mathcal{P}(T \setminus S)$. These two team propositions are clearly flat (as, e.g., $\{v_1\}, \dots, \{v_n\} \in \mathcal{P}(S)$ iff $\{v_1, \dots, v_n\} \subseteq S$ iff $\{v_1, \dots, v_n\} \in \mathcal{P}(S)$). Since L can express all flat team propositions, there are (flat) formulas α_S and $\alpha_{T\setminus S}$ in L (cf. formula (1) in Sect. 1) such that $\mathcal{P}(S) = [\![\alpha_S]\!]$ and $\mathcal{P}(T \setminus S) = [\![\alpha_{T\setminus S}]\!]$. We have that $\varphi \wedge (\alpha_S \vee \alpha_{T\setminus S}) \not\models (\varphi \wedge \alpha_S) \vee (\varphi \wedge \alpha_{T\setminus S})$.

To see why, first note that $T \models \varphi$. Moreover, $T \models \alpha_S \vee \alpha_{T\setminus S}$, since $T = S \cup (T \setminus S)$, $S \models \alpha_S$ (for $S \in \mathcal{P}(S)$) and $T\setminus S \models \alpha_{T\setminus S}$ (for $T\setminus S \in \mathcal{P}(T\setminus S)$). Thus, $T \models \varphi\wedge(\alpha_S \vee \alpha_{T\setminus S})$.

On the other hand, if $T \models (\varphi \wedge \alpha_S) \vee (\varphi \wedge \alpha_{T\setminus S})$, then there are T_1, T_2 such that $T = T_1 \cup T_2$, $T_1 \models \varphi \wedge \alpha_S$ and $T_2 \models \varphi \wedge \alpha_{T\setminus S}$. It follows that $T_1 \subseteq S$ and $T_2 \subseteq T \setminus S$. Since we also have $T = T_1 \cup T_2$, it must be that $T_1 = S$. But then $T_1 \models \varphi$ would imply $S \models \varphi$, which contradicts our assumption. □

Distributivity thus fails in any union closed language that properly extends the classical language $[\neg, \wedge, \vee]$ (such as propositional inclusion logic $[\neg, \wedge, \vee, \subseteq]$ or its weaker variant discussed above), as it contains non-downward closed formulas (e.g., $p \subseteq q$).

Our argument for the impossibility result below also uses a simple characterization of union closure in terms of the idempotence of disjunction $\vee$ (proof in Appendix C):

Lemma 3.5. *φ is union closed iff $\varphi \vee \varphi \models \varphi$.*

We are ready to prove another impossibility result, which assumes the Feeble Deduction Theorem. The main argument is due to Hardegree [8].

Theorem 3.6. *For any union and empty team closed language L that properly extends the classical language $[\neg, \wedge, \vee]$, there is no binary operator $>$ such that $L[>]$ is union closed and satisfies both Modus Ponens and the Feeble Deduction Theorem for $>$.*

Proof. Suppose that such an operator $>$ exists. Let φ, ψ, χ be formulas in L for which $\varphi \wedge (\psi \vee \chi) \not\models (\varphi \wedge \psi) \vee (\varphi \wedge \chi)$ with ψ, χ flat (such formulas exist by Proposition 3.4 and its proof). Since L is empty team closed, we have

$$\varphi \wedge \psi \models (\varphi \wedge \psi) \vee (\varphi \wedge \chi) \text{ and } \varphi \wedge \chi \models (\varphi \wedge \psi) \vee (\varphi \wedge \chi),$$

which imply, by the Feeble Deduction Theorem, that

$$\psi \models \varphi > (\varphi \wedge \psi) \vee (\varphi \wedge \chi) \text{ and } \chi \models \varphi > (\varphi \wedge \psi) \vee (\varphi \wedge \chi).$$

Since the $L[>]$-formula $\varphi > (\varphi \wedge \psi) \vee (\varphi \wedge \chi)$ is union closed, by Lemma 3.5, we derive

$$\psi \vee \chi \models (\varphi > (\varphi \wedge \psi) \vee (\varphi \wedge \chi)) \vee (\varphi > (\varphi \wedge \psi) \vee (\varphi \wedge \chi)) \models \varphi > (\varphi \wedge \psi) \vee (\varphi \wedge \chi).$$

Finally, by Modus Ponens, $\varphi \wedge (\psi \vee \chi) \models (\varphi \wedge \psi) \vee (\varphi \wedge \chi)$, which is a contradiction. □

We remark that the argument above actually depends only on the existence in L of three formulas used in the counterexample for distributivity. Languages of this kind are in general not expressively complete. One example is the weaker version of propositional inclusion logic discussed earlier. Another example is *first-order inclusion logic* ([6]), where Proposition 3.4 does not apply but other counterexamples for distributivity can be found.[3]

4 Impossibility in Convex Logics and Intersection Closed Logics

In this section, we prove sharper impossibility results for non-classical convex logics and intersection closed logics by adapting the argument from Theorem 3.6.

We first consider convex languages. A typical example, which is also expressively complete, is that given in [3], which is obtained by extending the classical language $[\bot, \wedge, \rightarrow]$ with the outer global disjunction $\mathbin{\bar{\triangledown}}$ and the epistemic might $\blacklozenge$, defined as

- $T \models \varphi \mathbin{\bar{\triangledown}} \psi$ iff there exists $S \supseteq T$ such that $S \models \varphi$ or $S \models \psi$.
- $T \models \blacklozenge\varphi$ iff there is a nonempty team $S \subseteq T$ such that $S \models \varphi$.

We can characterize convexity in terms of $\mathbin{\bar{\triangledown}}$ and $\blacklozenge$ (see Appendix C for the proof):

Lemma 4.7. *If φ is convex, then $\blacklozenge\varphi, \varphi \mathbin{\bar{\triangledown}} \varphi \models \varphi$; the converse holds if $\emptyset \not\models \varphi$.* [4]

Similar to the union closed context, in convex logics, conjunction does not distribute over the outer global disjunction $\mathbin{\bar{\triangledown}}$, even under a stronger assumption; specifically, $\varphi \wedge (\psi \mathbin{\bar{\triangledown}} \chi), \blacklozenge\psi \models (\varphi \wedge \psi) \mathbin{\bar{\triangledown}} (\varphi \wedge \chi)$ fails in general:

Example 4.8. *We construct a counterexample with φ classical. Consider the team $T = \{u, v\}$ with the valuations u, v satisfying $u(p, q) = (1, 1)$, $v(p, q) = (1, 0)$. Let $\varphi = p$, $\psi = q$ and $\chi = \blacklozenge\neg p$. It is easy to verify that T satisfies the antecedents $p \wedge (q \mathbin{\bar{\triangledown}} \blacklozenge\neg p)$ and $\blacklozenge q$, but not the consequent $(p \wedge q) \mathbin{\bar{\triangledown}} (p \wedge \blacklozenge\neg p)$.*

[3] For example, without going into details: $x \subseteq y \wedge (P(x) \vee P(y)) \not\models (x \subseteq y \wedge P(x)) \vee (x \subseteq y \wedge P(y))$.

[4] This can be easily strengthened to a full characterisation: φ is convex iff $\Diamond\varphi, \varphi \mathbin{\bar{\triangledown}} \varphi \models \varphi$, where $\Diamond$ is a closely related variant of $\blacklozenge$, defined as $T \models \Diamond\varphi$ iff there is a team $S \subseteq T$ such that $S \models \varphi$.

Next, we present our main impossibility theorem:

Theorem 4.9. *For any convex language L that properly extends the (convex) classical language with $\mathbin{\underline{\vee}}$ and $\blacklozenge$, there is no binary operator $>$ such that the language $L[>]$ is convex, and satisfies both Feeble Modus Ponens and the Deduction Theorem for $>$.*

Proof. Suppose that such a conditional $>$ exists. Let φ, ψ, χ be L-formulas such that $\varphi, \psi \mathbin{\underline{\vee}} \chi, \blacklozenge\psi \not\models (\varphi \wedge \psi) \mathbin{\underline{\vee}} (\varphi \wedge \chi)$ and φ is flat (such as those given in Example 4.8(1), where the flat formula $\neg p$ can be expressed in L with convexity-preserving connectives as it extends classical language). Clearly,

$$\varphi, \psi \models (\varphi \wedge \psi) \mathbin{\underline{\vee}} (\varphi \wedge \chi) \text{ and } \varphi, \chi \models (\varphi \wedge \psi) \mathbin{\underline{\vee}} (\varphi \wedge \chi),$$

which imply, by the Deduction Theorem, that

$$\psi \models \varphi > (\varphi \wedge \psi) \mathbin{\underline{\vee}} (\varphi \wedge \chi) \text{ and } \chi \models \varphi > (\varphi \wedge \psi) \mathbin{\underline{\vee}} (\varphi \wedge \chi).$$

By the monotonicity of $\blacklozenge$ and $\mathbin{\underline{\vee}}$, it follows that

$$\blacklozenge\psi \models \blacklozenge(\varphi > (\varphi\wedge\psi)\mathbin{\underline{\vee}}(\varphi\wedge\chi)) \text{ and } \psi\mathbin{\underline{\vee}}\chi \models (\varphi > (\varphi\wedge\psi)\mathbin{\underline{\vee}}(\varphi\wedge\chi)) \mathbin{\underline{\vee}} (\varphi > (\varphi\wedge\psi)\mathbin{\underline{\vee}}(\varphi\wedge\chi)).$$

Since $>$ preserves convexity, the formula $\varphi > (\varphi \wedge \psi) \mathbin{\underline{\vee}} (\varphi \wedge \chi)$ is convex. Thus, by Lemma 4.7 we obtain that $\psi \mathbin{\underline{\vee}} \chi, \blacklozenge\psi \models \varphi > (\varphi\wedge\psi) \mathbin{\underline{\vee}} (\varphi\wedge\chi)$. By Feeble Modus Ponens, $\varphi, (\psi \mathbin{\underline{\vee}} \chi), \blacklozenge\psi \models (\varphi \wedge \psi) \mathbin{\underline{\vee}} (\varphi \wedge \chi)$, which is a contradiction.

□

Next, we treat intersection closed logics. Unlike the other relatively well-understood closure properties and their corresponding logics, logics with intersection closure property have remained largely unexplored in the literature. To the best of our knowledge, the topic appears to have been addressed only in very recent unpublished work by Hägg-blom [7] and by the first author [4]. We therefore proceed in this section without assuming a (complete) syntax. Our argument, however, makes use of the *tensor conjunction* $\mathbin{\underline{\wedge}}$ from [9], defined as

- $T \models \psi \mathbin{\underline{\wedge}} \chi$ iff there are $R, S \supseteq T$ s. t. $T = R \cap S$, $R \models \psi$ and $S \models \chi$.

It is easy to verify that the tensor conjunction $\mathbin{\underline{\wedge}}$, as well as the usual conjunction $\wedge$, preserve intersection closure.

Intersection closure is characterised by the idempotence of $\mathbin{\underline{\wedge}}$ (the proof is given in Appendix C):

Lemma 4.10. *φ is intersection closed iff $\varphi \mathbin{\underline{\wedge}} \varphi \models \varphi$.*

Theorem 4.11. *Let S and T be such that $S \not\subseteq T$ and $T \not\subseteq S$. If L is a language that can express $\{S\}, \{T\}$ and $\{S \cap T\}$, then there is no binary operator $>$ such that $L[>]$ is intersection closed and satisfies both Modus Ponens and the Deduction Theorem for $>$.*

Proof. Suppose such a conditional $>$ exists. Let S, T be two distinct teams such that $S \cap T \neq S, T$. We then have

$$\theta_{S\cap T}, \theta_S \models (\theta_{S\cap T} \wedge \theta_S) \triangle (\theta_{S\cap T} \wedge \theta_T) \text{ and } \theta_{S\cap T}, \theta_T \models (\theta_{S\cap T} \wedge \theta_S) \triangle (\theta_{S\cap T} \wedge \theta_T),$$

as no team satisfies any of the two antecedents above. By Deduction Theorem,

$$\theta_S \models \theta_{S\cap T} > (\theta_{S\cap T} \wedge \theta_S) \triangle (\theta_{S\cap T} \wedge \theta_T) \text{ and } \theta_T \models \theta_{S\cap T} > (\theta_{S\cap T} \wedge \theta_S) \triangle (\theta_{S\cap T} \wedge \theta_T).$$

Put $\varphi = \theta_{S\cap T} > (\theta_{S\cap T} \wedge \theta_S) \triangle (\theta_{S\cap T} \wedge \theta_T)$, which is a formula closed under intersection, as $>$ preserves intersection closure. By Lemma 4.10, we have that $\theta_S \triangle \theta_T \models \varphi \triangle \varphi \models \varphi$. Then, by Modus Ponens, we arrive at $\theta_{S\cap T} \wedge (\theta_S \triangle \theta_T) \models (\theta_{S\cap T} \wedge \theta_S) \triangle (\theta_{S\cap T} \wedge \theta_T)$, which is impossible, as $S \cap T$ satisfies the antecedent but not the consequent. □

In contrast, languages that are both intersection and upward closed admit a well-behaved conditional, namely $\prec$; see Appendix D for a proof.

Let us remark that, as in the union closed case, the proofs of Theorems 4.9 and 4.11 rely only on the existence in L of three formulas: either φ, ψ, χ witnessing the failure of the strengthened distributivity, as in the proof of the former theorem, or $\theta_S, \theta_T, \theta_{S\cap T}$ as in the latter. The presence of the the operators $\blacklozenge$, $\mathbin{\bar{\triangledown}}$ or $\triangle$ in the language L is not substantial for the proofs either: For instance, the proof of Theorem 4.9 requires only that L contains formulas $\theta_\varphi, \theta_\psi, \theta_\chi$ in L equivalent to the formulas φ, ψ, χ in Example 4.8, respectively, together with formulas $\theta_{\psi \bar{\triangledown} \chi}$, $\theta_{\blacklozenge\psi}$, $\theta_{(\varphi\wedge\psi)\bar{\triangledown}(\varphi\wedge\chi)}$ equivalent to $\psi \mathbin{\bar{\triangledown}} \chi$, $\blacklozenge\psi$, and $(\varphi \wedge \psi) \mathbin{\bar{\triangledown}} (\varphi \wedge \chi)$, respectively.

5 Weak Conditionals

Having shown that certain classes of languages (union closed, convex, intersection closed) do not admit conditionals that are well-behaved with respect to stringent or even feeble requirements, a natural question is whether well-behaved conditionals can still exist in the remaining cases, or when we weaken the constraints further.

It has been claimed, e.g., by van Fraassen ([19]) that the essential features that warrant a binary connective $>$ being considered a conditional are Modus Ponens and *Introduction Rule*, a special case of the Deduction Theorem:

$$\text{If } \varphi \models \psi, \text{ then } \models \varphi > \psi.$$

In this regard, consider the following *maximal implication* $\hookrightarrow$ (introduced in [13]) and its dual *minimal implication* $\hookleftarrow\!\!\rightarrow$:

- $T \models \varphi \hookrightarrow \psi$ iff for all *maximal* $S \subseteq T$ such that $S \models \varphi$, we also have $S \models \psi$
- $T \models \varphi \hookleftarrow\!\!\rightarrow \psi$ iff for all *minimal* $S \supseteq T$ such that $S \models \varphi$, we also have $S \models \psi$.

The former is well-behaved in van Fraassen's sense for intersection closed languages, and even satisfies the Feeble Deduction theorem; it then witnesses that we cannot weaken the Deduction Theorem assumption in the impossibility result for intersection closed logics (whether the Modus Ponens aasumption can be relaxed remains an open problem). The latter is a van Fraassen conditional for union closed languages. Let us also remark that the *linear implication* $\multimap$ from [1], and the conditional $\rightsquigarrow$ from *relevance logic* ([2]) satisfy Modus Ponens and preserve union and downward closure:

- $T \models \varphi \multimap \psi$ iff for all S such that $S \models \varphi$, we also have $S \cup T \models \psi$
- $T \models \varphi \rightsquigarrow \psi$ iff for all S such that $S \models \varphi$, we have $T \cap S \models \psi$

However, the introduction rule fails for $\multimap$ in the worst possible way: $p \multimap p$ is not valid; similarly, $\blacklozenge p \rightsquigarrow \blacklozenge p$ is not valid either.

Alternatively, one may want to retain the Deduction Theorem fully. The following *epistemic indicative* $\circ\!\!\rightarrow$ preserves union closure and satisfies the Deduction Theorem, as well as Modus Ponens *for downward closed antecedents*, but it lacks transitivity:

- $T \models \varphi \circ\!\!\rightarrow \psi$ iff whenever $S \models \varphi$ for all $S \subseteq T$, we have $T \models \psi$

The existence of such a conditional shows *a fortiori* that requiring Feeble Modus Ponens and the Deduction Theorem does not yield an impossibility in the union closed case, differently from what we have seen in the convex case.

Another approach yet is to consider conditionals that satisfy both Modus Ponens and the Deduction Theorem partially. We propose two such conditionals here, both originated from an epistemic interpretation of teams (as descriptions of uncertainty among various possibilities):

- $T \models \varphi \rightarrowtail \psi$ iff whenever $S \subseteq T$ and $U \models \varphi$ for all $U \subseteq S$, we have $S \models \psi$.
- $T \models \varphi \bullet\!\!\rightarrow \psi$ iff whenever $S \models \varphi$ for all $S \subseteq T$, we have $S \models \psi$ for all $S \subseteq T$.

The former, which we shall call *epistemic counterfactual*, expresses the fact that "If we *knew* that φ, then we *would know* ψ", while the latter, called the *epistemic conditional* expresses "If we *know* that φ, then we *know* that ψ". Both conditionals satisfy Modus Ponens *for downward closed antecedents*, and the Deduction Theorem *for downward closed contexts*. As for preservation properties, $\bullet\!\!\rightarrow$ preserves union and upward closure. The conditional $\rightarrowtail$ preserves union, upward, and intersection closure, and convexity, and thus it testifies that the requirement of Feeble Modus Ponus plus the Feeble Deduction Theorem does not lead to an impossibility in the case of (union closed, intersection closed or) convex languages. Interestingly, both $\rightarrowtail$ and the relevant conditional $\rightsquigarrow$ coincide with the intuitionistic implication $\rightarrow$ over downward closed languages.

Tables 1 and 2 in Sect. E of the Appendix list some other typical desirable properties of conditionals that the above-mentioned ones satisfy or lack, such as (strong) transitivity, antecedent strengthening, importation, and exportation.

6 Concluding Remarks

In this paper, we have studied the possibility of having well-behaved conditionals in team logics with various closure properties, requiring that such conditionals preserve the closure property of the logic, and satisfy both Modus Ponens and the Deduction Theorem, or their weaker variants. We proved that the intuitionistic implication $\rightarrow$ is the unique well-behaved conditional for downward closed logics, and similarly for the dual of intuitionistic implication $\prec$ for upward closed logics. We obtained analogous characterizations for material implication $\twoheadrightarrow$ and its weaker variant $\twoheadrightarrow$ as well, from which we concluded that well-behaved conditionals do not exist for sufficiently expressive union closed, convex or intersection logics. We also showed that well-behaved conditionals satisfying weaker requirements typically fail to exist for these logics either.

Having ascertained that conditionals satisfying even weaker sets of requirements exist, a natural follow-up question is whether, given a natural list of requirements, such operators can be classified completely. A further question concerns how the addition of these "weak conditionals" affects the properties of a logic; e.g., what is the effect of adding a conditional that does not preserve flatness to the classical language?

Acknowledgments. We thank Samson Abramsky, Aleksi Anttila, Matilda Häggblom and Søren Knudstorp for helpful discussions, and an anonymous reviewer for very constructive suggestions. The first author's research was supported by the Research Council of Finland grant No. 349803.

APPENDIX

A Uniqueness of the Well-Behaved Conditionals for Downward and Upward Closed Languages

Proof of Theorem 2.1. We only give the proof of the left to right direction. Suppose L a downward closed language that can express all flat team propositions, and $L[>]$ is downward closed and satisfies both Modus Ponens and the Deduction Theorem for $>$. We show that $\varphi > \psi \equiv \varphi \rightarrow \psi$.

Suppose $T \models \varphi > \psi$. Let $S \subseteq T$ be such that $S \models \varphi$. By downward closure of $L[>]$, $S \models \varphi > \psi$ as well. Then, Modus Ponens for $>$ gives $S \models \psi$. Thus, $T \models \varphi \rightarrow \psi$.

Conversely, suppose $T \models \varphi \rightarrow \psi$. Consider the flat team proposition $\mathcal{P}(T)$. There exists a formula α_T in L such that $[\![\alpha_T]\!] = \mathcal{P}(T)$ (cf. formula (1) in Sect. 1). Note that $\alpha_T, \varphi \models \psi$. Indeed, for any team S such that $S \models \alpha_T$ and $S \models \varphi$, we have $S \subseteq T$, which implies $S \models \psi$, as $T \models \varphi \rightarrow \psi$. Now, $\alpha_T, \varphi \models \psi$ gives $\alpha_T \models \varphi > \psi$ by the Deduction Theorem for $L[>]$. Lastly, since $T \models \alpha_T$, we conclude that $T \models \varphi > \psi$, as required. □

A dual argument shows that the corresponding Theorem 2.1 holds for $\mathrel{-\!\!\prec}$ and upward closed languages that can express all team propositions of the form $Up(T)$, where in showing $T \models \varphi \mathrel{-\!\!\prec} \psi$ implies $T \models \varphi > \psi$, we now take a formula α_T^* in L such that $[\![\alpha_T^*]\!] = Up(T) = \{S : S \supseteq T\}$.

B Lack of Closure Properties for (Weak) Material Implication

Lemma B.1. *Neither* $\mathrel{-\!\!\triangleright}$ *nor* $\mathrel{-\!\!\blacktriangleright}$ *preserves union or intersection closure, or convexity.*

Proof. Consider the formulas $p \vee q$ and r, which have all the listed closure properties. Let u, v, w be valuations such that $u(p, q, r) = (0, 0, 0), v(p, q, r) = (1, 0, 0)$ and $w(p, q, r) = (0, 0, 1)$. Clearly, for $T = \{u, v\}$ and $S = \{v, w\}$, we have T and S satisfy both $p \vee q \mathrel{-\!\!\triangleright} r$ and $p \vee q \mathrel{-\!\!\blacktriangleright} r$, while $T \cap S = \{v\}$ satisfies neither, showing that none of the implications preserve intersection closure. Moreover, we have $\emptyset \models p \vee q \mathrel{-\!\!\triangleright} r$ and $\emptyset \models p \vee q \mathrel{-\!\!\blacktriangleright} r$. Since $\emptyset \subseteq \{v\} \subseteq T$, preservation of convexity fails for the two implications as well.

For the failure of preservation of union closure, consider the formulas $\blacklozenge p \wedge q$ and r, which are union closed (and convex). Let u, v be valuations such that $u(p, q, r) = (1, 1, 1)$ and $v(p, q, r) = (0, 1, 0)$. Clearly, both $\{u\}$ and $\{v\}$ satisfy $\blacklozenge p \wedge q \rightarrow r$ and $\blacklozenge p \wedge q \twoheadrightarrow r$, whereas their union $\{u, v\}$ satisfies neither implication. □

The first part of the proof above also shows that $\rightarrow$ or $\twoheadrightarrow$ does not preserve the combination of convexity and intersection closure; the second part of the proof also shows that none of them preserves the combination of convexity and union closure either.

C Proofs of Characterizations for Different Closure Properties

Proof of Lemma 3.5 *[union closure].* We only give the proof for the left to right direction. Suppose $T \models \varphi \vee \varphi$. Then, there exist R, S such that $T = R \cup S$, $R \models \varphi$ and $S \models \varphi$, which imply $T \models \varphi$, since φ is union closed. □

Proof of Lemma 4.7 *[convexity].* If φ is satisfied by no team, then φ is convex and $\blacklozenge\varphi, \varphi \mathbin{\vee\!\!\!\!\!\nabla} \varphi \models \varphi$ (as no team satisfies $\blacklozenge\varphi$ and $\varphi \mathbin{\vee\!\!\!\!\!\nabla} \varphi$).

Now, assume that φ is satisfied by some teams. Suppose φ is convex. Suppose $T \models \blacklozenge\varphi$ and $T \models \varphi \mathbin{\vee\!\!\!\!\!\nabla} \varphi$. Then there are R, S such that $\emptyset \neq R \subseteq T \subseteq S$, $R \models \varphi$ and $S \models \varphi$. By convexity, we conclude $T \models \varphi$.

For the converse direction, suppose $\emptyset \not\models \varphi$, and suppose φ is not convex. Then there are R, S, T such that $R \subseteq T \subseteq S$, $R \models \varphi$, $S \models \varphi$ and $T \not\models \varphi$. Clearly, $T \models \varphi \mathbin{\vee\!\!\!\!\!\nabla} \varphi$. By assumption, $R \neq \emptyset$, which then implies $T \models \blacklozenge\varphi$. This shows $\blacklozenge\varphi, \varphi \mathbin{\vee\!\!\!\!\!\nabla} \varphi \not\models \varphi$. □

Proof of Lemma 4.10 *[intersection closure].* Suppose φ is intersection closed, and $T \models \varphi \vartriangle \varphi$. Then, there are $R, S \models \varphi$ with $T = R \cap S$. Thus, $T \models \varphi$ by intersection closure.

Conversely, suppose $\varphi \vartriangle \varphi \models \varphi$. If $R, S \models \varphi$, then $R \cap S \models \varphi \vartriangle \varphi \models \varphi$. □

D Languages that Are both Intersection Closed and Upward Closed

At the end of Sect. 4 we mentioned the fact that languages that are closed both upward and under intersections do admit a well-behaved conditional, namely $\prec$. This follows from the fact that $\prec$ preserves the *conjunction* of intersection closure and upward closure (even though it does not preserve intersection closure alone).

Proposition D.13. *If φ is upward closed and ψ is intersection closed, then $\varphi \prec \psi$ is upward and intersection closed. In particular, $\prec$ preserves the property of being both upward and intersection closed.*

Proof. It follows immediately from the semantics that the formula $\varphi \prec \psi$ is always upward closed. For intersection closure, suppose $T, S \models \varphi \prec \psi$. Let $R \supseteq T \cap S$ be such that $R \models \varphi$; we must show that $R \models \psi$. By upward closure of φ, $R \cup T \models \varphi$ and $R \cup S \models \varphi$. Thus, since $T \models \varphi \prec \psi$ (resp. $S \models \varphi \prec \psi$) we obtain $R \cup T \models \psi$ (resp. $R \cup S \models \psi$). But, since $R \supseteq T \cap S$, we have $(R \cup T) \cap (R \cup S) = R \cup (T \cap S) = R$; thus, by intersection closure of ψ, $R \models \psi$. □

We already know that $\prec$ satisfies Modus Ponens and the Deduction Theorem relative to upward closed languages, thus a fortiori in languages that are both upward and intersection closed; thus, $\prec$ is well-behaved for this class of languages.

E Summary of the Weak Conditionals

Table 1 and Table 2 summarise the main properties of some of the most interesting weak conditionals identified in Sect. 5, where the relevant properties are defined as:

(Strong) transitivity: $\varphi > \psi, \psi > \chi \models \varphi > \chi$.
Weak transitivity: If $\models \varphi > \psi$ and $\models \psi > \chi$, then $\models \varphi > \chi$.
Intermediate transitivity: If $\models \varphi > \psi$, then $\psi > \chi \models \varphi > \chi$.
Antecedent strengthening: $\varphi > \psi \models (\varphi \wedge \chi) > \psi$.
Importation: $\varphi > (\psi > \chi) \models (\varphi \wedge \psi) > \chi$.
Exportation: $(\varphi \wedge \psi) > \chi \models \varphi > (\psi > \chi)$.
Monotonicity: If $\psi \models \psi'$, then $\varphi > \psi \models \varphi > \psi'$ and $\psi' > \varphi \models \psi > \varphi$.

These properties are often expected of conditionals, with an exception being the so-called *counterfactual conditionals* ([14, 16]).

We also include a conditional $\Rightarrow$, which is an object-language version of semantic entailment ($T \models \psi \Rightarrow \chi$ iff for all S, $S \models \psi$ implies $S \models \chi$), and a somewhat pathological example of a van Fraassen conditional for union closed languages.

In the tables, "ucl" abbreviates "union closed", "dwcl" abbreviates "downward closed" and "upcl" abbreviates upwards closed. A "yes" indicates that all conditionals formed using the operator $>$ indicated in the row have the property given by the column; "preserved" means that the operator preserves the property, i.e. $\psi > \chi$ has the property if ψ and χ have it; "no" means that $>$ does not even preserve the closure property. The marker "preserved (r)" means that $\psi > \chi$ has the given closure property if the consequent χ has it; the marker "preserved (l)" concerns the antecedent rather than the consequent. The row "generalizes $\rightarrow$" in Table 1 states whether $>$ coincides with the intuitionistic implication $\rightarrow$ when applied to downward closed antecedents.

For reasons of space, the simple proofs of the facts stated in the tables are omitted. We remark that some of the properties that we state to fail in general may hold in special cases: e.g., for $\hookrightarrow$, strong transitivity fails in general but holds in downward closed languages.

Table 1. Inferential properties

Conditional	$\Rightarrow$	$\rightarrowtail$	$\circ\!\!\rightarrow$	$\bullet\!\!\rightarrow$	$\hookrightarrow$	$\mathrel{\rotatebox{180}{$\hookleftarrow$}}$	$\leadsto$
Description	entailment	epistemic counterfactual	epistemic indicative	epistemic conditional	maximal implication	minimal implication	relevant
Modus Ponens	yes	yes for dwcl antecedent	yes for dwcl antecedent	yes for dwcl antecedent	yes	yes	yes
Deduction Theorem	introduction rule	yes for dwcl context	yes	yes for dwcl context	yes for dwcl context	yes for upcl context	dwcl antecedent and context
Transitivity	strong	strong	intermediate	strong	weak	weak	strong
Antecedent strengthening	yes	yes	yes	yes	for dwcl consequent	for upcl consequent	yes
Import	yes	yes	yes	yes	for dwcl consequent	for upcl consequent	yes
Export	no	yes	yes	yes	no	no	no
Monotonicity	yes	yes	yes	yes	if dwcl consequent	if upcl consequent	yes
Generalizes $\rightarrow$	no	yes	no	no	yes if antec. local	no	yes

Table 2. Closure properties

Conditional	$\Rightarrow$	$\rightarrowtail$	$\circ\!\!\rightarrow$	$\bullet\!\!\rightarrow$	$\hookrightarrow$	$\mathrel{\rotatebox{180}{$\hookleftarrow$}}$	$\leadsto$
Empty team closure	no	preserved	preserved (r)	preserved (r)	preserved (r)	no	preserved (r)
Flatness	yes except $\emptyset$	yes for ucl + $\emptyset$	no	no	preserved (r)	no	preserved (l)
Downward closure	yes	yes	no	no	preserved (r)	no	preserved (l)
Union closure	yes	preserved (r)	preserved (r)	preserved (r)	no	preserved	yes
Convexity	yes	yes	no	no	no	no	yes
Upward closure	yes	no	preserved (r)	preserved (r)	no	preserved (r)	preserved (r)
Intersection closure	yes	yes	no	no	preserved	no	preserved (r)

References

1. Abramsky, S., Väänänen, J.: From IF to BI: a tale of dependence and separation. Synthese **167**, 207–230 (2009)
2. Anderson, A.R., Dunn, J.M., Belnap, N.D.: The logic of relevance and necessity. Princeton University Press, Entailment (2017)
3. Anttila, A., Knudstorp, S.B.: Convex team logics. arXiv:2503.21850 (2025)
4. Barbero, F.: Characterizing intersection-closed logics (2026). manuscript
5. Ciardelli, I., Roelofsen, F.: Inquisitive logic. J. Philos. Log. **40**, 55–94 (2011)
6. Galliani, P.: Inclusion and exclusion dependencies in team semantics - on some logics of imperfect information. Ann. Pure Appl. Logic **163**(1), 68–84 (2012)
7. Häggblom, M.: Team logics with dual properties (2026). manuscript
8. Hardegree, G.M.: The conditional in quantum logic. Synthese **29**(1/4), 63–80 (1974)

9. Hella, L., Luosto, K., Väänänen, J.: Dimension in team semantics. Math. Struct. Comput. Sci., 1–45 (2024)
10. Hintikka, J., Sandu, G.: Informational independence as a semantical phenomenon. In: Fenstad, J.E., et al. (eds.) Logic, Methodology and Philosophy of Science VIII, pp. 571–589. Elsevier Science Publishers B.V. (1989)
11. Hodges, W.: Compositional semantics for a language of imperfect information. Logic J. IGPL **5**, 539–563 (1997)
12. Jauch, J.-M., Piron, C.: What is "quantum-logic". In: Freund, P.G.O. (ed.), pp. 166-81 of Quanta. Chicago University of Chicago Press (1970)
13. Kontinen, J., Nurmi, V.: Team logic and second-order logic. In: Ono, H., Kanazawa, M., de Queiroz, R. (eds.) Logic, Language, Information and Computation, vol. 5514, pp. 230–241. Springer, Berlin, Heidelberg (2009). https://doi.org/10.1007/978-3-642-02261-6_19
14. Lewis, D.: Counterfactuals. Blackwell Publishers, Oxford (1973)
15. Mann, A.L., Sandu, G., Sevenster, M.: Independence-Friendly Logic - A Game-Theoretic Approach, vol. 386. London Mathematical Society lecture note series. Cambridge University Press (2011)
16. Starr, W., Kocurek, A.: Counterfactuals. In: Zalta, E.N., Nodelman, U. (eds.) The Stanford Encyclopedia of Philosophy. Metaphysics Research Lab, Stanford University, Winter 2025 edition (2025)
17. Väänänen, J.: Dependence logic: a new approach to independence friendly logic, vol. 70. London Mathematical Society Student Texts. Cambridge University Press (2007)
18. Väänänen, J.: Modal dependence logic. In: Apt, K., van Rooij, R. (eds.) New Perspectives on Games and Interaction, vol. 5. Texts in Logic and Games, pp. 237–254. Amsterdam University press (2008)
19. van Fraassen, B.C.: Semantic analysis of quantum logic. In: Hooker, C.A. (eds.) Contemporary Research in the Foundations and Philosophy of Quantum Theory: Proceedings of a Conference Held at the University of Western Ontario, London, Canada, vol. 2, pp. 80–113. Springer (1973). https://doi.org/10.1007/978-94-010-2534-8_3
20. Yang, F.: Expressing second-order sentences in intuitionistic dependence logic. Stud. Logica. **101**(2), 323–342 (2013)
21. Yang, F.: Propositional union closed team logics. Ann. Pure Appl. Logic **173**(6), 103102 (2022)
22. Yang, F.: There Are (Other) Ways to Negate in Propositional Team Semantics. In: Sano, K., Hatano, R., Ono, H. (eds.) Exploring negation, modality and proof, Logic in Asia: Studia Logica Library. Springer, Singapore (2026). https://doi.org/10.1007/978-981-96-8566-0_1
23. Yang, F., Väänänen, J.: Propositional logics of dependence. Ann. Pure Appl. Logic **167**(7), 557–589 (2016)

Decidability of MSO Reparameterization over Countable Chains

Alexander Rabinovich(✉)

Tel Aviv University, Tel Aviv, Israel
rabinoa@tauex.tau.ac.il
https://www.tau.ac.il/ rabinoa/

Abstract. Interpretations are a fundamental tool in mathematical logic, allowing structures to be encoded within other structures via logical definitions. We study *MSO multidimensional point interpretations*, where elements of an interpreted structure are represented by tuples of elements of the host structure, and address the problem of simplifying such interpretations by reducing their representation dimension.

To formalize simplification, we use the notion of *reparameterization*. Our main result shows that, over the class of countable labelled linear orders, it is decidable whether a given *MSO* formula admits a d-dimensional reparameterization. As a consequence, every interpretation whose domain admits such a reparameterization is equivalent to a d-dimensional point interpretation.

1 Introduction

The notion of interpretation was first carefully defined and developed in the foundational work of Tarski, Mostowski, and Robinson [9]. Interpretations are a fundamental tool in mathematical logic, playing a central role in the foundations of mathematics, as well as in the philosophy of science.

Consider Monadic Second-Order[1] (*MSO*) d-dimensional *(point) interpretations* of a structure $\mathfrak{A}$ in a structure $\mathfrak{B}$. Under such an interpretation, each element of $\mathfrak{A}$ is represented within $\mathfrak{B}$ by a d-tuple of elements of $\mathfrak{B}$.

A central problem is whether a given interpretation can be simplified, for instance by reducing the dimension of the representation. The domain of the interpreted structure is specified by an *MSO* formula $\varphi(x_1, \ldots, x_m)$ over $\mathfrak{B}$. To formalize this notion of simplification, we use the notion of *reparameterization*, introduced in [3] for *MSO*-definable relations.

Throughout, $\bar{x}$ and $\bar{y}$ denote tuples of first-order variables.

Definition 1.1 (Reparameterization). *Let $\varphi(\overline{x})$ be an MSO formula and let C be a class of structures. A formula $G(\overline{x}, \overline{y})$ is a (functional)* reparameterization *of φ over C if the following conditions hold:*

[1] Let us recall that monadic second-order logic is an extension of first-order logic by set variables (see Sect. 2.2 for a formal definition).

P. Johann and R. de Queiroz (Eds.): WoLLIC 2026, LNCS 16757, pp. 67–80, 2027.
https://doi.org/10.1007/978-3-032-33486-2_5

Same domain: *Over* $\mathcal{C}$, $\varphi(\overline{x}) \equiv \exists \overline{y}\, G(\overline{x}, \overline{y})$.
Functional: *G defines the graph of a partial function, that is,* $\forall \overline{x}\, \exists^{\leq 1} \overline{y}\, G(\overline{x}, \overline{y})$.
Bounded preimage: *There exists* $N \in \mathbb{N}$ *such that, for every* $\mathcal{M} \in \mathcal{C}$ *and every parameter tuple* $\overline{y}$,

$$\left|\{\, \overline{x} \mid \mathcal{M} \models G(\overline{x}, \overline{y}) \,\}\right| \leq N.$$

We refer to $\overline{x}$ *as the* domain variables *and to* $\overline{y}$ *as the* image variables *of* G. *The* dimension *of* G *is the number of variables in* $\overline{y}$.

Intuition. A reparameterization replaces the original parameters $\overline{x}$ by auxiliary parameters $\overline{y}$, while preserving the interpreted domain. The bounded preimage condition ensures that each choice of $\overline{y}$ corresponds to only a uniformly bounded number of $\overline{x}$.

If $\varphi(\bar{x})$ admits a reparameterization with d image variables, then any interpretation whose domain is defined by φ can be reduced to a d-dimensional point interpretation (see Proposition 3.2).

Bojańczyk [2] studied *polyregular functions*, namely string-to-string functions defined by MSO interpretations. He proved that it is decidable whether an *MSO* formula admits a d-dimensional reparameterization over finite words. In this work, we generalize this result to arbitrary countable labelled chains.

The paper is organized as follows. In Sect. 2 we recall standard notions concerning chains and monadic second-order logic, and introduce the basic tools of the composition method used throughout the paper. In Sect. 3 we recall the notion of interpretation and motivate the reparameterization problem by showing how d-dimensional reparameterizations yield d-dimensional interpretations. Section 4 contains our main result, showing that it is decidable whether an *MSO* formula admits a d-dimensional reparameterization over the class of countable chains. In Sect. 5, following Bojańczyk [2], we study the growth rate of *MSO* interpretations. Extending results of [2,3], we show that the growth rate is polynomial, with degree equal to the minimal reparameterization dimension.

A full version of this paper is available on arXiv [6].

2 Preliminaries

Here we recall standard notions concerning chains and monadic second-order logic [4,5,10], and introduce the basic tools of the composition method [4,8] used throughout the paper.

2.1 Chains

A *k-chain* is a structure $\mathcal{M} = (M, <, \overline{P})$, where $(M, <)$ is a linear order and $\overline{P} = (P_1, \ldots, P_k)$ is a k-tuple of unary (monadic) predicates on M. When k is clear from the context, we simply refer to $\mathcal{M}$ as a *chain* or a *labelled chain*.

An interval I is a subset $I \subseteq M$ such that if $b, c \in I$ and $b < d < c$ then $d \in I$. We denote by $\mathcal{M} \restriction I$ the induced substructure on I.

2.2 Monadic Second-Order Logic

We work in monadic second-order logic (*MSO*) over the signature $\{<, P_1, \dots, P_k\}$, where each P_i is a unary (monadic) predicate symbol. First-order variables $x, y, \dots$ range over elements of the domain, and second-order variables $X, Y, \dots$ range over subsets of the domain. The atomic formulas are $x < y$, $x = y$, $P_i(x)$, and $X(x)$. Formulas are built from atomic formulas using Boolean connectives and the quantifiers $\exists x$, $\forall x$, $\exists X$, and $\forall X$.

Definition 2.1 (Definability). *Let $\psi(z_1, \dots, z_m)$ be an MSO formula and let $\mathcal{M}$ be a structure with domain D. The relation* defined *by ψ in $\mathcal{M}$ is the set*

$$\psi^{\mathcal{M}} := \{(a_1, \dots, a_m) \in D^m \mid \mathcal{M} \models \psi(a_1, \dots, a_m)\}.$$

*A relation $R \subseteq D^m$ is said to be MSO-*definable *in $\mathcal{M}$ if there exists an MSO formula $\psi(z_1, \dots, z_m)$ such that $R = \psi^{\mathcal{M}}$.*

We use standard abbreviations. In particular, $\exists^{\geq N} x\, \varphi(x)$ expresses that there are at least N distinct elements satisfying $\varphi(x)$.

2.3 Types

The *quantifier rank* $\mathrm{qr}(\varphi)$ of an *MSO* formula φ is the maximal nesting depth of quantifiers. For $r, k \in \mathbb{N}$, let $\mathfrak{Form}_k^r$ be the set of *MSO* sentences of quantifier rank at most r over the signature $\sigma_k = \{<, P_1, \dots, P_k\}$.

For chains $\mathfrak{A}$ and $\mathfrak{B}$, write $\mathfrak{A} \equiv_k^r \mathfrak{B}$ if $\mathfrak{A}$ and $\mathfrak{B}$ satisfy the same formulas in $\mathfrak{Form}_k^r$. This is an equivalence relation with finitely many classes.

Lemma 2.2 (Hintikka). *For every $r, k \in \mathbb{N}$ there exists a finite, effectively computable set $H_k^r \subseteq \mathfrak{Form}_k^r$ such that:*

1. *The disjunction $\bigvee_{\tau \in H_k^r} \tau$ is valid.*
2. *If $\tau, \tau' \in H_k^r$ are distinct, then $\tau \wedge \tau'$ is unsatisfiable.*
3. *Moreover, given $\varphi \in \mathfrak{Form}_k^r$, one can effectively compute a set $H_\varphi \subseteq H_k^r$ such that φ is equivalent to the disjunction of the formulas in H_φ.*

By (1) and (2), every σ_k-structure $\mathfrak{A}$ satisfies a unique sentence $\tau \in H_k^r$. We denote this sentence by $\mathrm{type}_k^r(\mathfrak{A})$ and call it the (r,k)-*type* of $\mathfrak{A}$. Moreover, $\mathrm{type}_k^r(\mathfrak{A})$ effectively determines which sentences in $\mathfrak{Form}_k^r$ are satisfied in $\mathfrak{A}$.

When k is clear from the context, we write $\mathrm{type}^r(\mathfrak{A})$ and call it the r-*type* of $\mathfrak{A}$. For an interval I of a chain $\mathfrak{A}$, we write $\mathrm{type}^r(I)$ for the r-type of the induced substructure $\mathfrak{A} \restriction I$.

2.4 Concatenation of Chains and Sum of Types

Given ℓ-chains $\mathfrak{A}$ and $\mathfrak{B}$, their *sum* (or *concatenation*) $\mathfrak{A} + \mathfrak{B}$ is obtained by placing $\mathfrak{A}$ before $\mathfrak{B}$. More generally, for a finite sequence of ℓ-chains $\mathfrak{A}_1, \dots, \mathfrak{A}_n$, we write $\sum_{i=1}^n \mathfrak{A}_i$ for their sum [8]. The next proposition implies that the r-type of the concatenation of two chains is determined by their r-types.

Proposition 2.3 (Sum of types). *For every r there is a computable operation $+$ on r-types such that*

$$\mathrm{type}^r(\mathfrak{A} + \mathfrak{B}) = \mathrm{type}^r(\mathfrak{A}) + \mathrm{type}^r(\mathfrak{B}).$$

The following lemma is a standard consequence of composition methods for *MSO* over linear orders [8]; in particular, it follows from Proposition 2.3.

Lemma 2.4 (Local normal form). *Let*

$$\varphi(x_1, \dots, x_m) \wedge \bigwedge_{i<m} x_i < x_{i+1}$$

be an MSO formula of quantifier rank q. For every $r \geq q + 2$, the formula φ is equivalent to a (finite) positive Boolean combination of formulas asserting the r-types of the induced subchains on the intervals

$$(-\infty, x_1), \quad [x_i, x_{i+1}), \quad \text{and} \quad [x_m, \infty).$$

Moreover, this Boolean combination is computable from φ.

3 Interpretations and Reparameterizations

In this section we recall the notion of interpretation and show that if the universe formulas admit d-dimensional reparameterizations, then the interpretation is equivalent to a d-dimensional interpretation. These results are not needed for the computability of d-dimensional reparameterizations and serve only to motivate the reparameterization problem. Throughout this section we consider *MSO* over arbitrary relational signatures; its syntax and semantics are defined in the natural way. Readers interested primarily in the decidability results may skim this section on first reading.

Definition 3.1 (MSO interpretation). *An* MSO (many-dimensional point) interpretation *is a function*

$$f : \mathcal{C} \to \mathcal{D}$$

between two classes of structures, where all structures in $\mathcal{C}$ (respectively, $\mathcal{D}$) are over a fixed relational signature. The interpretation is defined as follows.

All formulas mentioned below are MSO formulas over the signature of the input class $\mathcal{C}$. All free variables are first-order (element) variables, but the formulas may quantify over sets.

1. ***Components.*** *There is a finite set Q whose elements are called the* components *of the interpretation. Each component $q \in Q$ is associated with a* dimension $\dim(q) \in \{0, 1, 2, \dots\}$.

2. ***Universe formulas.*** *For each component* $q \in Q$*, there is an associated* universe formula $\varphi_q(\bar{x})$*, where the tuple* $\bar{x}$ *has length* $\dim(q)$*. These formulas define the universe/domain of the output structure as follows. For an input structure* $\mathfrak{A} \in \mathcal{C}$ *with universe* A*, the universe of* $f(\mathfrak{A})$ *is the disjoint union*

$$\coprod_{q \in Q} \{\bar{a} \in A^{\dim(q)} \mid \mathfrak{A} \models \varphi_q(\bar{a})\}.$$

3. ***Relation interpretations.*** *Let* R *be a relation symbol in the vocabulary of the output class* $\mathcal{D}$ *of arity* ℓ*. For every choice of components* $q_1, \ldots, q_\ell \in Q$*, there is an MSO formula*

$$\varphi^R_{q_1,\ldots,q_\ell}(\bar{x}_1, \ldots, \bar{x}_\ell),$$

where each tuple $\bar{x}_i$ *has length* $\dim(q_i)$*. For every input structure* $\mathfrak{A} \in \mathcal{C}$ *and tuples* $\bar{a}_i \in A^{\dim(q_i)}$*, we have*

$$\mathfrak{A} \models \varphi^R_{q_1,\ldots,q_\ell}(\bar{a}_1, \ldots, \bar{a}_\ell)$$

if and only if, in the structure $f(\mathfrak{A})$*, the relation* R *holds on the* ℓ*-tuple whose* i*-th coordinate is* $\bar{a}_i$ *from component* q_i*.*

An interpretation is said to be *m-dimensional* if all its universe formulas use at most m free variables. Two interpretations

$$f, h \colon \mathcal{C} \to \mathcal{D}$$

are *equivalent* if for every $\mathfrak{A} \in \mathcal{C}$ the structures $f(\mathfrak{A})$ and $h(\mathfrak{A})$ are isomorphic.

Proposition 3.2. *Let* $\mathcal{C}$ *be a class of structures equipped with an MSO-definable linear order. Assume that for each component* q *of an interpretation* f *over* $\mathcal{C}$*, the corresponding universe formula* φ_q *admits a reparameterization of dimension* d*. Then* f *is equivalent to a* d*-dimensional interpretation* h*. Moreover, there exists an MSO formula that uniformly defines, in every* $\mathfrak{A} \in \mathcal{C}$*, an isomorphism between* $f(\mathfrak{A})$ *and* $h(\mathfrak{A})$*.*

Proof (Proof Sketch). For each component q, let $G_q(\bar{x}, \bar{y})$ be an *MSO*-definable reparameterization of the domain formula $\varphi_q(\bar{x})$, where $|\bar{y}| \leq d$. Assume that there exists a constant N_q such that for every input structure $\mathcal{A}$ and every tuple $\bar{y}$, the set

$$\{\bar{x} \mid \mathcal{A} \models \varphi_q(\bar{x}) \wedge G_q(\bar{x}, \bar{y})\}$$

has size at most N_q.

We construct an equivalent d-dimensional interpretation whose components are pairs (q, i), where q ranges over the original components and $1 \leq i \leq N_q$.

For each such pair (q, i), we define the corresponding domain formula $\psi_{q,i}(\bar{y})$ by $\exists \bar{x} \; \Big(G_q(\bar{x}, \bar{y}) \;\; \wedge \;\; \bar{x} \text{ is the } i\text{-th tuple in the lexicographic order of this set}\Big)$. Since the lexicographic order on tuples is *MSO*-definable, the formula $\psi_{q,i}$ is an *MSO* formula; by construction, it has at most d free variables. By construction, the disjoint union of the components (q, i) recovers exactly the universe defined by φ_q.

Relation formulas in the new interpretation are obtained by replacing the original variables by their corresponding reparameterizations. For simplicity, consider a binary relation symbol R of the output signature. For components (q_1, i_1) and (q_2, i_2), define $\psi^R_{(q_1,i_1),(q_2,i_2)}(\bar{y}_1, \bar{y}_2)$ to assert that there exist tuples $\bar{x}_1, \bar{x}_2$ such that $\bar{x}_j$ is the i_j-th tuple satisfying $G_{q_j}(\bar{x}_j, \bar{y}_j)$ for $j = 1, 2$, and $\varphi^R_{q_1,q_2}(\bar{x}_1, \bar{x}_2)$ holds. The resulting d-dimensional interpretation is canonically isomorphic to the original one.

4 Reparameterization

The following theorem is our main result. It generalizes Lemma II.7 of Bojańczyk [2] from finite words to arbitrary countable chains.

Theorem 4.1 (Decidability of m-dimensional reparameterizations). *Let $\mathcal{C}$ be an MSO-definable class of countable chains, and let $\varphi(\bar{x})$ be an MSO formula with first-order free variables $\bar{x} = (x_1, \dots, x_n)$. There is an algorithm which, given $m \in \mathbb{N}$, decides whether there exists an MSO formula $G(\bar{x}, \bar{y})$ with $\bar{y}$ an m-tuple of first-order variables, and a number $N \in \mathbb{N}$ such that, over $\mathcal{C}$,*

$$\varphi(\bar{x}) \;\equiv\; \exists \bar{y}\, G(\bar{x}, \bar{y}) \qquad \textit{and} \qquad \big|\{\, \bar{x} \mid \mathcal{M} \models G(\bar{x}, \bar{y}) \,\}\big| \;\leq\; N$$

for all $\mathcal{M} \in \mathcal{C}$ and all tuples $\bar{y}$ of elements of $\mathcal{M}$. Moreover, whenever the answer is positive, an m-dimensional functional reparameterization can be effectively constructed from φ and an MSO definition of $\mathcal{C}$.

Below we consider the reparameterization problem over the class of countable chains. If $\mathcal{C}$ is a class of countable chains definable by a formula ψ, then the reparameterization problem for φ over $\mathcal{C}$ is reducible to the reparameterization problem for $\varphi \wedge \psi$ over the class of all countable chains.

4.1 Pumpability and Dimension Bounds

In this subsection we study the connection between pumpability and the minimal dimension of a reparameterization. We first establish in Lemma 4.2 a pumping criterion for formulas with one free variable, characterizing the existence of arbitrarily many realizations in terms of idempotent types. We then introduce in Lemma 4.4 the notion of a pumpable pair of types and show how non-pumpable pairs allow the elimination of variables, yielding lower-dimensional reparameterizations. Finally, Lemma 4.6 shows that if all adjacent pairs are pumpable, then the dimension cannot be reduced.

Lemma 4.2. *There exist constants $B, q \in \mathbb{N}$, computable from $\varphi(x)$, such that the following are equivalent:*

1. *The formula $\exists^{\geq B} x\, \varphi(x)$ is satisfiable.*
2. *For every N, the formula $\exists^{\geq N} x\, \varphi(x)$ is satisfiable.*
3. *There exist satisfiable q-types τ, τ_1, and τ_2 such that:*
   - *τ is idempotent (i.e., $\tau + \tau = \tau$),*
   - *$\tau_1 + \tau = \tau_1$,*
   - *$\tau + \tau_2 = \tau_2$, and*
   - *the conjunction $\mathit{type}^q((-\infty, x)) = \tau_1 \wedge \mathit{type}^q([x, \infty)) = \tau_2$ implies $\varphi(x)$.*

Proof. The implication (2) $\implies$ (1) is trivial.

(1) $\implies$ (3). Let q be any number that exceeds the quantifier rank of φ by 2. By Lemma 2.2 and Lemma 2.4, the formula $\varphi(x)$ is equivalent to a disjunction of formulas of the form

$$\mathit{type}^q((-\infty, x)) = \tau_1 \wedge \mathit{type}^q([x, \infty)) = \tau_2.$$

Without loss of generality, we may assume that φ is of this form.

We aim to find a constant B for formulas of the above form.

Let H be the number of q-types (over the signature of φ). By Ramsey's theorem, there exists a constant B such that every coloring of the edges of the complete graph on B vertices using H colors contains a monochromatic triangle. We claim this value of B suffices.

Suppose $a_1 < \cdots < a_B$ are elements in some chain $\mathcal{M}$ such that $\mathcal{M} \models \varphi(a_i)$ for all i. For each pair $i < j$, define the color $\mathsf{col}(i, j)$ as the q-type of the interval $[a_i, a_j)$. By Ramsey's theorem, there exist indices $i < j < k$ such that

$$\mathsf{col}(i, j) = \mathsf{col}(j, k) = \mathsf{col}(i, k) = \tau.$$

It follows that $\tau + \tau = \tau$, i.e., τ is idempotent.

By assumption, the type τ_1 of $(-\infty, a_i)$ equals that of $(-\infty, a_j)$, so $\tau_1 + \tau = \tau_1$. Similarly, the type τ_2 of $[a_k, \infty)$ equals that of $[a_j, \infty)$, so $\tau + \tau_2 = \tau_2$. Thus, condition (3) of the lemma holds. Hence, we have established (1) $\implies$ (3).

Let us prove that (3) implies (2). Let L, I, and U be chains with q-types τ_1, τ, and τ_2, respectively. Since $q \geq 2$, every q-type determines whether the corresponding structures have a minimal element. In particular, all structures of type τ_2 have a minimal element. Since $\tau + \tau_2 = \tau_2$, it follows that all structures of type τ also have a minimal element. Hence, I has a minimal element.

For $N \in \mathbb{N}$, define the structure

$$\mathcal{M}_N := L + \underbrace{I + \cdots + I}_{N \text{ copies}} + U.$$

Then the minimal element of each copy of I satisfies $\varphi(x)$ in $\mathcal{M}_N$. Thus, $\exists^{\geq N} x\, \varphi(x)$ holds in $\mathcal{M}_N$ for all N. $\square$

Definition 4.3 (Pumpable pair of types). *We say that a pair of q-types (τ_b, τ_e) is* pumpable *if there exists a satisfiable idempotent q-type τ such that:*

$$\tau_b + \tau = \tau_b \quad \textit{and} \quad \tau + \tau_e = \tau_e.$$

Let $\tau_0, \ldots, \tau_k$ be a sequence of q-types, and define the formula

$$\begin{aligned}\varphi(x_1, \ldots, x_k) := x_1 < x_2 < \cdots < x_k \wedge \\ \quad type^q((-\infty, x_1)) = \tau_0 \wedge type^q([x_k, \infty)) = \tau_k \wedge \\ \quad \bigwedge_{i=1}^{k-1} type^q([x_i, x_{i+1})) = \tau_i.\end{aligned} \tag{1}$$

If the pair (τ_{i-1}, τ_i) is not pumpable, then the variable x_i can be eliminated as explained in the following Lemma.

Lemma 4.4. *Assume that φ is as in Equation (1), and that the pair (τ_i, τ_{i+1}) is not pumpable. Then:*

$$G_i(x_1, \ldots, x_k, y_1, \ldots, y_{k-1}) := \varphi(x_1, \ldots, x_k) \wedge \bigwedge_{j<i} y_j = x_j \wedge \bigwedge_{j>i} y_j = x_{j-1}$$

defines a $(k-1)$-dimensional functional reparameterization of φ.

Proof. Follows from Lemma 4.2. □

Remark 4.5. In the reparameterization constructed in Lemma 4.4, each image variable is equal to one of the domain variables.

The next lemma treats the case in which all pairs are pumpable, and shows that in this situation the dimension cannot be reduced.

Lemma 4.6. *Assume that $\varphi(x_1, \ldots, x_k)$ is as in Eq. (1), and that all pairs (τ_i, τ_{i+1}) are pumpable. Then:*

1. *For every $N \in \mathbb{N}$ and every proper subset $I \subsetneq \{1, \ldots, k\}$, there exists a structure $\mathcal{M}_N$ and at least N distinct tuples that satisfy φ and agree on all coordinates x_i for $i \in I$.*
2. *If G is a reparameterization of φ, then G must use at least k image variables.*
3. *For every $N \in \mathbb{N}$, there exists a structure $\mathcal{M}_N$ and a subset $S \subseteq \mathcal{M}_N$ of size $2Nk$ such that:*

$$\{(a_1, \ldots, a_k) \in S^k \mid \mathcal{M}_N \models \varphi(a_1, \ldots, a_k)\}$$

has cardinality at least $(2N)^k$.

Proof. (1) follows from (2).
(2) Assume toward a contradiction that there exists a reparameterization G of φ with $l < k$ image variables. Let $r - 2$ be greater than the quantifier rank of both φ and G. By Lemma 2.4, the formulas φ and G are equivalent to Boolean combinations of formulas asserting the r-types of the induced subchains on the relevant intervals.

Let τ_i' be an idempotent q-type witnessing that the pair (τ_i, τ_{i+1}) occurring in the representation of φ as in Eq. (1) is pumpable, that is,

$$\tau_i + \tau_i' = \tau_i \quad \text{and} \quad \tau_i' + \tau_{i+1} = \tau_{i+1}.$$

There is a satisfiable idempotent r-type σ_i such that $\sigma_i \to \tau_i'$. Let U_i be a chain of r-type σ_i (and hence of q-type τ_i'), and let L_i be a chain of type τ_i. Define the structure $\mathcal{M} := \mathcal{M}_N$ by

$$\mathcal{M} := L_0 + \sum_i (U_i \times 2N + L_{i+1}),$$

where $U_i \times 2N$ denotes the concatenation of $2N$ consecutive copies of U_i.

Let a_i be the first element of the N-th copy of U_i. By construction,

$$\mathcal{M} \models \varphi(a_1, \ldots, a_k).$$

Hence, there exist elements $b_1, \ldots, b_\ell$ such that

$$\mathcal{M} \models G(a_1, \ldots, a_k, b_1, \ldots, b_\ell).$$

We say that a_i and b_j are *close* if b_j lies in $U_i \times 2N$; otherwise, we say that a_i and b_j are *far*. Since $\ell < k$, by the pigeonhole principle there exists some a_i that is far from every b_j.

For $m = 2, \ldots, 2N$, let a_i^m be the first element of the m-th copy of U_i. Since the r-type $\sigma_i := \mathit{type}^r(U_i)$ is idempotent, for every formula ψ of quantifier rank at most $r - 2$, and every tuple $\bar{c}$ that is far from a_i, we have

$$\mathcal{M} \models \psi(\bar{c}, a_i) \quad \text{iff} \quad \mathcal{M} \models \psi(\bar{c}, a_i^m).$$

It follows that all tuples

$$(a_1, \ldots, a_i^m, \ldots, a_k), \qquad m = 2, \ldots, 2N,$$

are mapped by G to the same tuple $(b_1, \ldots, b_\ell)$. Hence, the preimage of $(b_1, \ldots, b_\ell)$ under G has size at least $2N - 1$.

This contradicts the bounded preimage condition in the definition of reparameterization. Therefore, G cannot be a valid reparameterization of φ.
(3) Let $\mathcal{M} = \mathcal{M}_N$ be the structure defined as in the proof of (2), where for each $i = 1, \ldots, k$, the structure contains $2N$ consecutive copies of a chain U_i of type σ_i and hence of τ_i'.

For each $i = 1, \ldots, k$, define the set

$$S_i := \left\{ l_i^j \;\middle|\; l_i^j \text{ is the first element in the } j\text{-th copy of } U_i \right\}.$$

Note that $|S_i| = 2N$. Define $S := \bigcup_{i=1}^{k} S_i$. Then $|S| \leq 2Nk$.

Now consider any tuple $(a_1, \ldots, a_k)$ such that $a_i \in S_i$ for all i. By construction, each a_i lies at the beginning of a block of type U_i positioned to satisfy the formula φ. Therefore, $\mathcal{M} \models \varphi(a_1, \ldots, a_k)$.

Since there are $2N$ choices for each $a_i \in S_i$, the total number of such tuples is $(2N)^k$. This shows that $\left|\{(a_1, \ldots, a_k) \in S^k \mid \mathcal{M} \models \varphi(a_1, \ldots, a_k)\}\right| \geq (2N)^k$, as required. □

4.2 Computability of a Minimal Reparameterization

Definition 4.7 (Minimal reparameterization). *A reparameterization $G(\bar{x}, \bar{y})$ of a formula $\varphi(\bar{x})$ is called* minimal *if it uses the smallest possible number of image variables among all reparameterizations of φ.*

Proposition 4.8. *Let $G(\overline{x}, \overline{y})$ be a reparameterization of a formula $\varphi(\overline{x})$. Then: There exists an algorithm which, given a d-dimensional reparameterization of φ (respectively, of $\exists \overline{x}\, G$), constructs a d-dimensional reparameterization of $\exists \overline{x}\, G$ (respectively, of φ).*

Proof. Assume that $F(\overline{x}, \overline{u})$ is a d-dimensional reparameterization of $\varphi(\overline{x})$. Then we can define a reparameterization of $\exists \overline{x}\, G(\overline{x}, \overline{y})$ by:

$$\exists \overline{x}\, (F(\overline{x}, \overline{u}) \ \wedge\ \overline{x} \text{ is the lexicographically minimal tuple such that } G(\overline{x}, \overline{y}))\,.$$

That is, for each tuple $\overline{y}$, we select the lexicographically minimal tuple $\overline{x}$ such that $G(\overline{x}, \overline{y})$ holds, and apply the original reparameterization F to that tuple.

Note that, by the definition of reparameterization, there are only finitely many tuples $\overline{x}$ such that $G(\overline{x}, \overline{y})$ holds. Therefore, the lexicographically minimal such $\overline{x}$ exists.

This construction yields a d-dimensional reparameterization of $\exists \overline{x}\, G$.

Conversely, assume that $H(\overline{y}, \overline{u})$ is a d-dimensional reparameterization of the formula $\exists \overline{x}\, G(\overline{x}, \overline{y})$. Then we can define a reparameterization of $\varphi(\overline{x})$ by:

$$\exists \overline{y}\, (G(\overline{x}, \overline{y}) \ \wedge\ H(\overline{y}, \overline{u}))\,.$$

That is, for each $\overline{x}$ satisfying φ, we compute the image of $\overline{x}$ by first obtaining $\overline{y}$ via G, and then applying the reparameterization H to $\overline{y}$. This defines a d-dimensional reparameterization of φ. □

Lemma 4.9. *Let $\psi_1(\bar{x}), \ldots, \psi_k(\bar{x})$ be formulas. Assume that for each j the formula $\psi_j(\bar{x})$ admits a d_j-dimensional reparameterization. Then one can effectively construct a d-dimensional reparameterization of $\bigvee_{j=1}^{k} \psi_j(\bar{x})$, where $d := \max_{1 \leq j \leq k} d_j$.*

Proof. Assume $G_j(\overline{x}, \overline{y})$ is a d_j-dimensional reparameterization of ψ_j. Let $d = \max_j d_j$. Define the guarded disjunction

$$G(\overline{x}, \overline{y}) := \bigvee_{j} \left(\left(\bigwedge_{i<j} \neg\psi_i(\overline{x}) \right) \wedge \psi_j(\overline{x}) \wedge G_j(\overline{x}, \overline{y}) \right).$$

This formula selects the appropriate G_j for the first ψ_j (in index order) that is satisfied by $\overline{x}$. By construction, G is a d-dimensional reparameterization of $\bigvee_j \psi_j$. □

Theorem 4.1 follows from the next proposition.

Proposition 4.10. *A minimal reparameterization of an MSO formula is computable.*

Proof. We proceed by induction on the number k of free variables in the formula.

Base case: $k = 0$.
In this case, φ is a sentence with no free variables. The minimal dimension of a reparameterization is 0, and the trivial reparameterization is clearly computable.

Inductive step: Assume that for all formulas with fewer than k free variables, a minimal reparameterization is computable.

Let φ be a formula with k free variables. We can effectively compute a disjunction $\bigvee_i \varphi_i$ equivalent to φ, where each φ_i is of the form described in Eq. (1).

Suppose first that for every disjunct φ_i, the corresponding sequence of types $(\tau_0^i, \dots, \tau_k^i)$ contains at least one non-pumpable pair. Then, by Lemma 4.4, each such φ_i admits a $(k-1)$-dimensional reparameterization G_i, computable from φ_i. By taking the guarded disjunction of these reparameterizations (as in the proof of Lemma 4.9), we obtain a $(k-1)$-dimensional reparameterization $G(\overline{x}, \overline{y})$ of φ, computable from φ.

By the inductive hypothesis, we can compute a minimal reparameterization of the formula $\exists \overline{x}\, G(\overline{x}, \overline{y})$. Then, by Proposition 4.8, we can compute a minimal reparameterization of φ.

Now suppose there exists a disjunct φ_i whose sequence of types $(\tau_0^i, \dots, \tau_k^i)$ contains only pumpable pairs. Then, by Lemma 4.6, every reparameterization G_i of φ_i has dimension at least k.

Note that if G is a reparameterization of $\bigvee_i \varphi_i$, then $G \wedge \varphi_i$ is a reparameterization of φ_i. Hence, any reparameterization of φ must have dimension at least k. It follows that the trivial reparameterization $G(\overline{x}, \overline{y}) := \varphi(\overline{x}) \wedge \bigwedge_j y_j = x_j$ is minimal and computable. □

Remark 4.11. By the construction above, there exists a reparameterization $G(\overline{x}, \overline{y})$ of $\varphi(\overline{x})$ over $\mathcal{C}$ of *minimal dimension* (i.e., with $|\overline{y}|$ minimal) such that each image variable y_j is always equal to one of the domain variables.

5 Growth Rate

Bojańczyk [2] introduced the notion of the *growth rate* of a string-to-string function as the function that maps an input length $n \in \{0, 1, \dots\}$ to the maximal size of an output produced on inputs of length at most n.

This notion was later generalized by Gallot et al. [3], who showed that the output size of an *MSO* set interpretation from finite trees to relational structures grows either polynomially or exponentially in the input size, with a computable degree $k \in \mathbb{N} \cup \{\infty\}$.

In this section, we define the growth rate of an *MSO* interpretation over arbitrary structures, including infinite ones. We show that the growth rate of an *MSO point* interpretation is polynomial, with degree equal to the minimal reparameterization dimension.

Let $\varphi(x_1, \ldots, x_k)$ be an *MSO* formula, and let S be a subset of a structure $\mathcal{M}$. Define: $I(S, \mathcal{M}) := \{\overline{a} \in S^k \mid \mathcal{M} \models \varphi(\overline{a})\}$. Let the growth function $g_\varphi(n, \mathcal{M})$ be defined as:

$$g_\varphi(n, \mathcal{M}) := \max \{|I(S, \mathcal{M})| \mid S \subseteq M,\ |S| \leq n\}.$$

Note that $g_\varphi(n, \mathcal{M})$ is bounded above by n^k.

For a class $\mathcal{C}$ of structures, define:

$$g_\varphi(n, \mathcal{C}) := \max_{\mathcal{M} \in \mathcal{C}} g_\varphi(n, \mathcal{M})$$

The following theorem generalizes Bojańczyk's theorem [2, Theorem II.3] from finite words to arbitrary countable chains.

Theorem 5.1. *Let $\varphi(\bar{x}) \in MSO$ and let $\mathcal{C}$ be an MSO-definable class of labelled linear orders. Then there exists a natural number $d \in \mathbb{N}$ such that $g_\varphi(n, \mathcal{C}) = \Theta(n^d)$. Furthermore, the degree d coincides with the minimal reparameterization dimension of φ over $\mathcal{C}$, and is therefore computable.*

Proof (Proof sketch). Upper bound. By Remark 4.11, there exists a minimal reparameterization $G(\bar{x}, \bar{y})$ of φ over $\mathcal{C}$ such that $|\bar{y}| = d$ and, whenever $\bar{x} \in S^k$ satisfies φ, the corresponding tuple $\bar{y}$ also belongs to S^d.

For a fixed structure $\mathcal{M} \in \mathcal{C}$ and a set $S \subseteq M$ of size at most n, the set of possible parameter tuples $\bar{y}$ therefore has cardinality at most $|S|^d \leq n^d$. By the bounded preimage property of reparameterizations, each such $\bar{y}$ corresponds to at most N tuples $\bar{x}$. This yields the upper bound $g_\varphi(n, \mathcal{C}) = O(n^d)$.

Lower bound. If $d = k$, i.e., if the minimal reparameterization of $\varphi(\bar{x})$ has the same number of image and domain variables, then the lower bound follows directly from Lemma 4.6(3).

Assume now that $d < k$, and let $G(\bar{x}, \bar{y})$ be a minimal reparameterization of φ. The construction used in the proof of Lemma 4.6(3), applied to $\exists \bar{x}\, G(\bar{x}, \bar{y})$, yields a lower bound of $\Omega(n^d)$. A refinement of this construction, combined with the additional properties of the reparameterization G, then yields the same lower bound $\Omega(n^d)$ for φ; see [6] for details. □

6 Conclusion and Further Results

Bojańczyk [2] studied reparameterizations of *MSO*-definable relations over finite words and proved that it is decidable whether an m-dimensional point *MSO* interpretation admits a d-dimensional point *MSO* reparameterization. In this paper, we extend this decidability result to arbitrary countable labelled chains.

In many situations, however, one considers *MSO* interpretations that are more general than point interpretations. In *finite-set* and *set* interpretations, elements of the interpreted structure are represented by tuples of finite sets or arbitrary sets, respectively.

Interpretations of $\mathfrak{A}$ *in* $\mathfrak{B}$. We distinguish three standard flavours of d-dimensional *MSO* interpretations of a structure $\mathfrak{A}$ in a structure $\mathfrak{B}$. In each case, an element of $\mathfrak{A}$ is encoded inside $\mathfrak{B}$ by a d-tuple:

Set interpretations (*MSO*, d-dimensional): each element of $\mathfrak{A}$ is represented by a d-tuple of arbitrary subsets of $\mathfrak{B}$.

Finite-set interpretations (*MSO*, d-dimensional): each element of $\mathfrak{A}$ is represented by a d-tuple of finite subsets of $\mathfrak{B}$.

Point interpretations (*MSO*, d-dimensional): each element of $\mathfrak{A}$ is represented by a d-tuple of elements of $\mathfrak{B}$.

A natural question is whether a given interpretation can be simplified; for instance, whether a set or finite-set interpretation is equivalent to a point interpretation.

Gallot, Lhote, and Nguyen [3] studied *finite-set-to-point* reparameterizations over finite words and trees and proved that it is decidable whether a finite-set interpretation admits a point reparameterization.

In [7] we extended this decidability result to arbitrary countable labelled chains: given an *MSO* formula φ with free finite-set variables, it is decidable whether φ admits a point reparameterization.

Over linear orders, a canonical class of simple subsets is given by *cuts*, i.e., downward-closed sets. Cuts correspond to points in the Dedekind completion and form a structurally robust family of subsets. The analogue of our main result, Theorem 4.1, also holds when first-order domain and image variables are replaced by variables interpreted as cuts.

Finally, building on the techniques of [1], we also proved in [7] that it is decidable whether an *MSO* formula φ with free set variables admits a many-dimensional finite-set reparameterization over Dedekind-complete countable labelled chains.

Acknowledgements. We thank the anonymous reviewers for their careful reading and valuable comments and suggestions, which helped improve the presentation of this paper.

References

1. Barany, V., Kaiser, L., Rabinovich, A.: Expressing cardinality quantifiers in monadic second-order logic over chains. J. Symb. Log. **76**(2), 603–619 (2011)
2. Bojańczyk, M.: On the growth rates of polyregular functions. In: Symposium on Logic in Computer Science (LICS), pp. 1–13. IEEE (2023)
3. Gallot, P., Lhote, N., Nguyên, L.T.O.: The structure of polynomial growth for tree automata/transducers and MSO set queries. To appear in TheoretiCS (2025). https://doi.org/10.48550/arXiv.2501.10270

4. Gurevich, Y.: Monadic second-order theories. In: Barwise, J., Feferman, S. (eds.) Model-Theoretic Logics, pp. 479–506. Springer (1985)
5. Rabin, M.O.: Decidability of second-order theories and automata on infinite trees. Trans. Am. Math. Soc. **141**, 1–35 (1969)
6. Rabinovich, A.: Decidability of MSO reparameterization over countable chains. arXiv:2605.18248 (2026)
7. Rabinovich, A.: From sets to points: simplifying MSO interpretations via reparameterizations. In: ICALP 2026, Leibniz International Proceedings in Informatics (LIPIcs), pp. 163:1–163:20. Schloss Dagstuhl – Leibniz-Zentrum für Informatik (2026). https://doi.org/10.4230/LIPIcs.ICALP.2026.189
8. Shelah, S.: The monadic theory of order. Ann. Math. **102**(3), 379–419 (1975)
9. Tarski, A., Mostowski, A., Robinson, R.M.: Undecidable Theories. North-Holland, Amsterdam (1953)
10. Thomas, W.: Automata on infinite objects. In: Formal Models and Semantics, pp. 133–191. Elsevier (1990)

A Natural Axiomatization of Büchi Arithmetic

Konstantin Kovalyov(✉)

Steklov Mathematical Institute of Russian Academy of Sciences, Moscow, Russia
kovalyov.ka@mi-ras.ru

Abstract. We investigate Büchi Arithmetic BA_k—the elementary theory of the natural numbers equipped with addition and the function mapping a number x to the greatest power of k dividing x. BA_k is known to be decidable and to enjoy a few important properties, in particular, a first-order structure is automatic iff it is interpretable in BA_k. We propose a natural axiomatization of this theory based on a comprehension schema restricted to bounded formulas, interpreting natural numbers as finite (multi)sets of powers of k via their base-k expansions. The completeness proof for this axiomatization proceeds through a formalization of the Büchi–Bruyère Theorem on the equivalence of definability in Büchi Arithmetic and recognizability by finite automata.

1 Introduction

Base-k Büchi arithmetic, denoted BA_k, is the elementary theory of the structure $(\mathbb{N}, 0, S, +, V_k, \leq)$, where $k \geq 2$ is a fixed integer. For $x > 0$, $V_k(x)$ denotes the largest power of k dividing x, and $V_k(0) = 0$. It is useful to think about $V_k(x)$ as the position of the least significant non-zero digit of the base-k expansion of x. The structure $(\mathbb{N}, 0, S, +, V_k, \leq)$ is *automatic* and, moreover, it interprets every automatic structure (see [1, Theorem 4.5]). The theory BA_k is well known for the following fundamental result.

Theorem 1 ([2,3]). *A set $A \subseteq \mathbb{N}^m$ is definable in BA_k if and only if the set of base-k expansions of the elements of A is recognizable by a finite automaton. Moreover, the construction of a finite automaton from a defining formula is effective; consequently, BA_k is decidable.*

Büchi Arithmetic has been the subject of extensive investigation, particularly in connection with problems of definability, complexity, and interpretability. A central theme in this area is the relationship between Büchi Arithmetic and Presburger Arithmetic, which also highlights the close link with recognizability by finite automata. This connection is made precise by a classical result due to A. Cobham and A. Semenov.

Theorem 2 ([4,5]). *For $A \subseteq \mathbb{N}^m$, the following are equivalent:*

(i) *A is definable in Presburger Arithmetic;*

P. Johann and R. de Queiroz (Eds.): WoLLIC 2026, LNCS 16757, pp. 81–96, 2027.
https://doi.org/10.1007/978-3-032-33486-2_6

(ii) *A is definable in* BA_k *for all* $k \geq 2$;
(iii) *A is definable in* BA_k *and* BA_l *for some multiplicatively independent* $k, l \geq 2$.

This result has been substantially extended in subsequent work, most notably in [6] and, more recently, in [7]. Namely, for multiplicatively independent $k, l \geq 2$, if X and Y are not definable in Presburger Arithmetic, X is definable in BA_k, and Y is definable in BA_l, then the theory of the expansion of Presburger Arithmetic with the predicates for X and Y is undecidable.

From the point of view of computational complexity, BA_k has a complicated behavior as the following results describe.

Theorem 3 (follows from[8]). BA_k *is not Kalmar elementary. That is,* BA_k *cannot be decided in*

$$\exp_2(\exp_2(\ldots\exp_2(n)\ldots))$$

steps for any fixed number of nested exponentiations (here $\exp_2(n) = 2^n$*).*

Note that this bound is, in a sense, sharp: for a formula of length n with m quantifier alternations, the method from Theorem 1 runs in

$$\underbrace{\exp_2(\exp_2(\ldots\exp_2(}_{m \text{ times}}\mathrm{poly}(n))\ldots))$$

steps. Despite this extreme worst-case complexity, certain fragments of BA_k admit more feasible decision procedures.

Theorem 4 ([9]). *The existential fragment of* BA_k *is* NP*-complete.*

Nevertheless, some purely logical questions about Büchi Arithmetic remain open. In particular, no natural axiomatization of this theory is known. In our earlier work [10,11], we suggested a simple axiomatization of BA_k based on bounds for witnesses for existential quantifiers. However, the axioms are not very natural, and it would be difficult to verify whether an arbitrary structure is a model of these axioms. The following related negative result was obtained by A. Zapryagaev [12].

Theorem 5. *The theory axiomatized as follows is not complete:*

(i) *axioms of Presburger Arithmetic;*
(ii) $V_2(x) = 0 \leftrightarrow x = 0$;
(iii) $\neg\exists y\ (x = y + y) \rightarrow V_2(x) = 1$;
(iv) $x = t + t \rightarrow V_2(x) = V_2(t) + V_2(t)$.

The absence of an adequate axiomatization of BA_k makes the study of model-theoretic and interpretability questions difficult. For instance, no explicit construction of a nonstandard model of BA_k is currently known.

In this paper, we provide a natural axiomatization of BA_k based on basic properties of $+$ and V_k, together with a comprehension scheme restricted to Δ_0-formulas (see below for the definition of Δ_0-formulas). Here, natural numbers are interpreted as finite (multi)sets of powers of k via their base-k expansions (see below). Alternatively, the comprehension scheme can be replaced by an induction scheme for powers of k (see Remark 1). The main idea is to express, by means of a Δ_0-formula, the existence of a run of a finite automaton (cf. [13,14]) and to formalize within this axiomatization a proof of Theorem 1.

Let us now describe our axiomatization in detail. Fix a natural number $k \geq 2$ as the base for Büchi Arithmetic. For each $n \in \mathbb{N}$, we denote by $\underline{n}$ the term

$$\underbrace{S(S(\ldots S}_{n \text{ times}}(0)\ldots))$$

called the *numeral* corresponding to n. For a term t and $n \in \mathbb{N}$, we denote by nt the term

$$\underbrace{t + (t + (\ldots (t}_{n \text{ times}} + 0)\ldots)).$$

A formula φ is said to be *bounded*, or a Δ_0*-formula*, if every quantifier occurring in φ is of the form $\exists x \leq t$ or $\forall x \leq t$, where x does not occur in t. We denote by Δ_0 the set of bounded $\mathcal{L}_{\mathsf{BA}}$-formulas. We denote by Π_1 the set of formulas of the form $\forall \vec{x}\, \theta$, where $\theta \in \Delta_0$. Finally, we write $\varphi(x_1, \ldots, x_n)$ to indicate that the free variables of φ are among $\{x_1, \ldots, x_n\}$.

We introduce the following formulas:

$$P_k(d) \; :\Longleftrightarrow \; (d > 0) \wedge (V_k(d) = d),$$
$$x \equiv_k y \; :\Longleftrightarrow \; \exists z \leq x + y \; (x = y + kz \vee y = x + kz),$$

and, for each $a \in \{0, \ldots, k-1\}$, a formula

$$(x)_d = a \; :\Longleftrightarrow \; P_k(d) \wedge \exists y < d \, \exists z \leq x \, \Big((x = y + ad + z) \wedge (z = 0 \vee V_k(z) > d)\Big).$$

Here P_k defines the set of powers of k, and $(x)_d = a$ expresses that the coefficient before d in the base-k expansion of x is equal to a. We write $\exists^{P_k} d \, \varphi$ and $\forall^{P_k} d \, \varphi$ as abbreviations for $\exists d \, (P_k(d) \wedge \varphi)$ and $\forall d \, (P_k(d) \rightarrow \varphi)$, respectively. Also, we will sometimes write $d \in P_k$ instead of $P_k(d)$ when convenient.

Definition 1. *A theory* T_k *consists of the universal closures of the following formulas:*

(Add) *axioms of discretely ordered commutative cancelative monoids;*
(Ord0) $x \geq 0$*;*
(Ord1) $x \leq y \leftrightarrow \exists z \leq y \; (z + x = y)$*;*
(Mod) $\bigvee_{a=0}^{k-1} (x \equiv_k \underline{a})$*;*
(V0) $V_k(0) = 0$, $V_k(\underline{1}) = \underline{1}$*;*
(V1) $V_k(kx) = kV_k(x)$, $P_k(d) \rightarrow \bigwedge_{a=1}^{k-1} (V_k(ad) = d)$*;*
(V2) $(x > 0 \wedge y > 0 \wedge V_k(x) < V_k(y)) \rightarrow V_k(x + y) = V_k(x)$*;*
(V3) $x > 0 \rightarrow \exists y \leq x \; \bigvee_{a=1}^{k-1} \left(x = y + aV_k(x) \wedge (V_k(y) > V_k(x) \vee y = 0)\right)$*;*

(V4) $x > 0 \to \exists^{P_k} d \leq x \ (d \leq x < kd)$;
(V5) $V_k(V_k(x)) = V_k(x)$;
(Comp) $P_k(d) \to \exists x < d \ \forall^{P_k} d' < d \ \Big(\big((x)_{d'} = 1 \wedge \varphi(d', \vec{y}) \big) \vee \big((x)_{d'} = 0 \wedge \neg\varphi(d', \vec{y}) \big) \Big)$ *for every* Δ_0*-formula* $\varphi(d, \vec{y})$.

Let us clarify the meaning of some of the axioms. Axiom (Ord1) states that subtraction is well-defined. Axiom (V3) asserts that, for $x > 0$, there exists a coefficient before $V_k(x)$ in the k-expansion of x. Axiom scheme (Comp) corresponds to *comprehension* when we interpret numbers as finite sets of powers of k. In Sect. 3, we prove the completeness of T_k (see Theorem 6).

2 Preliminaries

We fix a natural number $k \geq 2$ as the base of Büchi arithmetic. By $\mathcal{L}_{\mathsf{BA}}$ we denote the language of Büchi arithmetic, namely $(0, S, +, V_k, \leq)$. We denote the standard model $(\mathbb{N}, 0, S, +, V_k, \leq)$ simply by $\mathbb{N}$. The theory BA_k is the elementary theory of $(\mathbb{N}, 0, S, +, V_k, \leq)$.

By a *finite automaton* (FA for short) over a finite alphabet Σ we mean a tuple $A = (\Sigma, Q, q_0, F, \Delta)$, where

(i) Q is a finite set of states;
(ii) $q_0 \in Q$ is the initial state;
(iii) $F \subseteq Q$ is the set of accepting states;
(iv) $\Delta \subseteq Q \times \Sigma \times Q$ is the transition relation.

Given a finite automaton A, we denote by $L(A)$ the language recognized by A, namely

$$L(A) := \{w \in \Sigma^* \mid \text{some accepting state is reachable from } q_0 \text{ when } A \text{ reads } w\}.$$

A finite automaton $A = (\Sigma, Q, q_0, F, \Delta)$ is called a *deterministic finite automaton* (DFA for short) if Δ is a total function $Q \times \Sigma \to Q$. Given a DFA A, a state $q \in Q$, and a word $w \in \Sigma^*$, there exists a unique state $q' \in Q$ reached from q after A reads w; we denote this state by $A(q, w)$.

A language $L \subseteq \Sigma^*$ is said to be *recognizable* if there exists a FA (or, equivalently, a DFA) A such that $L = L(A)$.

We denote by Σ_k the alphabet $\{0, \ldots, k-1\}$. We say that a word $w \in \Sigma_k^*$ is a *k-expansion* of $a \in \mathbb{N}$ if

$$\sum_{i<|w|} w_i k^i = a.$$

Similarly, we say that a word $w \in (\Sigma_k^m)^*$ is a *k-expansion* of $(a_1, \ldots, a_m) \in \mathbb{N}^m$ if

$$\sum_{i<|w|} (w_i)_j k^i = a_j$$

for every $j = 1, \ldots, m$. Here w_i denotes the i-th symbol of w (that is, an element of Σ_k^m), and $(w_i)_j$ denotes the j-th component of w_i (that is, an element of Σ_k).

Given a set $A \subseteq \mathbb{N}^m$, we denote by $[A]_k$ the language consisting of all k-expansions of elements of A. We say that $A \subseteq \mathbb{N}^m$ is *k-recognizable* if the language $[A]_k$ is recognizable (as a language over Σ_k^m).

Given finite automata $A = (\Sigma_k^m, Q, q_0, F, \Delta)$ and $A' = (\Sigma_k^m, Q', q_0', F', \Delta')$, we use the following notation:

- $A \times A'$ denotes the product automaton of A and A', that is,

$$A \times A' = (\Sigma_k^m, Q \times Q', (q_0, q_0'), F \times F', \Delta''),$$

  where

$$\Delta'' := \{((q, q'), \vec{a}, (q_1, q_1')) \mid (q, \vec{a}, q_1) \in \Delta \text{ and } (q', \vec{a}, q_1') \in \Delta'\};$$

- $\mathrm{pr}(A)$ denotes the finite automaton obtained from A by removing the last digit from the label of each transition;
- A^{+n} denotes the finite automaton $(\Sigma_k^{m+n}, Q, q_0, F, \Delta^{+n})$, where

$$\Delta^{+n} := \{(q, (\vec{a}, \vec{b}), q') \in Q \times \Sigma_k^{m+n} \times Q \mid (q, \vec{a}, q') \in \Delta\};$$

- $\overline{A} := (\Sigma_k^m, Q, q_0, Q \setminus F, \Delta)$ denotes the automaton obtained from A by complementing the set of accepting states;
- $\det(A)$ denotes the determinization of A, with $\mathcal{P}(Q)$ as the set of states.

The following facts are well known:

- $L(A \times A') = L(A) \cap L(A')$;
- $L(\mathrm{pr}(A)) = \{u \in (\Sigma_k^{m-1})^* \mid \exists w \in L(A) \text{ such that } u = \mathrm{pr}(w)\}$, where $\mathrm{pr}(w)$ is obtained from w by removing the last digit from each symbol of w;
- $L(A^{+n}) = L(A) \times (\Sigma_k^n)^*$;
- if A is a DFA, then $L(\overline{A}) = \overline{L(A)}$;
- $L(\det(A)) = L(A)$ and $\det(A)$ is a DFA.

3 Completeness of T_k

This section is devoted to proving the following theorem.

Theorem 6. *The theory* T_k *axiomatizes* BA_k*. In particular,* BA_k *admits a* Π_1*-axiomatization.*

Before proving this theorem, we need some auxiliary results. The following lemma establishes some basic facts about V_k and $(x)_d$. The scheme (Comp) is not used in this lemma.

Lemma 1. *The following are provable in* T_k*:*

(i) $x > 0 \to P_k(V_k(x))$;
(ii) $V_k(x) \leq x$;
(iii) $x > 0 \to \bigvee_{a=1}^{k-1} \left((x)_{V_k(x)} = a\right)$;
(iv) $\left(x > 0 \wedge P_k(d) \wedge d < V_k(x)\right) \to (x)_d = 0$;
(v) $\bigwedge_{a' \neq a} \Big(\left(x > 0 \wedge (x)_d = a\right) \to \neg\left((x)_d = a'\right)\Big)$ *for all* $a \in \{0, \ldots, k-1\}$;
(vi) $x \not\equiv_k 0 \to V_k(x) = \underline{1}$;
(vii) $\left(d > \underline{1} \wedge P_k(d)\right) \to \exists^{P_k} d' \left(d = kd'\right)$;
(vii) $\left(x > 0 \wedge y > 0 \wedge V_k(x) \leq V_k(y)\right) \to V_k(x+y) \geq V_k(x)$.

Proof. We argue in T_k.

(i) Let $x > 0$. By (V3), there exist y and $a \in \{1, \ldots, k-1\}$ such that $x = y + aV_k(x)$ and either $V_k(y) > V_k(x)$ or $y = 0$. This implies that $V_k(x) > 0$ since if $V_k(x) = 0$, then $x = y$ and $V_k(x) = V_k(y)$, which implies that $y = 0$ and, hence, $x = 0$, a contradiction. Next, by (V5), we have $V_k(V_k(x)) = V_k(x)$ and, since $V_k(x) > 0$, we obtain $P_k(V_k(x))$.
(ii) The case $x = 0$ is immediate. Suppose $x > 0$. By (V3), we have $x \geq aV_k(x)$ for some $a \in \{1, \ldots, k-1\}$, and thus $x \geq V_k(x)$.
(iii) This follows directly from (V3) together with part (i).
(iv) Take $y = 0$ and $z = x$ in the definition of "$(x)_d = a$".
(v) Let $x > 0$ and $P_k(d)$. Suppose, towards a contradiction, that $(x)_d = a$ and $(x)_d = a'$ for distinct $a, a' \in \{0, \ldots, k-1\}$. Without loss of generality assume $a < a'$. Then x can be represented as $x = y + ad + z$ and $x = y' + a'd + z'$, where $y, y' < d$, and either $z = 0$ or $V_k(z) > d$, and similarly either $z' = 0$ or $V_k(z') > d$. Consider the following cases.
   (a) Case $y = y'$. By cancellation,
   $$z = (a' - a)d + z'.$$
   This implies $z > 0$, hence $V_k(z) > d$. By (V1), we obtain $V_k((a'-a)d) = d$. If $z' = 0$, then $V_k(z) = d$, contradicting $V_k(z) > d$. If $z' > 0$, then $V_k(z') > d$ and by (V2) we have $V_k((a'-a)d + z') = V_k((a'-a)d) = d$, again contradicting $V_k(z) > d$.
   (b) Case $y < y'$. Denote by $y' - y$ the unique (positive) element w such that $w + y = y'$, which exists by (Ord1). By cancellation,
   $$z = (y' - y) + (a' - a)d + z'.$$
   Hence $z > 0$, so $V_k(z) > d$. By item (ii), $V_k(y' - y) \leq y' - y < d$, and by (V1), $V_k((a'-a)d) = d$. Thus, by (V2), $V_k((y'-y) + (a'-a)d) = V_k(y'-y) < d$. If $z' > 0$, then $V_k(z') > d$, and again by (V2), $V_k((y'-y) + (a'-a)d + z') < d$. If $z' = 0$, then we trivially have $V_k((y'-y) + (a'-a)d + z') < d$. In both cases this contradicts $V_k(z) > d$.

(c) Case $y' > y$. By cancellation,

$$(y - y') + z = (a' - a)d + z'.$$

By (ii), $V_k(y-y') < d$, while by (V1) and (V2) we have $V_k((a'-a)d+z') = d$ and $V_k((y-y')+z) = V_k(y-y') < d$, contradicting $V_k((a'-a)d+z') = d$.

(vi) Let $x \not\equiv_k 0$. By (Mod) there exist y and $a \in \{1, \ldots, k-1\}$ such that $x = ky + \underline{a}$. By (V0) and (V1), we have

$$V_k(\underline{a}) = V_k(a\underline{1}) = V_k(\underline{1}) = \underline{1}.$$

If $y = 0$ we are done. Assume $y > 0$. Then by (V1) and (i), $V_k(ky) = kV_k(y) \geq k$, hence, by (V2),

$$V_k(x) = V_k(ky + \underline{a}) = V_k(\underline{a}) = \underline{1}.$$

(vii) Let $d > \underline{1}$ and $P_k(d)$. If $d \not\equiv_k 0$, then (vi) we obtain that $V_k(d) = \underline{1} < d$, which contradicts $P_k(d)$. Hence, there is d' such that $d = kd'$. We claim that $P_k(d')$. Indeed,

$$kd' = d = V_k(d) = V_k(kd') = kV_k(d'),$$

where the last equality follows from (V1). Hence, we obtain $d' = V_k(d')$. Moreover, since $d > 0$, we have $d' > 0$. So $P_k(d')$ holds.

(viii) Fix $x, y > 0$ such that $V_k(x) \leq V_k(y)$. If $V_k(x) < V_k(y)$, the statement follows immediately from (V2). Thus assume $V_k(x) = V_k(y)$ and suppose, towards a contradiction, that $V_k(x+y) < V_k(x)$. We first claim that $V_k((k-1)z) = V_k(z)$ for any $z > 0$. Indeed, if $V_k(z) < V_k((k-1)z)$, then by (V2),

$$kV_k(z) = V_k(kz) = V_k((k-1)z + z) = V_k(z),$$

a contradiction. If $V_k(z) > V_k((k-1)z)$, then by (V2),

$$kV_k(z) = V_k(kz) = V_k((k-1)z + z) = V_k((k-1)z) < V_k(z),$$

a contradiction. This proves the claim. Applying the claim with $z = x + y$, we obtain $V_k((k-1)(x+y)) = V_k(x+y) < V_k(x) = V_k(y)$. Hence, by two applications of (V2),

$$V_k((k-1)(x+y) + x + y) = V_k((k-1)(x+y)) = V_k(x+y).$$

Consequently,

$$kV_k(x+y) = V_k(k(x+y)) = V_k((k-1)(x+y) + x + y) = V_k(x+y),$$

and $kV_k(x+y) = V_k(x+y)$ which is impossible. This contradiction completes the proof.

□

The following proposition and corollary show that the least element principle on P_k and the induction principle on P_k are provable in T_k. This is the only essential use of the scheme (Comp).

Proposition 1. *Let $\varphi(d, \vec{y})$ be a Δ_0-formula. Then the formula*

$$\exists^{P_k} d\ \varphi(d, \vec{y}) \rightarrow \exists^{P_k} d\ \Big(\varphi(d, \vec{y}) \wedge \forall^{P_k} d' < d\ \neg\varphi(d', \vec{y})\Big)$$

is provable in T_k.

Proof. We argue in T_k. Let $d \in P_k$ be such that $\varphi(d, \vec{y})$ holds. By (Comp), there exists $x < kd$ such that for every $d' < kd$, $d' \in P_k$, we have $(x)_{d'} = 1$ if $\varphi(d', \vec{y})$ and $(x)_{d'} = 0$ otherwise. Since $(x)_d = 1$, it follows that $x > 0$. Let $d_0 := V_k(x)$. By items (iii) and (v) of Lemma 1, we have $(x)_{d_0} = 1$, and therefore $\varphi(d_0, \vec{y})$ holds. Moreover, by Lemma 1(iv), we have $(x)_{d'} = 0$ for all $d' \in P_k$ with $d' < d_0$, and hence $\neg\varphi(d', \vec{y})$ for all such d'. □

Corollary 1. *Let $\varphi(d, \vec{y})$ be a Δ_0-formula. Then the formula*

$$\varphi(\underline{1}, \vec{y}) \wedge \forall^{P_k} d\ (\varphi(d, \vec{y}) \rightarrow \varphi(kd, \vec{y})) \rightarrow \forall^{P_k} d\ \varphi(d, \vec{y})$$

is provable in T_k.

Proof. The proof is standard; just apply Proposition 1 and Lemma 1(vii). □

We denote by $x|_d = y$ the following BA_k-formula:

$$P_k(d) \wedge (y < d) \wedge \exists z \leq x\ \Big(x = y + z \wedge \big(z = 0 \vee V_k(z) \geq d\big)\Big).$$

Intuitively, $x|_d$ represents the sum of the first $\log_k d$ summands in the k-expansion of x, namely

$$(x)_1 + (x)_k \cdot k + \cdots + (x)_{d/k} \cdot (d/k).$$

Equivalently, $x|_d$ can be described as the remainder of x modulo d.

The following lemma provides us some basic properties of $x|_d$.

Lemma 2. *The following are provable in T_k:*

(i) $\forall^{P_k} d\ \forall^{P_k} d'\ (d' \leq d \vee kd \leq d')$;
(ii) $\forall x\ \forall^{P_k} d\ \exists y \leq x\ (x|_d = y)$;
(iii) $\forall x\ \forall y\ \forall y'\ \forall^{P_k} d\ (x|_d = y \wedge x|_d = y' \rightarrow y = y')$;
(iv) $\forall x\ \forall^{P_k} d\ (x < d \rightarrow x|_d = x)$;
(v) $\forall x\ \forall^{P_k} d\ \forall^{P_k} d' < d\ \Big(\bigvee_{a=0}^{k-1} \big((x)_{d'} = a \wedge (x|_d)_{d'} = a\big)\Big)$.

Proof. We argue in T_k.

(i) Using Corollary 1, we prove by induction on $d \in P_k$ the Δ_0-formula

$$\forall^{P_k} d' < kd \; (d' \leq d).$$

The base case $d = \underline{1}$ is immediate. For the inductive step, assume $\forall^{P_k} d' < kd \; (d' \leq d)$, and let us show that $\forall^{P_k} d' < k^2 d \; (d' \leq kd)$. Suppose, towards a contradiction, that there exists $d' \in P_k$ such that $kd < d' < k^2 d$. By Lemma 1(vii), there exists $d'' \in P_k$ such that $d' = kd''$. This implies $d < d'' < kd$, contradicting the induction hypothesis. By Corollary 1, the desired statement follows.

(ii) Fix x. We prove by induction on $d \in P_k$ the Δ_0-formula

$$\exists y \leq x \; (x|_d = y).$$

The base case $d = \underline{1}$ is immediate: take $y = 0$ and $z = x$ in the definition of $x|_d = y$. For the inductive step, assume $\exists y \leq x \; (x|_d = y)$ and let us prove $\exists y' \leq x \; (x|_{kd} = y')$. Fix $y \leq x$ such that $x|_d = y$. By the definition of $x|_d = y$, there exists $z \leq x$ such that $x = y + z$ and either $z = 0$ or $V_k(z) \geq d$. If $z = 0$, we may take $y' = y$, and we are done. Suppose $V_k(z) \geq d$. Then $z > 0$. By (V3) together with Lemma 1(iv), there exist z' and $a \in \{0, \ldots, k-1\}$ such that $z = ad + z'$ and $z' = 0$ or $V_k(z') > d$. Now one can take $y' = y + ad$ and z' as witnesses that $x|_{kd} = y'$.

(iii) Fix x, y, y' and d such that $x|_d = y$ and $x|_d = y'$. Then there exist $z, z' \leq x$ such that

$$x = y + z \wedge \bigl(z = 0 \vee V_k(z) \geq d\bigr) \quad \text{and} \quad x = y' + z' \wedge \bigl(z' = 0 \vee V_k(z') \geq d\bigr).$$

Without loss of generality, assume that $y \leq y'$. Then $z' \leq z$ and $y' - y = z - z'$. Suppose $y' - y \neq 0$. Then $0 < y' - y \leq y' < d$, and hence $V_k(y' - y) \leq y' - y < d$. We claim that $V_k(z - z') \geq d$. Indeed, if $V_k(z - z') < d$, then by (V2), $V_k(z) = V_k((z - z') + z') = V_k(z - z') < d$, a contradiction. Hence $V_k(z - z') \geq d$, contradicting $V_k(y' - y) < d$. Therefore $y' - y = 0$ and $y = y'$.

(iv) This follows immediately from the definition of $x|_d = y$ by taking $z = 0$.

(v) Fix x, $d \in P_k$, and $d' \in P_k$ such that $d' < d$. By items (ii) and (iii), there exist unique y and z such that $x = y + z$, $y < d$ and $z = 0$ or $V_k(z) \geq d$, that is, $x|_d = y$. By Lemma 1, there exists a unique $a \in \{0, \ldots, k-1\}$ such that $(y)_{d'} = a$. Thus we can write $y = t + ad' + u$ for some $t < d'$ and with $u = 0$ or $V_k(u) > d'$. We claim that $(x)_{d'} = a$. Indeed, $x = y + z = t + ad' + u + z$. It is sufficient to show that $u + z = 0$ or $V_k(u + z) > d'$. The cases of $u = 0$ or $z = 0$ are immediate. Otherwise, assume $u, z > 0$, that is, $V_k(u) > d'$ and $V_k(z) \geq d > d'$. By Lemma 1(viii), it follows that $V_k(u + z) > d'$, as required.

□

The rest of this section is organized as follows. First, we express runs of automata in the language of BA_k and prove some natural facts about automata, formalized in T_k (Lemma 3). Next, we prove in T_k that the standard DFAs for 0, S, $+$, V_k, and $\leq$ recognize the corresponding predicates (Lemma 4 and Corollary

2). These results imply the formalized version of Theorem 1, namely Theorem 7, which is crucial for us. After these steps, one can easily derive Theorem 6. Now let us proceed with this plan.

Denote $\Sigma_k := \{0, \dots, k-1\}$. Let $A = (\Sigma_k^m, Q, q_0, F, \Delta)$ be a finite automaton, where $\Delta \subseteq Q \times \Sigma_k^m \times Q$ is the set of transitions. For any $q_1 \in Q$, we define the following Δ_0-formula $W_{A,q_1}(x_1, \dots, x_m, d)$:

$$
\begin{aligned}
P_k(d) \wedge \exists (w_q)_{q\in Q} < kd \Big(& \forall^{P_k} d' \leq d \bigvee_{q\in Q} ((w_q)_{d'} = 1 \wedge \bigwedge_{q'\neq q} ((w_{q'})_{d'} = 0)) \wedge \\
& ((w_{q_0})_{\underline{1}} = 1) \wedge ((w_{q_1})_d = 1) \wedge \\
& \forall^{P_k} d' < d \bigwedge_{q\in Q} ((w_q)_{d'} = 1 \to \bigvee_{(q,\vec{a},q')\in\Delta} ((w_{q'})_{kd'} = 1 \wedge \bigwedge_{i=1}^{m} (x_i)_{d'} = a_i))\Big).
\end{aligned}
$$

Here, by $\exists (w_q)_{q\in Q} < kd \dots$ we mean a block of $|Q|$ bounded existential quantifiers. This formula expresses that the automaton A can reach the state q_1 by reading the k-expansion of $(x_1, \dots, x_m)$ in exactly $\log_k d$ steps. The numbers w_q encode a run of the automaton: the condition $(w_q)_{d'} = 1$ means that the state at step $\log_k d'$ of the run is q. The first row of the formula ensures that $(w_q)_{q\in Q}$ encodes a sequence of exactly $\log_k d + 1$ states, with exactly one active state at each position. The second row specifies that the run starts in the initial state q_0 and ends in the state q_1. Finally, the third row guarantees that all transitions along the run are consistent with the transition relation Δ and with the digits of the k-expansion of $(x_1, \dots, x_m)$.

Lemma 3. *Let $A = (\Sigma_k^m, Q, q_0, F, \Delta)$ and $A' = (\Sigma_k^m, Q', q_0', F', \Delta')$ be finite automata. Then the following are provable in T_k:*

(i) $\forall \vec{x}\ \forall^{P_k} d\ \bigwedge_{q\in Q, q'\in Q'} \Big(W_{A\times A',(q,q')}(\vec{x}, d) \leftrightarrow W_{A,q}(\vec{x}, d) \wedge W_{A',q'}(\vec{x}, d)\Big)$;

(ii) $\forall \vec{x}\ \forall^{P_k} d\ \bigwedge_{q\in Q} \Big(W_{A,q}(\vec{x}, d) \leftrightarrow \bigvee_{H\subseteq Q, q\in H} W_{\det(A),H}(\vec{x}, d)\Big)$;

(iii) $\forall \vec{x}\ \forall^{P_k} d\ \bigwedge_{q\in Q} \Big(W_{\mathrm{pr}(A),q}(\vec{x}, d) \leftrightarrow \exists y < d\ W_{A,q}(\vec{x}, y, d)\Big)$;

(iii') $\forall \vec{x}\ \forall^{P_k} d\ \bigwedge_{q\in Q} \Big(W_{\mathrm{pr}(A),q}(\vec{x}, d) \leftrightarrow \exists y\ W_{A,q}(\vec{x}, y, d)\Big)$;

(iv) $\forall \vec{x}\ \forall \vec{y}\ \forall^{P_k} d\ \bigwedge_{q\in Q} \Big(W_{A,q}(\vec{x}, d) \leftrightarrow W_{A^{+n},q}(\vec{x}, \vec{y}, d)\Big)$;

Moreover, if A is a DFA, then the following is provable in T_k:

(v) $\forall \vec{x}\ \forall^{P_k} d\ \bigvee_{q\in Q} \Big(W_{A,q}(\vec{x}, d) \wedge \bigwedge_{q'\neq q} \neg W_{A,q'}(\vec{x}, d)\Big)$.

Proof. The proof of (i), (ii), (iii), (iv), (v) is straightforward. Fix $\vec{x}$ (and $\vec{y}$ in (iv)) and apply induction on d. Statement (iii') follows from (iii), since

$$W_{A,q}(\vec{x}, y, d) \leftrightarrow W_{A,q}(\vec{x}, y|_d, d)$$

is provable in T_k by Lemma 2(v). We prove (iii) as an illustration in Appendix A. □

Now construct DFAs A_0, A_S, A_+, A_{V_k}, and $A_\leq$ recognizing the predicates

$$x = 0, \quad S(x) = y, \quad x + y = z, \quad V_k(x) = y, \quad x \leq y,$$

respectively (see below). Accepting states are indicated by double circles. In each automaton, there is an implicit sink state q_{sink} required to make the transition function total (it is omitted from the diagrams to save space). Unless stated otherwise, a and b range over $\{0, \ldots, k-1\}$.

Automaton A_0:

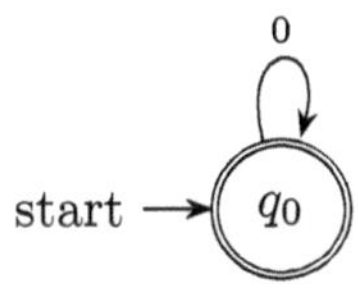

Automaton A_S:

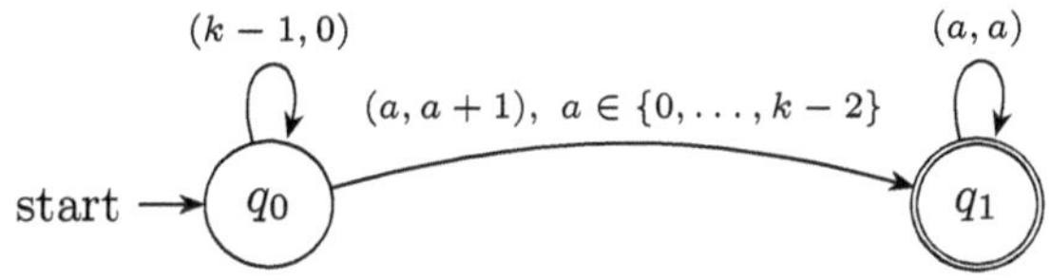

Automaton A_+:

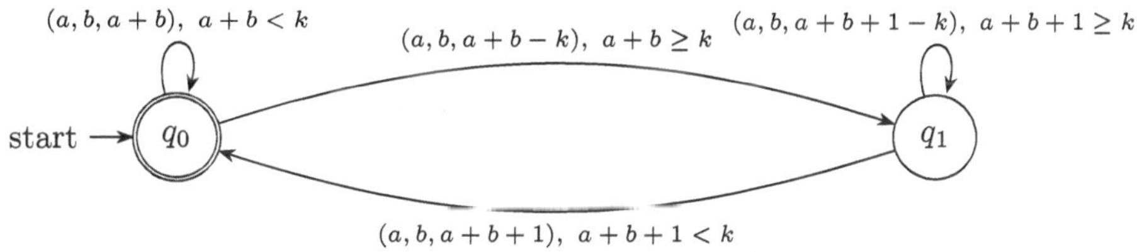

Automaton A_{V_k}:

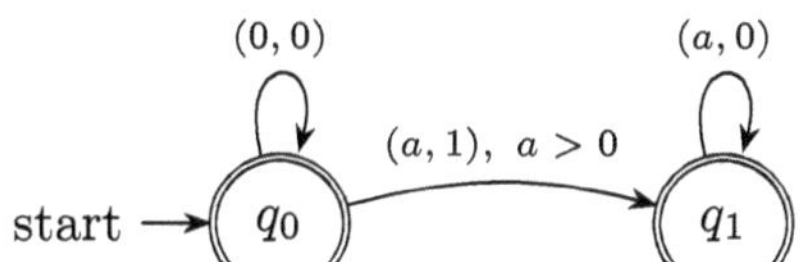

Automaton $A_\leq$:

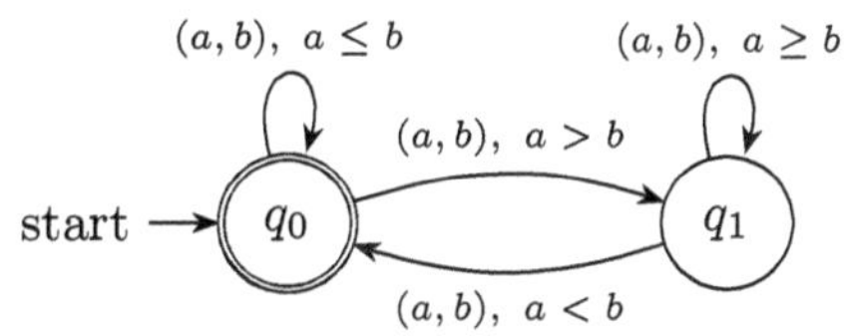

Lemma 4. *The following are provable in* T_k*:*

(i) $\forall x\ \forall^{P_k} d\ \Big(x|_d = 0 \leftrightarrow W_{A_0, q_0}(x, d)\Big)$;

(ii) $\forall x\ \forall y\ \forall^{P_k} d\Big(\big(x|_d = d - 1 \wedge y|_d = 0 \leftrightarrow W_{A_S, q_0}(x, y, d)\big) \wedge \big(S(x|_d) = y|_d \leftrightarrow W_{A_S, q_1}(x, y, d)\big)\Big)$;

(iii) $\forall x\ \forall y\ \forall z\ \forall^{P_k} d\ \Big(\big(x|_d + y|_d = z|_d \leftrightarrow W_{A_+, q_0}(x, y, z, d)\big) \wedge \big(x|_d + y|_d = z|_d + d \leftrightarrow W_{A_+, q_1}(x, y, d)\big)\Big)$;

(iv) $\forall x\ \forall y\ \forall^{P_k} d\ \Big(\big(x|_d = 0 \wedge y|_d = 0 \leftrightarrow W_{A_{V_k}, q_0}(x, y, d)\big) \wedge \big(V_k(x|_d) = y|_d \leftrightarrow W_{A_{V_k}, q_1}(x, y, d)\big)\Big)$;

(v) $\forall x\ \ \forall y\ \ \forall^{P_k} d\ \Big(\big(x|_d\ \leq\ y|_d\ \leftrightarrow\ W_{A_\leq, q_0}(x, y, d)\big) \wedge \big(x|_d\ >\ y|_d\ \leftrightarrow W_{A_\leq, q_1}(x, y, d)\big)\Big)$.

Proof. The proof is standard and proceeds by induction on d. For an illustration, see the proof of (iii) in Appendix B. □

Next, we want to get rid of the quantifiers on d in the formulas from Lemma 4. In order to do this, let us introduce the function $g_n : \mathbb{N}^n \to \mathbb{N}$ that maps $(x_1, \ldots, x_n)$ to the least power of k strictly greater than each of $x_1, \ldots, x_n$. Clearly, the graph of $g_n(x_1, \ldots, x_n) = d$ is definable by the quantifier-free formula

$$\Big(\bigwedge_{i=1}^{n}(x_i = 0) \wedge d = \underline{1}\Big) \vee \Big(P_k(d) \wedge \bigvee_{i=1}^{n}\big(\bigwedge_{j=1}^{n}(x_i \geq x_j) \wedge (x_i < d) \wedge (d \leq kx_i)\big)\Big).$$

Hence all occurrences of g_n can be eliminated using a bounded quantifier. We will write simply g instead of g_n when the arity is clear from the context. Note that by Lemma 2(iv) we have

$$\mathsf{T}_k \vdash \forall \vec{x}\ \forall^{P_k} d\ (d \geq g(\vec{x}) \to \bigwedge_{i=1}^{n}(x_i|_d = x_i)).$$

Corollary 2. *The following are provable in* T_k*:*

(i) $\forall x\ \Big(x = 0 \leftrightarrow W_{A_0,q_0}(x, g(x))\Big)$;

(ii) $\forall x\ \forall y\ \Big(S(x) = y \leftrightarrow W_{A_S,q_1}(x, y, g(x, y))\Big)$;

(iii) $\forall x\ \forall y\ \forall z\ \Big(x + y = z \leftrightarrow W_{A_+,q_0}(x, y, z, g(x, y, z))\Big)$;

(iv) $\forall x\ \forall y\ \Big(V_k(x) = y \leftrightarrow \bigvee_{i=1,2} W_{A_{V_k},q_i}(x, y, g(x, y))\Big)$;

(v) $\forall x\ \forall y\ \Big(x \leq y \leftrightarrow W_{A_\leq,q_0}(x, y, g(x, y))\Big)$.

Proof. Substitute $g(\ldots)$ for d in Lemma 4. □

The following result is crucial for us.

Theorem 7. *For any formula* $\varphi(\vec{x})$*, there exists a DFA* A *such that*

$$\mathsf{T}_k \vdash \forall \vec{x}\ \Big(\varphi(\vec{x}) \leftrightarrow \bigvee_{q \in F} W_{A,q}(\vec{x}, g(\vec{x}))\Big).$$

Here, F *denotes the set of accepting states of* A*.*

Proof. We may assume that all atomic formulas are simple (i.e., they contain no nested occurrences of function symbols) and that the only logical connectives are $\neg$, $\wedge$, and $\exists$.

The proof proceeds by induction on φ. The base case of atomic formulas is handled in Corollary 2.

Let $\varphi = \neg\psi$ and let A be a DFA for ψ, which exists by the induction hypothesis. Then, by Lemma 3(v) $\overline{A}$ is a DFA for ψ.

Let $\varphi = (\psi_0 \wedge \psi_1)$. By the induction hypothesis, there exist DFAs A_0 and A_1 for ψ_0 and ψ_1, respectively. After possibly adding dummy variables and applying Lemma 3(iv), we may assume that φ, ψ_0, and ψ_1 share the same set of free variables and that A_0 and A_1 share the same alphabet (namely, Σ_k^m, where φ has m free variables). Hence, by Lemma 3(i), the product $A_0 \times A_1$ is a DFA for φ.

Finally, let $\varphi = \exists y\, \psi$ and let A be a DFA for ψ. If y does not occur freely in ψ, then A is already a DFA for φ. If y occurs freely in ψ, then by Lemma 3(ii, iii'), $\det(\mathrm{pr}(A))$ is a DFA for φ. □

The following proposition is proved in the standard manner, see [15, Theorem 1.8].

Proposition 2. *If φ is a Δ_0-sentence and $\mathbb{N} \models \varphi$, then $\mathsf{T}_k \vdash \varphi$.*

Proof of Theorem 6. Let φ be a sentence, such that $\mathbb{N} \models \varphi$. By Theorem 7, there is Δ_0-sentence θ such that $\mathsf{T}_k \models \varphi \leftrightarrow \theta$ and, by Proposition 2, $\mathsf{T}_k \vdash \theta$. Hence, $\mathsf{T}_k \vdash \varphi$. □

Remark 1. It is clear from the proof that the only essential use of the comprehension schema is to derive the least element schema. Hence, BA_k can alternatively be axiomatized using the induction scheme from Corollary 1 together with the axioms (Add), (Ord0), (Ord1), (Mod), (V0), (V1), (V2), (V3), (V4), and (V5).

However, it remains unknown whether BA_k is finitely axiomatizable. We leave the following questions open.

Question 1. (1) Is BA_k finitely axiomatizable?
(2) Is BA_k finitely axiomatizable over Presburger Arithmetic?
(3) Is it possible to replace the induction scheme for Δ_0-formulas with a quantifier-free induction scheme in the axiomatization of BA_k?
(4) Does BA_k admit a *finite* expansion by definable functions or predicates that admits quantifier elimination?

Acknowledgments. This work was supported by the Theoretical Physics and Mathematics Advancement Foundation ≪BASIS≫.

Disclosure of Interests. The author has no competing interests to declare that are relevant to the content of this article.

Appendix A Proof of Lemma 3(iii)

Lemma 3(iii). *Let $A = (\Sigma_k^m, Q, q_0, F, \Delta)$ and $A' = (\Sigma_k^m, Q', q_0', F', \Delta')$ be finite automata. Then the following is provable in T_k:*

(iii) $\forall \vec{x}\ \forall^{P_k} d \ \bigwedge_{q \in Q} \Big(W_{\mathrm{pr}(A),q}(\vec{x}, d) \leftrightarrow \exists y < d\ W_{A,q}(\vec{x}, y, d) \Big).$

Proof. We argue in T_k. Fix $\vec{x}$ and argue by induction on d:

$$\bigwedge_{q\in Q}\Big(W_{\mathrm{pr}(A),q}(\vec{x},d)\leftrightarrow \exists y<d\; W_{A,q}(\vec{x},y,d)\Big).$$

Consider the base case of $d=\underline{1}$. If $W_{\mathrm{pr}(A),q}(\vec{x},d)$ holds, then by definition of $W_{\mathrm{pr}(A),q}$ we must have $q=q_0$. Hence we have $W_{A,q}(\vec{x},0,d)$. The backward implication is immediate from the definitions.

For the inductive step, suppose

$$\bigwedge_{q\in Q}\Big(W_{\mathrm{pr}(A),q}(\vec{x},d)\leftrightarrow \exists y<d\; W_{A,q}(\vec{x},y,d)\Big).$$

Denote by $\vec{a}$ the tuple $\Big((x_i)_d\Big)_{i=1,\dots,|\vec{x}|}$. If $W_{\mathrm{pr}(A),q}(\vec{x},kd)$ holds, then the definition of $W_{\mathrm{pr}(A),q}$ implies that $W_{\mathrm{pr}(A),q'}(\vec{x},d)$ for some $q'\in Q$ such that $(q',\vec{a},q)$ is a transition of $\mathrm{pr}(A)$. By the induction hypothesis there exists $y<d$ such that $W_{A,q}(\vec{x},y,d)$. The definition of $\mathrm{pr}(A)$ implies that there is $b\in\{0,\dots,k-1\}$ such that $(q',(\vec{a},b),q)$ is a transition of A. Now it is easy to see that $W_{A,q}(\vec{x},y+bd,kd)$ holds.

The backward implication is immediate, since if $(w_q)_{q\in Q}$ are witnesses for $W_{A,q}(\vec{x},y,d)$, then the same $(w_q)_{q\in Q}$ witness for $W_{\mathrm{pr}(A),q}(\vec{x},d)$. □

Appendix B Proof of Lemma 4 (iii)

Lemma 4(iii). *The following is provable in* T_k*:*

(iii) $\forall x\,\forall y\,\forall z\,\forall^{P_k} d\,\Big(\big(x|_d+y|_d=z|_d\leftrightarrow W_{A_+,q_0}(x,y,z,d)\big)\wedge\big(x|_d+y|_d=z|_d+d\leftrightarrow W_{A_+,q_1}(x,y,d)\big)\Big)$.

Proof. As before, we argue in T_k. Fix x,y,z. The base case of $d=\underline{1}$ is trivial, since $x|_{\underline{1}}=y|_{\underline{1}}=z|_{\underline{1}}=0$ and by definition $W_{A_+,q_0}(x,y,z,\underline{1})$ holds. At the same time, $W_{A_+,q_1}(x,y,z,\underline{1})$ does not hold. For the inductive step, suppose that

$$\big(x|_d+y|_d=z|_d\leftrightarrow W_{A_+,q_0}(x,y,z,d)\big)\wedge\big(x|_d+y|_d=z|_d+d\leftrightarrow W_{A_+,q_1}(x,y,d)\big).$$

We first show that $x|_{kd}+y|_{kd}=z|_{kd}\leftrightarrow W_{A_+,q_0}(x,y,z,kd)$. Suppose $x|_{kd}+y|_{kd}=z|_{kd}$. We need to prove that $W_{A_+,q_0}(x,y,z,kd)$ holds. There exist unique $a,b,c\in\{0,\dots,k-1\}$ such that

$$x|_{kd}=x|_d+ad,\quad y|_{kd}=y|_d+bd,\quad z|_{kd}=z|_d+cd,$$

where $a=(x)_d$, $b=(y)_d$, and $c=(z)_d$. Then we have

$$z|_d+cd=z|_{kd}=x|_{kd}+y|_{kd}=x|_d+y|_d+(a+b)d.$$

We claim that either $c = a + b$ or $c = a + b + 1$. Suppose, for a contradiction, that $c \leq a + b - 1$ or $c \geq a + b + 2$. In the case $c \leq a + b - 1$ we have

$$x|_d + y|_d + (a + b)d \geq (c + 1)d > z|_d + cd,$$

a contradiction. In the case $c \geq a + b + 2$ we have

$$z|_d + cd \geq (a + b + 2)d > x|_d + y|_d + (a + b)d,$$

also a contradiction. Hence, $c = a + b$ or $c = a + b + 1$. In the first case, we have $x|_d + y|_d = z|_d$, and by the induction hypothesis, $W_{A_+,q_0}(x, y, z, d)$ holds. Consequently, $W_{A_+,q_0}(x, y, z, kd)$ holds as well. The other forward implication is treated in a similar manner.

Now assume that $W_{A_+,q_0}(x, y, z, kd)$,holds. We prove that $x|_{kd} + y|_{kd} = z|_{kd}$. Choose $a, b, c \in \{0, \dots, k - 1\}$ such that $x|_{kd} = x|_d + ad$, $y|_{kd} = y|_d + bd$ and $z|_{kd} = z|_d + cd$. $W_{A_+,q_0}(x, y, z, kd)$ implies that either $W_{A_+,q_0}(x, y, z, d)$ and $c = a + b$ or $W_{A_+,q_1}(x, y, z, d)$ and $c = a + b + 1$. In the first case, by the induction hypothesis we have $x|_d + y|_d = z|_d$. Therefore, $(x|_d + ad) + (y|_d + bd) = (z|_d + cd)$, which shows that $x|_{kd} + y|_{kd} = z|_{kd}$. The second case is treated in an analogous way.

We now show that $x|_{kd} + y|_{kd} = z|_{kd} + kd \leftrightarrow W_{A_+,q_1}(x, y, kd)$. Assume first that $x|_{kd} + y|_{kd} = z|_{kd} + kd$. We prove that $W_{A_+,q_1}(x, y, z, kd)$ holds. Choose $a, b, c \in \{0, \dots, k-1\}$ such that $x|_{kd} = x|_d + ad$, $y|_{kd} = y|_d + bd$ and $z|_{kd} = z|_d + cd$. Then we have

$$z|_d + (c + k)d = z|_{kd} + kd = x|_{kd} + y|_{kd} = x|_d + y|_d + (a + b)d.$$

We claim that either $c = a + b - k$ or $c = a + b + 1 - k$. Suppose, towards a contradiction, that $c \leq a + b - 1 - k$ or $c \geq a + b + 2 - k$. If $c \leq a + b - 1 - k$, then

$$x|_d + y|_d + (a + b)d \geq (c + 1 + k)d > z|_d + (c + k)d,$$

which contradicts the above equality. If $c \geq a + b + 2 - k$, then

$$z|_d + (c + k)d \geq (a + b + 2)d > x|_d + y|_d + (a + b)d,$$

again a contradiction. Hence, $c = a + b - k$ or $c = a + b + 1 - k$. In the first case, we have $x|_d + y|_d = z|_d$ and by the induction hypothesis $W_{A_+,q_0}(x, y, z, d)$ holds. Therefore, $W_{A+,q_1}(x, y, z, kd)$. The second case is treated analogously.

The implication $W_{A_+,q_1}(x, y, z, kd) \rightarrow x|_{kd} + y|_{kd} = z|_{kd} + kd$ is proved in the same way as $W_{A_+,q_0}(x, y, z, kd) \rightarrow x|_{kd} + y|_{kd} = z|_{kd}$. □

References

1. Blumensath, A., Grädel, E.: Finite presentations of infinite structures: automata and interpretations. Theory Comput. Syst. **37**(6), 641–674 (2004)
2. Büchi, J.R.: Weak second-order arithmetic and finite automata. Math. Log. Q. **6**(1–6), 66–92 (1960)
3. Bruyère, V., Hansel, G., Michaux, C., Villemaire, R.: Logic and p-recognizable sets of integers. Bull. Belgian Math. Soc. - Simon Stevin **1**(2), 191–238 (1994)
4. Cobham, A.: On the base-dependence of sets of numbers recognizable by finite automata. Math. Syst. Theory **3**(2), 186–192 (1969)
5. Semenov, A.L.: Presburgerness of predicates regular in two number systems. Sib. Math. J. **18**(2), 289–300 (1977)
6. Bès, A.: Undecidable extensions of Büchi arithmetic and Cobham-Semënov theorem. J. Symb. Log. **62**(4), 1280–1296 (1997)
7. Hieronymi, P., Schulz, C.: A strong version of Cobham's theorem. In: Proceedings of the 54th Annual ACM SIGACT Symposium on Theory of Computing, pp. 1172–1179. Association for Computing Machinery, Rome (2022)
8. Meyer, A.R.: Weak monadic second order theory of succesor is not elementary-recursive. Log. Colloq. Lect. Notes Math. **453**, 132–154 (1975)
9. Guépin, F., Haase, C., Worrell, J.: On the existential theories of Büchi arithmetic and linear p-adic fields. In: 2019 34th Annual ACM/IEEE Symposium on Logic in Computer Science (LICS), pp. 1–10. IEEE, Vancouver (2019)
10. Kovalyov, K.: Axiomatization of Büchi arithmetic. arXiv:2411.03043, math.LO (2024)
11. Kovalyov, K.: On axiomatization of Büchi arithmetic (in Russian). Proceedings of MIPT **17**(2(66)), 42–49 (2025)
12. Zapryagaev, A.: Some properties of Büchi arithmetics. arXiv:2310.16019, math.LO (2023)
13. Villemaire, R.: The theory of $\langle \mathbb{N}, +, V_k, V_l \rangle$ is undecidable. Theoret. Comput. Sci. **106**(2), 337–349 (1992)
14. Haase, C., Różycki, J.: On the expressiveness of Büchi arithmetic. In: Kiefer, S., Tasson, C. (eds.) FOSSACS 2021. LNCS, vol. 12650, pp. 310–323. Springer, Cham (2021). https://doi.org/10.1007/978-3-030-71995-1_16
15. Hájek, P., Pudlák, P.: Metamathematics of First-Order Arithmetic. Cambridge University Press, Cambridge (2017)

Two Generalizations of Shininess

Guilherme V. Toledo(✉) and Yoni Zohar

Bar-Ilan University, Ramat Gan, Israel
guivtoledo@gmail.com

Abstract. Shininess is one of the main theory combination methods in Satisfiability Modulo Theories. We present two infinite families of generalizations of it: one involving a property between gentleness and shininess, which helps us see gentleness itself as a variation of shininess; and another having no further computability requirements on the weaker theory, in addition dropping the need for smoothness. We prove these methods sharp, and compare them with existing methods.

1 Introduction

SAT, standing for satisfiability, is the area of computer science which studies the efficiency of methods that decide whether a Boolean formula is satisfiable. Extending on this, Satisfiability Modulo Theories, or **SMT** for short, automatizes the process of establishing whether a first-order formula is satisfied, now with respect to a first-order theory. In this context, if a theory is the combination of other two, we would like to combine the algorithms of the latter into an algorithm for the former: there is a variety of methods to accomplish this, and the sub-field in SMT that deals with this problem is called *theory combination*.

There are three combination methods that have become widespread. First and foremost, the Nelson–Oppen method [8], requiring the two theories to be combined to be decidable and stably infinite.[1] In a close second place, the polite method, which requires one theory to be decidable and strongly polite while the other is allowed to be simply decidable [6,10]; it is known, thanks to [2,3] that, for decidable theories, strong politeness is equivalent to shininess [11], a property that is more difficult to implement but is easier to understand. This is the method used by some of the most robust SMT-solvers, such as cvc5 [1]. And, finally, the gentle method [5], which requires a theory to be gentle and the other to be decidable and have computable finite spectra [15].

These methods are all *sharp* [9], e.g.: a decidable theory that can be combined with all decidable theories must be strongly polite or, equivalently, shiny. The machinery necessary to prove sharpness of combination methods, involving the notions of test theories and a Galois connection, also provides a reasonably effective approach to finding new combination methods. We showcase this feature by producing two infinite families of methods closely resembling shiny combination.

[1] All technical properties of theories, as well as other notions, will be formally reviewed in the next section.

P. Johann and R. de Queiroz (Eds.): WoLLIC 2026, LNCS 16757, pp. 97–110, 2027.
https://doi.org/10.1007/978-3-032-33486-2_7

$$\neq(x_1,\ldots,x_n) = \bigwedge_{i=1}^{n-1}\bigwedge_{j=i+1}^{n} \neg(x_i = x_j) \qquad \psi_{\leq n} = \exists\, x_1,\ldots,x_n.\, \forall\, y.\, \bigvee_{i=1}^{n} y = x_i$$

$$\psi_{\geq n} = \exists\, x_1,\ldots,x_n.\ \neq(x_1,\ldots,x_n) \qquad \psi_{=n} = \psi_{\geq n} \wedge \psi_{\leq n}$$

Fig. 1. Cardinality formulas

The first is inspired by a method from [9] involving the notions of n-decidability and n-shininess. It offers a new way of understanding gentleness as a variation of shininess, helping contextualize that method. The second comes from dropping smoothness from the definition of shininess, a quite restrictive and often undesirable requirement, which imposes no computability requisites other than decidability on the weaker theory to be combined (much like the Nelson–Oppen and strongly polite combination methods).

We start with some basic notions necessary for the rest of the paper in Sect. 2. Sections 3 and 4 give two sets of generalizations of shininess. In Sect. 5 we prove that these new combination results are sharp, in the sense that they cannot be theoretically strengthened. A brief conclusion and plans for future work can be found in Sect. 6.

2 Preliminaries

We denote $\mathbb{N}\setminus\{0\}$ by $\mathbb{N}^*$, for any $S\subseteq\mathbb{N}$ the set $S\cup\{\aleph_0\}$ by S_ω, and $\{n\in\mathbb{N}_\omega : p\leq n\leq q\}$ by $[p,q]$.

2.1 First-Order Logic

We review standard definitions and notations regarding first-order logic. For more details, see, e.g., [4]. A **signature** Σ is a countable[2] set of function and predicate symbols with fixed arities and containing equality. Two signatures are **disjoint** if they share only the equality symbol; Fixed a countably infinite set of variables, we define literals, formulas and sentences (formulas with no free variables) as usual; let $QF(\Sigma)$ be the set of quantifier-free Σ-formulas.

A **Σ-interpretation** $\mathcal{A}$ is a non-empty set $dom(\mathcal{A})$ (its **domain**) equipped with functions $f^{\mathcal{A}}$ and predicates $P^{\mathcal{A}}$ over $dom(\mathcal{A})$ of the same arity as their corresponding symbols, and values $x^{\mathcal{A}}\in dom(\mathcal{A})$ assigned to all variables x. We define the truth-value of a formula φ in an interpretation $\mathcal{A}$ in the usual way, and if that value is true we write $\mathcal{A}\vDash\varphi$. In Fig. 1 the formula $\neq(x_1,\ldots,x_n)$ states the variables x_1 through x_n all take different values (for $n\geq 2$, when $n=1$ we can take it to be any tautology); the formulas $\psi_{\geq n}$, $\psi_{=n}$ and $\psi_{\leq n}$ state that there are at least, exactly, and at most n elements in the domain, respectively.

[2] A set is called *countable* if its cardinality is either finite or $\aleph_0$.

A Σ-**theory** $\mathcal{T}$ is a set of Σ-sentences, called its **axioms**, and if an interpretation satisfies all of them it is said to be a $\mathcal{T}$-**interpretation**. A formula is $\mathcal{T}$-**satisfiable** if there is at least one $\mathcal{T}$-interpretation that satisfies it. A Σ-theory $\mathcal{T}$ is **decidable** when there is an algorithm that takes a quantifier-free Σ-formula and returns whether or not it is $\mathcal{T}$-satisfiable. Given signatures Σ_1 and Σ_2, $\Sigma_1 \sqcup \Sigma_2$ is their disjoint union, which is the union of their symbols after renaming them to avoid overriding; and given a Σ_1-theory $\mathcal{T}_1$ and a Σ_2-theory $\mathcal{T}_2$, their **disjoint combination** $\mathcal{T}_1 \sqcup \mathcal{T}_2$ is the $\Sigma_1 \sqcup \Sigma_2$-theory with axiomatization equal to the union of $\mathcal{T}_1$ and $\mathcal{T}_2$ (after possible renaming).

The **spectrum** $Spec_{\mathcal{T}}(\varphi)$ of a formula φ in a theory $\mathcal{T}$ is the subset of $\mathbb{N}_\omega$ of those n such that there exists a $\mathcal{T}$-interpretation $\mathcal{A}$ with $\mathcal{A} \vDash \varphi$ and $|dom(\mathcal{A})| = n$. We often make use of the Löwenheim–Skolem theorem as stated below.

Theorem 1 (**[7, Theorems 2.3.4 and 2.3.7]**). *Let Δ be a set of formulas over a countable signature, and let $\kappa \geq \aleph_0$. Then, Δ is satisfied by an interpretation of size κ if and only if it is satisfied by an interpretation of size $\aleph_0$.*

The following is a classical result we make use of, obtained as an immediate corollary from compactness.

Corollary 1. *If $\aleph_0 \notin Spec_{\mathcal{T}}(\phi)$, then $Spec_{\mathcal{T}}(\phi)$ is finite.*

2.2 Theory Combination and Its Galois Connection

$\mathcal{T}$ is said to have **computable finite spectra**[3] [15] when there is an algorithm that takes a quantifier-free formula ϕ and an $n \in \mathbb{N}^*$, returning whether $n \in Spec_{\mathcal{T}}(\phi)$. A theory $\mathcal{T}$ is **stably infinite** [8] if $Spec_{\mathcal{T}}(\phi) \neq \varnothing$, for a quantifier-free ϕ, implies $\aleph_0 \in Spec_{\mathcal{T}}(\phi)$. A theory $\mathcal{T}$ is **smooth** when, for every quantifier-free ϕ, $\mathcal{T}$-interpretation $\mathcal{A} \vDash \phi$ and $\kappa \geq |dom(\mathcal{A})|$, there is a $\mathcal{T}$-interpretation $\mathcal{B} \vDash \phi$ with $|dom(\mathcal{B})| = \kappa$. $\mathcal{T}$ has the **finite model property** when, for every $\mathcal{T}$-satisfiable quantifier-free formula ϕ, $Spec_{\mathcal{T}}(\phi) \cap \mathbb{N}^* \neq \varnothing$. And, if $\mathcal{T}$ is decidable, its **minimal model function** is the function $\mathrm{minmod}_{\mathcal{T}}$ that takes a quantifier-free formula ϕ and returns $\min Spec_{\mathcal{T}}(\phi)$, if that set is not empty (and any value in $\mathbb{N}_\omega$ otherwise). A theory is then said to be **shiny** [11] when it is smooth, has the finite model property, and its minimal model function is computable.

Proposition 1. *A theory is shiny if and only if there is an algorithm that takes a quantifier-free formula ϕ and returns an $n \in \mathbb{N}$ such that $Spec_{\mathcal{T}}(\phi) = \varnothing$ if $n = 0$, or $Spec_{\mathcal{T}}(\phi) = [n, \aleph_0]$ otherwise.*

Proof. Suppose $\mathcal{T}$ is shiny: if ϕ is not $\mathcal{T}$-satisfiable we return 0; if it is, we make $n = \mathrm{minmod}_{\mathcal{T}}(\phi)$. This value is in $\mathbb{N}$ because $\mathcal{T}$ has the finite model property; and $Spec_{\mathcal{T}}(\phi) = [n, \aleph_0]$ because $\mathcal{T}$ is smooth. For the converse, we make $\mathrm{minmod}_{\mathcal{T}}(\phi) = n$; $\mathcal{T}$ has the finite model property because this value is always in $\mathbb{N}$; and it is smooth because $Spec_{\mathcal{T}}(\phi) = [n, \aleph_0]$ (Theorem 1).

[3] Papers [9,12–15] include many examples for all properties discussed here.

A theory $\mathcal{T}$ is **gentle** ([5], though we use the equivalent definition of [15]) when there is an algorithm that takes a quantifier-free formula ϕ and returns a pair (S, b), where $S \subset \mathbb{N}^*$ is finite and b is a Boolean, such that: if b is true, $Spec_{\mathcal{T}}(\phi) = S$; and if b is false, $Spec_{\mathcal{T}}(\phi) = \mathbb{N}_\omega \setminus S$. Using the notations for sets[4] of theories found in Table 1(where, essentially, $\mathfrak{T}_X$ means the set of decidable theories with property X) we present the following proposition, whose proof can be found in Proposition 6.1 of [9]. It says that for decidable theories, shininess implies gentleness, that in turn implies having computable finite spectra.

Table 1. Notations for sets of theories.

Symbol	Description (decidable and ...)	Definition
$\mathfrak{T}$	–	Section 2
$\mathfrak{T}_{\text{shiny}}$	Shiny	
$\mathfrak{T}_{gentle}$	Gentle	
$\mathfrak{T}_{\text{SI}}$	Stably infinite	
$\mathfrak{T}_{\text{CFS}}$	Computable finite spectra	
$\mathfrak{T}_{\text{S-d}}$	S-decidable	Section 3
$\mathfrak{T}_{\text{S-s}}$	S-shiny	
$\mathfrak{T}_{\text{S-r}}$	S-restricted	Section 4
$\mathfrak{T}_{\text{S-f}}$	S-final	

Proposition 2. $\mathfrak{T}_{shiny} \subseteq \mathfrak{T}_{gentle} \subseteq \mathfrak{T}_{CFS} \subseteq \mathfrak{T}$.

One important tool in what is to come is the following result from [5,9].

Lemma 1 (Fontaine's lemma). *$\mathcal{T}_1 \sqcup \mathcal{T}_2$ is decidable iff the following problem is decidable: given conjunctions of literals φ_1 and φ_2, determine whether $Spec_{\mathcal{T}_1}(\varphi_1) \cap Spec_{\mathcal{T}_2}(\varphi_2) = \varnothing$.*

Two theories are **combinable** if their disjoint union is decidable, and two sets of theories are combinable if any theory in the first is combinable with any theory in the second; if one of these sets is a singleton, we may simply say the theory it contains is combinable with the other set. For each $X \subseteq \mathfrak{T}$, let $G(X)$ be the set of all decidable theories that are combinable with X, that is, the largest set of decidable theories that is combinable with X.

If $X \subseteq Y$, as every theory combinable with Y is also combinable with X, we get $G(Y) \subseteq G(X)$; and X is combinable with Y iff Y is combinable with X, meaning $X \subseteq G(Y)$ iff $Y \subseteq G(X)$. Both these facts make G an **antitone Galois connection** with respect to $\subseteq$. A **combination theorem** typically says two sets

[4] These, in principle, would constitute proper classes. But, we can select all symbols for our signatures from a countable pool of symbols to ensure these are sets.

of theories are combinable, meaning $X \subseteq G(Y)$ and $Y \subseteq G(X)$. Such a theorem is *sharp* if, in fact, $X = G(Y)$ and $Y = G(X)$. In this case $G(G(X)) = X$ and $G(G(Y)) = Y$, meaning, in lattice-theoretic terms, that X and Y are **closed**; for an arbitrary X, $G(G(X))$ is its **closure**, the least closed set containing X.

3 First Generalization

We now provide a new combination method, which generalizes shiny combination, and requires the following properties, that parameterize shininess and decidability by a computable set S.

Definition 1. *Take a computable set $S \subseteq \mathbb{N}^*$.*

1. *A decidable theory $\mathcal{T}$ is S-decidable when there is an algorithm that takes a quantifier-free formula ϕ and an $n \in \mathbb{N}^*$ and returns: whether $n \in Spec_{\mathcal{T}}(\phi)$ if $n \in S$; and an arbitrary Boolean value otherwise.*
2. *A decidable theory $\mathcal{T}$ is S-shiny if there is an algorithm that takes a quantifier-free formula ϕ and returns a pair (n, S_0), where $n \in \mathbb{N}$ and S_0 is a finite subset of S (possibly empty), such that: if $n = 0$, $Spec_{\mathcal{T}}(\phi) = S_0$; if $n \neq 0$, $Spec_{\mathcal{T}}(\phi) = S_0 \cup [n, \aleph_0]$.*

Remark 1. n-decidability and n-shininess were defined in [9] for any $n \in \mathbb{N}^*$. The former corresponds to $\{n\}$-decidability, the latter to $\{n\}$-shininess.

Now, it was shown in [15] that every shiny theory is decidable. This also holds for the new generalizations.

Proposition 3. *An S-shiny theory is S-decidable.*

Proof. Suppose $\mathcal{T}$ is S-shiny, and that we are given a quantifier-free ϕ and an $m \in S$: we want to return whether $m \in Spec_{\mathcal{T}}(\phi)$. As $\mathcal{T}$ is S-shiny, there is an algorithm that takes ϕ and returns a pair (n, S_0) such that $S_0 \subseteq S$ is finite, if $n = 0$ then $Spec_{\mathcal{T}}(\phi) = S_0$, and otherwise $Spec_{\mathcal{T}}(\phi) = S_0 \cup [n, \aleph_0]$. If $n = 0$, $m \in Spec_{\mathcal{T}}(\phi)$ iff $m \in S_0$; otherwise $m \in Spec_{\mathcal{T}}(\phi)$ iff $m \in S_0$ or $m \geq n$. This procedure may be seen in Algorithm 1.

Algorithm 1. Pseudocode for showing $\mathcal{T}$ is S-decidable if it is S-shiny.

```
function SD(φ,m)
    (n, S0) ← computed for T and φ, according to Definition 1
    if m ∈ S0 then return true
    else
        if n < 0 then
            if m ≥ n then return true
        return false
```

First, we show that these notions are indeed generalizations of decidable and shiny theories, in particular when S is taken to be the empty set. Additionally, we show that when S is taken to be the entire set $\mathbb{N}^*$, we get computable finite spectra and gentleness. This shows gentle and shiny theory combination are two ends of a spectrum: gentleness is the weakest form of S-shininess, and shininess the strongest; reciprocally, having computable finite spectra is the strongest form of S-decidability, and decidability itself the weakest.

Proposition 4. *$\mathfrak{T}_{\varnothing\text{-}d} = \mathfrak{T}$, $\mathfrak{T}_{\mathbb{N}^*\text{-}d} = \mathfrak{T}_{CFS}$, $\mathfrak{T}_{\mathbb{N}^*\text{-}s} = \mathfrak{T}_{gentle}$, and $\mathfrak{T}_{\varnothing\text{-}s} = \mathfrak{T}_{shiny}$.*

Proof. $\mathfrak{T}_{\varnothing\text{-d}} = \mathfrak{T}$ should be clear, as no condition is imposed on its theories other than being decidable. If a theory $\mathcal{T}$ is in $\mathfrak{T}_{\mathbb{N}^*\text{-d}}$ then there is an algorithm that takes a quantifier-free formula ϕ and an $n \in \mathbb{N}^*$ and returns whether $n \in Spec_{\mathcal{T}}(\phi)$, what corresponds precisely to the definition of having computable finite spectra.

That $\mathfrak{T}_{\varnothing\text{-s}} = \mathfrak{T}_{\text{shiny}}$ follows from the fact that in a $\varnothing$-shiny theory $\mathcal{T}$ there is an algorithm that takes a quantifier-free formula ϕ and returns a pair $(n, \varnothing)$ such that: either $n = 0$ and $Spec_{\mathcal{T}}(\phi) = \varnothing$ (meaning ϕ is not $\mathcal{T}$-satisfiable); or $n \in \mathbb{N}^*$ and $Spec_{\mathcal{T}}(\phi) = [n, \aleph_0]$, as expected of a shiny theory by Proposition 1.

Finally, it is clear $\mathbb{N}^*$-shiny theories are gentle. And if a theory $\mathcal{T}$ is gentle we either have $Spec_{\mathcal{T}}(\phi)$ finite, when we output $(0, Spec_{\mathcal{T}}(\phi))$, which is compatible with being an $\mathbb{N}^*$-shiny theory as $Spec_{\mathcal{T}}(\phi) \subseteq \mathbb{N}$; or $Spec_{\mathcal{T}}(\phi)$ is cofinite, and from gentleness we get $S = \mathbb{N}_{\omega} \setminus Spec_{\mathcal{T}}(\phi)$. In this case take the greatest element n not in $Spec_{\mathcal{T}}(\phi)$, and we have $Spec_{\mathcal{T}}(\phi)$ equals the union of $[1, n] \setminus S$ and $[n+1, \aleph_0]$, also compatible with $\mathcal{T}$ being $\mathbb{N}$-shiny as certainly $[1, n] \setminus S \subseteq \mathbb{N}$, when we output $(n+1, [1, n] \setminus S)$.

The following theorem is the main result of this section. It generalizes the shiny combination theorem, according to which the disjoint combination of a shiny theory with a decidable theory is itself decidable [11].

Theorem 2. *If $\mathcal{T}_1$ is S-decidable and $\mathcal{T}_2$ is S-shiny for some S, and both $\mathcal{T}_1$ and $\mathcal{T}_2$ are decidable, then $\mathcal{T}_1 \sqcup \mathcal{T}_2$ is decidable.*

Proof (sketch). By Lemma 1, it suffices to show a decision procedure that decides, given conjunctions of literals ϕ_1 and ϕ_2 whether $Spec_{\mathcal{T}_1}(\phi_1) \cap Spec_{\mathcal{T}_2}(\phi_2)$ is empty. This decision procedure is shown in Algorithm 2.

Algorithm 2. Pseudocode for determining non-emptyness of $Spec_{\mathcal{T}_1}(\phi_1) \cap Spec_{\mathcal{T}_2}(\phi_2)$ when $\mathcal{T}_1$ is S-decidable and $\mathcal{T}_2$ is S-shiny.

function SD+SS(ϕ_1, ϕ_2)
  if ϕ_2 is not $\mathcal{T}_2$-satisfiable **then return** false
  $(n, S_0) \leftarrow$ computed for ϕ_2 and $\mathcal{T}_2$, according to Definition 1.
  if $n \neq 0$ and $\phi_1 \wedge \neq(x_1, \dots, x_n)$ is $\mathcal{T}_1$-satisfiable **then** ▷ $x_1, \dots, x_n$ are fresh
    return true
  for $m \in S_0$ **do**
    if $m \in Spec_{\mathcal{T}_1}(\phi_1)$ **then**
      return true
  return false

We now study how S-decidability and S-shininess change with S.

Proposition 5. *1. If $S \subsetneq T$, then $\mathfrak{T}_{T\text{-}d} \subsetneq \mathfrak{T}_{S\text{-}d}$ and $\mathfrak{T}_{S\text{-}s} \subsetneq \mathfrak{T}_{T\text{-}s}$.*
2. If S and T are incomparable (i.e. $S \nsubseteq T$ and $T \nsubseteq S$), so are $\mathfrak{T}_{S\text{-}d}$ and $\mathfrak{T}_{T\text{-}d}$, and also $\mathfrak{T}_{S\text{-}d}$ and $\mathfrak{T}_{T\text{-}d}$.

Thus, the collections of S-decidable and S-shiny theories, for computable $S \subseteq \mathbb{N}^*$, have the structure of the computable subsets of $\mathbb{N}^*$, and its dual. More precisely, we have Fig. 2: the Galois connection G is simply the reflection over the dashed line. Below it we find the many variations of S-shininess, having the structure of the computable subsets of $\mathbb{N}^*$, with shininess at the bottom and gentleness on top. Above the dashed line we find the variations of S-decidability, having the structure of the dual of the computable subsets of $\mathbb{N}^*$, with computable finite spectra at the bottom and decidability at the top.

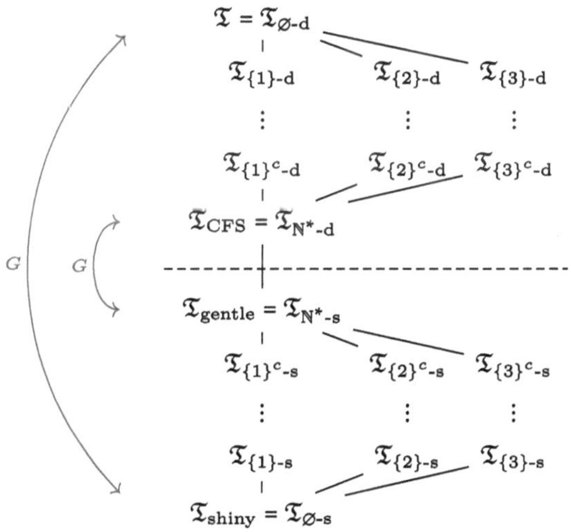

Fig. 2. The rich universe of S-decidable and S-shiny theory combination. For readability, $\{n\}^c$ denotes $\mathbb{N}^* \setminus \{n\}$.

We conclude the first generalization of shininess with some examples:

Example 1. 1. Consider a one-sorted variant of the very popular SMT-LIB theory of bit-vectors, where the single domain includes all bit-vectors of the same width. The set X of all possible sizes of models is comprised of all the powers of two, a decidable set. Thus, this variant is X-decidable, and can be combined with any X-shiny theory, thanks to Theorem 2.
2. The first-order theory of fields only has finite models of cardinalities in the set $Y = \{p^n : n \in \mathbb{N}^*, p \text{is prime}\}$, which is again decidable, and is therefore Y-decidable.
3. Given a finite field of cardinality p^n, the theory of vector spaces over this field only has finite models of cardinality in $Z = \{kp^n : k \in \mathbb{N}\}$, also decidable, and is therefore Z-decidable.

Algorithm 3. Pseudocode for determining non-emptiness of $Spec_{\mathcal{T}_1}(\phi_1) \cap Spec_{\mathcal{T}_2}(\phi_2)$ when $\mathcal{T}_1$ is S-restricted and $\mathcal{T}_2$ is S-final.

function SR+SF(ϕ_1, ϕ_2)
    if ϕ_2 is not $\mathcal{T}_2$-satisfiable **then return** false
    $n \leftarrow$ computed for ϕ_2 and $\mathcal{T}_2$, according to Definition 2.
    if $\phi_1 \wedge \neq(x_1, \dots, x_n)$ is $\mathcal{T}_1$-satisfiable **then**   ▷ $x_1, \dots, x_n$ are fresh
        return true
    return false

4 Second Generalization

We now present our second generalization of the shiny combination theorem. It allows one to combine two sets of theories: the first, weaker set, has no requirement on the existence of algorithms for it (other than decidability, of course). The second requires an algorithm for computing a variant of a spectra.

Definition 2. *Take a computable, infinite set* $S \subseteq \mathbb{N}^*$.

1. *A decidable theory* $\mathcal{T}$ *is* S*-restricted if, for every quantifier-free formula* ϕ, $Spec_{\mathcal{T}}(\phi) \setminus S \neq \emptyset$ *implies* $\aleph_0 \in Spec_{\mathcal{T}}(\phi)$.
2. *A decidable theory is* S*-final if there is an algorithm that takes a quantifier-free formula* ϕ *and returns* 0 *if* ϕ *is not* $\mathcal{T}$*-satisfiable, and otherwise an* $n \in \mathbb{N}^*$, *not necessarily in* S, *such that* $Spec_{\mathcal{T}}(\phi) \cap S_\omega = [n, \aleph_0] \cap S_\omega$.

Let us first see relations between these properties and others.

Proposition 6. *1.* $\mathfrak{T}_{S\text{-}f} \subseteq \mathfrak{T}_{SI} \subseteq \mathfrak{T}_{S\text{-}r}$, *for any* S.
2. $\mathfrak{T}_{\mathbb{N}^*\text{-}r} = \mathfrak{T}$, *and* $\mathfrak{T}_{\mathbb{N}^*\text{-}f} = \mathfrak{T}_{shiny}$.

Proof. 1. Suppose $\mathcal{T}$ is S-final, and take a quantifier-free ϕ: if ϕ is not $\mathcal{T}$-satisfiable we have nothing to prove; otherwise our algorithm gives an $n \in \mathbb{N}^*$ such that $Spec_{\mathcal{T}}(\phi) \cap S_\omega = [n, \aleph_0] \cap S_\omega$, and since $\aleph_0 \in S_\omega$, $\mathcal{T}$ is stably infinite. If $\mathcal{T}$ is stably infinite we get that if $Spec_{\mathcal{T}}(\phi)$ is not empty then $\aleph_0 \in Spec_{\mathcal{T}}(\phi)$, meaning $\mathcal{T}$ is trivially S-restricted.
2. An $\mathbb{N}^*$-restricted theory imposes no further requirements on the theory other than being decidable, as we cannot have $Spec_{\mathcal{T}}(\phi) \setminus \mathbb{N}^*$ not empty unless $Spec_{\mathcal{T}}(\phi)$ already contains $\aleph_0$. $\mathbb{N}^*$-finality implies there is an algorithm that takes a quantifier-free ϕ and returns 0 if ϕ is not $\mathcal{T}$-satisfiable, and otherwise an $n \in \mathbb{N}^*$ such that $Spec_{\mathcal{T}}(\phi) = [n, \aleph_0]$, exactly the notion of shininess in Proposition 1.

□

Now, we present our second new combination theorem: its proof follows that of Theorem 2, but this time using Algorithm 2.

Theorem 3. *Let* $\mathcal{T}_1$ *be* S*-restricted, and* $\mathcal{T}_2$ *be* S*-final. Then* $\mathcal{T}_1 \sqcup \mathcal{T}_2$ *is decidable.*

Example 2. The first example of a finitely witnessable (property related to politeness) theory that is not strongly finitely witnessable (property related to strong politeness, equivalent to shininess over decidable theories) was $\mathcal{T}_{even}^{\infty}$: this theory has only interpretations of even size, or infinite ones. Yet, in a sense, it is a surprisingly well-behaved theory: if S is the set of positive even numbers, then it should not be too hard to prove that $Spec_{\mathcal{T}_{even}^{\infty}}(\phi) = [n, \aleph_0] \cap S_\omega$, where n is the minimal size of any first-order model of ϕ, which we assume to be quantifier-free. This is almost the definition of shininess, except for the pesky intersection with S_ω. Using the notions just defined, $\mathcal{T}_{even}^{\infty}$ is seen in fact to be S-shiny, and thus combinable with any S-restricted theory.

As we did for S-decidability and S-shininess, we analyze how the sets of S-restricted and S-final theories change as S changes.

Proposition 7. *1. If $S \subsetneq T$, $\mathfrak{T}_{S\text{-}r} \subsetneq \mathfrak{T}_{T\text{-}r}$, and $\mathfrak{T}_{T\text{-}f} \subsetneq \mathfrak{T}_{S\text{-}f}$.*
2. If S and T are incomparable, so are $\mathfrak{T}_{S\text{-}r}$ and $\mathfrak{T}_{T\text{-}r}$, and $\mathfrak{T}_{S\text{-}f}$ and $\mathfrak{T}_{T\text{-}f}$ (Fig. 3).

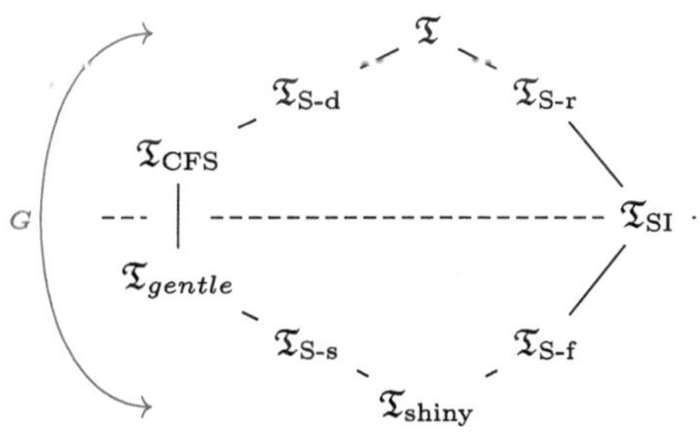

Fig. 3. The general picture involving the notions defined in this paper: notice how Fig. 2 is a more detailed version of the left side of the diagram.

5 Sharpness of the New Methods

We now set out to prove that the new combination Theorems 2 and 3 are sharp. For the former, this means every theory combinable with all S-decidable theories must be S-shiny, and that every theory combinable with all S-shiny theories must be S-decidable. Similar sharpness results are proven for the latter. We utilize the method of *test theories*, introduced in [9].

5.1 Test Theories

The idea behind test theories goes more or less as follows: we want to prove that if a theory $\mathcal{T}$ is combinable with every theory of X, then it admits some

Table 2. Test theories and their properties; $S \subseteq \mathbb{N}^*$; for the first and last theories, $m<n$; for the last, $n \notin S$. We define $P_{\neq} = \{P_i \rightarrow \neg P_j : i \neq j\}$ and $M_{\mathcal{T}}(\phi) = 1 + \max Spec_{\mathcal{T}}(\phi)$ to make the table more readable.

Theory	Details
$\mathcal{T}_n^m$	Axiomatization: $\{\psi_{=n} \vee \psi_{=m}\} \cup \{P_k \rightarrow \psi_{=m} : k \in U\} \cup P_{\neq}$
	Properties: Decidable, S-decidable (if $n \notin S$), S-restricted (if $m, n \in S$)
	$m \notin Spec_{\mathcal{T}}(\phi), n \in Spec_{\mathcal{T}}(\phi) \Rightarrow [\phi \wedge P_k$ is $\mathcal{T} \sqcup \mathcal{T}_n^m$-SAT $\Leftrightarrow k \notin U]$
$\mathcal{T}_=^P$	Axiomatization: $\{P_n \rightarrow \psi_{=n} : n \in \mathbb{N}^*\}$
	Properties: Decidable, S-decidable (for any S)
	$\phi \wedge P_n$ is $\mathcal{T} \sqcup \mathcal{T}_=^P$-SAT $\Leftrightarrow n \in Spec_{\mathcal{T}}(\phi)$
$\mathcal{T}_\leq^S$	Axiomatization: $\{P_n \rightarrow \psi_{\leq F(n)} : F(n) \in \mathbb{N}\} \cup \{\neg\psi_{=n} : n \notin S\} \cup P_{\neq}$
	Properties: Decidable, $\overline{S}$-decidable, S-restricted
	$Spec_{\mathcal{T}}(\phi) \neq \varnothing, S \cap Spec_{\mathcal{T}}(\phi) = \varnothing \Rightarrow [\phi \wedge P_k$ is $\mathcal{T} \sqcup \mathcal{T}_\leq^S$-SAT $\Leftrightarrow F(k) = \aleph_0]$
$\mathcal{T}_=^S$	Axiomatization: $\{P_n \rightarrow \psi_{=n} : n \in S\} \cup \{\neg P_n : n \notin S\} \cup P_{\neq}$
	Properties: Decidable, S-shiny, S-restricted
	$k \in S \Rightarrow [\phi \wedge P_k$ is $\mathcal{T} \sqcup \mathcal{T}_=^S$-SAT $\Leftrightarrow k \in Spec_{\mathcal{T}}(\phi)]$
$\mathcal{T}_{S-r}^{m,n}$	Axiomatization: $\{\neg\psi_{=k} : k \notin S \cup \{n\}\} \cup \{\psi_{=n} \vee \psi_{\geq m}\} \cup \{\psi_{=n} \rightarrow \neg P_k : k \notin U\} \cup P_{\neq}$
	Properties: Decidable, S-final
	$n \in Spec_{\mathcal{T}}(\phi), m = M_{\mathcal{T}}(\phi) \Rightarrow [\phi \wedge P_k$ is $\mathcal{T} \sqcup \mathcal{T}_{S-r}^{m,n}$-SAT $\Leftrightarrow k \in U]$

property; this could be done by looking at all $\mathcal{T} \sqcup \mathcal{T}'$, for $\mathcal{T}' \in X$. But considering all theories of X is rarely feasible, and is certainly not very effective. So, from X, we select special theories, *test theories*, such that the satisfiability problem of the combination of $\mathcal{T}$ and a test theory directly relates to properties from $\mathcal{T}$. In this sense, the set of test theories will be a very difficult set of theories to combine with $\mathcal{T}$, as being combinable with them forces $\mathcal{T}$ to have a given property.

We need 5 sets of test theories, three found in [9], and two new. Let $\Sigma_P^{\mathbb{N}}$ be the signature with no function symbols, and nullary predicate symbols $\{P_n : n \in \mathbb{N}^*\}$: all of our test theories will be $\Sigma_P^{\mathbb{N}}$-theories, and are described in Table 2, which relies on an undecidable set $U \subseteq \mathbb{N}^*$, and a function $F : \mathbb{N}^* \rightarrow \mathbb{N}^* \cup \{\aleph_0\}$ such that $\{(m, n) \in \mathbb{N}^{*2} : n \leq F(m)\}$ is decidable, but $\{n \in \mathbb{N}^* : F(n) = \aleph_0\}$ is not.[5]

The three test theories from [9] are $\mathcal{T}_n^m$, $\mathcal{T}_=^P$ and $\mathcal{T}_\leq^S$. $\mathcal{T}_n^m$ is a $\Sigma_P^{\mathbb{N}}$-theory with only interpretations of size m or n, and where P_k only has interpretations of size m whenever $k \in U$; so $Spec_{\mathcal{T}_n^m}(P_k) = \{n, m\}$ if $k \notin U$, and $\{m\}$ otherwise. A $\mathcal{T}_=^P$-interpretation where P_n is true must have exactly n elements; so $Spec_{\mathcal{T}_=^P}(P_n) = \{n\}$. The theory $\mathcal{T}_\leq^S$ has only interpretations of cardinality in S_ω, and if P_n is true and $F(n)$ is finite, then we have at most $F(n)$ elements; so $Spec_{\mathcal{T}}(P_n) = S \cap [1, F(n)]$ if $F(n)$ is finite, and S_ω otherwise.

The two new test theories are $\mathcal{T}_=^S$ and $\mathcal{T}_{\mathrm{S-r}}^{m,n}$. The theory $\mathcal{T}_=^S$ is similar to $\mathcal{T}_=^P$, with a twist: if P_n is true (what can only happen for $n \in S$) then the interpretation has size n. So, $Spec_{\mathcal{T}_=^S}(P_n) = \varnothing$ if $n \notin S \subseteq \mathbb{N}^*$, and $\{n\}$ otherwise.

[5] An example for F assumes an enumeration of Turing machines, takes the index of a machine, and returns the number of steps it takes to halt, or $\aleph_0$ if it doesn't.

Algorithm 4. Pseudocode for showing $\mathcal{T}$ is S-shiny if $\mathcal{T} \in G(\mathfrak{T}_{\text{S-d}})$.

1: **function** SS(ϕ)
2:     $k \leftarrow 1$
3:     $S_0 \leftarrow \varnothing$
4:     **while** True **do**
5:         **if** $k \in Spec_{\mathcal{T}}(\phi)$ **then**
6:             **if** $k \notin S$ **then return** (k, S_0)
7:             $S_0 \leftarrow S_0 \cup \{k\}$
8:             $k \leftarrow k + 1$
9:         **else**
10:             **if** $\phi \wedge \neq(x_1, \ldots, x_k)$ is not $\mathcal{T}$-satisfiable **then return** $(0, S_0)$
11:             $k \leftarrow k + 1$

The theory $\mathcal{T}_{\text{S-r}}^{m,n}$ is quite similar to $\mathcal{T}_n^m$, and will be used to test whether the spectrum of a formula is entirely contained in a computable, infinite set $S \subseteq \mathbb{N}^*$. It depends on two numbers m and n, with $m<n$ and $n \notin S$, and its interpretations must: have cardinality in S or equal to n; have cardinality n or at least m; and, if they have cardinality n, then P_k can only be true if $k \in U$. To summarize it, $Spec_{\mathcal{T}_{\text{S-r}}^{m,n}}(P_k) = S_\omega \cap (\{n\} \cup [m, \aleph_0])$ if $k \in U$, and $S_\omega \cap [m, \aleph_0]$ otherwise.

Theorem 4. *Table 2 is correct: each theory satisfies the properties listed for it.*

5.2 Sharpness for S-Shininess

We now prove that Theorem 2 is sharp, that is: Given S, all decidable theories that can be combined with all S-shiny theories must be S-decidable, and all decidable theories that can be combined with all S-decidable theories must be S-shiny. Formally, we utilize operator G from Sect. 2.2, and the test theories $\mathcal{T}_=^S$ to prove $G(\mathfrak{T}_{\text{S-s}}) \subseteq \mathfrak{T}_{\text{S-d}}$, and $\mathcal{T}_=^P$, $\mathcal{T}_\leq^S$ and $\mathcal{T}_n^m$ to prove $G(\mathfrak{T}_{\text{S-d}}) \subseteq \mathfrak{T}_{\text{S-s}}$.

Theorem 5. $G(\mathfrak{T}_{S\text{-}s}) \subseteq \mathfrak{T}_{S\text{-}d}$ *and* $G(\mathfrak{T}_{S\text{-}d}) \subseteq \mathfrak{T}_{S\text{-}s}$.

Proof. 1. Suppose that $\mathcal{T} \in G(\mathfrak{T}_{\text{S-s}})$, and take a quantifier-free formula ϕ: since $\mathcal{T}_=^S$ is decidable and S-shiny (see Theorem 4), for any $n \in S$ we have $n \in Spec_{\mathcal{T}}(\phi)$ if and only if $\phi \wedge P_n$ is $\mathcal{T} \sqcup \mathcal{T}_=^S$-satisfiable, a problem for which we have an algorithm since $\mathcal{T} \sqcup \mathcal{T}_=^S$ is decidable; we thus have $\mathcal{T}$ is S-decidable.

2. Suppose now that $\mathcal{T} \in G(\mathfrak{T}_{\text{S-d}})$. First we show that $\mathcal{T}$ must have computable finite spectra. $\mathcal{T}_=^P$ is decidable and S-decidable by Theorem 4; this means $\mathcal{T} \sqcup \mathcal{T}_=^P$ is decidable, and $k \in Spec_{\mathcal{T}}(\phi)$ (for a quantifier-free ϕ) if and only if $\phi \wedge P_k$ is $\mathcal{T} \sqcup \mathcal{T}_=^P$-satisfiable, proving $\mathcal{T}$ indeed has computable finite spectra. We now prove $\mathcal{T}$ is S-shiny by showing, in Algorithm 4, the algorithm that outputs (n, S_0). Checking (for $k \in \mathbb{N}^*$) whether $k \in S$ in line 5 is possible because S is computable, whether $k \in Spec_{\mathcal{T}}(\phi)$ in line 4 is possible because we just proved $\mathcal{T}$ has computable finite spectra, and whether $\phi \wedge \neq(x_1, \ldots, x_k)$ is $\mathcal{T}$-satisfiable in line 10 is possible because $\mathcal{T}$ is decidable. We notice that S_0 is nothing but $Spec_{\mathcal{T}}(\phi) \cap [1, k-1]$. Now, to see that our algorithm stops, there

are two cases to consider: whether $Spec_{\mathcal{T}}(\phi) \setminus S$ is empty or not.
If it is empty, and $Spec_{\mathcal{T}}(\phi)$ is infinite, using Corollary 1 we get $\aleph_0 \in Spec_{\mathcal{T}}(\phi)$, and that leads to a contradiction: $Spec_{\mathcal{T}}(\phi) \setminus S = \varnothing$, $\aleph_0 \notin S$ and $\aleph_0 \in Spec_{\mathcal{T}}(\phi)$ cannot be simultaneously true. So, if $Spec_{\mathcal{T}}(\phi) \setminus S$ is empty, $Spec_{\mathcal{T}}(\phi)$ must be finite (and contained in S), and eventually we will find a k such that $k \notin Spec_{\mathcal{T}}(\phi)$ and $\phi \wedge \neq(x_1, \dots, x_k)$ is not $\mathcal{T}$-satisfiable, when our algorithm must stop. In that case it returns $(0, S_0)$ for $S_0 = Spec_{\mathcal{T}}(\phi) \cap [1, k-1]$, which is a finite subset of S and equals $Spec_{\mathcal{T}}(\phi)$.
So now we assume $Spec_{\mathcal{T}}(\phi) \setminus S \neq \varnothing$: we will then prove $Spec_{\mathcal{T}}(\phi)$ has a finite value not in S, and our algorithm will stop when it finds the first such value, and will output (k, S_0) for $S_0 = Spec_{\mathcal{T}}(\phi) \cap [1, k-1]$ a finite subset of S; second, we will prove that the existence of a finite value k in $Spec_{\mathcal{T}}(\phi)$ that is not in S implies $[k, \aleph_0] \subseteq Spec_{\mathcal{T}}(\phi)$, so the spectrum indeed has the form suggested by the algorithm as $Spec_{\mathcal{T}}(\phi)$ equals the union of $Spec_{\mathcal{T}}(\phi) \cap [1, k-1]$ and $[k, \aleph_0]$.
Suppose, then, that $Spec_{\mathcal{T}}(\phi) \setminus S \neq \varnothing$ but $(Spec_{\mathcal{T}}(\phi) \setminus S) \cap \mathbb{N} = \varnothing$. We then have that $Spec_{\mathcal{T}}(\phi) \setminus S = \{\aleph_0\}$, and therefore $\phi \wedge P_i$ is $\mathcal{T} \sqcup \mathcal{T}_{\leq}^{\overline{S}}$-satisfiable if and only if $F(i) = \aleph_0$, an undecidable problem. This leads to a contradiction, as $\mathcal{T}_{\leq}^{\overline{S}}$, for $\overline{S} = \mathbb{N}^* \setminus S$, is decidable and has no interpretations with sizes in S, thus being S-decidable (see Theorem 4). Next, suppose $n \in Spec_{\mathcal{T}}(\phi) \setminus S$ is finite and there is an $n < m < \aleph_0$ such that $m \notin Spec_{\mathcal{T}}(\phi)$. Then $\phi \wedge P_i$ is $\mathcal{T} \sqcup \mathcal{T}_n^m$-satisfiable iff $i \notin U$, an undecidable problem. This too leads to a contradiction, as $\mathcal{T}_n^m$ is decidable and S-decidable (Theorem 4).

□

5.3 Sharpness for *S*-Finality

We now prove that Theorem 3 is sharp, namely: given S, every decidable theory that can be combined with all S-final theories must be S-restricted, and every decidable theory that can be combined with all S-restricted theories must be S-final. Again, we utilize operator G from Sect. 2, the test theory $\mathcal{T}_{\text{S-r}}^{m,n}$ to prove $G(\mathfrak{T}_{\text{S-f}}) \subseteq \mathfrak{T}_{\text{S-r}}$, and $\mathcal{T}_{\leq}^{S}$, $\mathcal{T}_{=}^{S}$ and $\mathcal{T}_n^m$ to prove $G(\mathfrak{T}_{\text{S-r}}) \subseteq \mathfrak{T}_{\text{S-f}}$.

Theorem 6. *$G(\mathfrak{T}_{S\text{-}f}) \subseteq \mathfrak{T}_{S\text{-}r}$ and $G(\mathfrak{T}_{S\text{-}r}) \subseteq \mathfrak{T}_{S\text{-}f}$.*

Proof. 1. Suppose that $\mathcal{T} \in G(\mathfrak{T}_{\text{S-f}})$ is not S-restricted, that is, there are a quantifier-free formula ϕ, an $n \in Spec_{\mathcal{T}}(\phi) \setminus S$ and a maximum element of $Spec_{\mathcal{T}}(\phi)$; define $m = 1 + \max Spec_{\mathcal{T}}(\phi)$. We state that $\mathcal{T}_{\text{S-r}}^{m,n}$ is decidable and S-final, so $\mathcal{T} \sqcup \mathcal{T}_{\text{S-r}}^{m,n}$ should be decidable; yet $\phi \wedge P_k$ is $\mathcal{T} \sqcup \mathcal{T}_{\text{S-r}}^{m,n}$-satisfiable if and only if $k \in U$, leading to a contradiction.
2. Suppose that $\mathcal{T} \in G(\mathfrak{T}_{\text{S-r}})$: first we prove that, if ϕ is $\mathcal{T}$-satisfiable (otherwise we just return 0), there is a finite number in $Spec_{\mathcal{T}}(\phi) \cap S_\omega$, for any quantifier-free formula ϕ. Were that not the case we would get $\phi \wedge P_k$ is $\mathcal{T} \sqcup \mathcal{T}_{\leq}^{S}$ if and only if $F(k) = \aleph_0$, what contradicts the fact that $\mathcal{T}_{\leq}^{S}$ is S-restricted.
Next we show how the least element of $Spec_{\mathcal{T}}(\phi) \cap S_\omega$ can be calculated: using that $\mathcal{T}_{=}^{S}$ is decidable and S-restricted, we simply search for the first $k \in S$ such

that $\phi \wedge P_k$ is $\mathcal{T} \sqcup \mathcal{T}_{=}^{S}$-satisfiable, which must be finite by what we have seen above. Finally, suppose $n \in Spec_{\mathcal{T}}(\phi) \cap S$ but, for some $n < m < \aleph_0$ in S (which we can always find as S is infinite), $m \notin Spec_{\mathcal{T}}(\phi)$. Then $\phi \wedge P_k$ is $\mathcal{T} \sqcup \mathcal{T}_n^m$-satisfiable if and only if $k \notin U$, contradicting the fact that $\mathcal{T}_n^m$ is decidable and S-restricted.

□

6 Conclusion and Future Work

We have presented two infinite families of sharp combination methods resembling shininess. One motivates gentleness as simply one extreme of a range of properties, the other extreme being shininess itself. The other requires very little from the weaker theory to be combined, not unlike Nelson–Oppen and polite theory combination. This is in line with [9], which suggests that new combination methods should also be proven sharp given the new techniques available to researchers in the area.

Directions for future work are many: the Galois connection of theory combination makes finding new combination methods much easier; but perhaps more interesting than finding new methods would be trying to generalize those we have at hand to the many-sorted case, a task currently being carried out.

Acknowledgments. This research was supported in part by Defense Advanced Research Projects Agency (DARPA) contract FA875024-2-1001, U.S.-Israel Binational Science Foundation (BSF) grant 2024049, and Israel Science Foundation (ISF) grants number 619/21 and 209/25.

References

1. Barbosa, H., et al.: cvc5: a versatile and industrial-strength SMT solver. In: Fisman, D., Rosu, G. (eds.) TACAS 2022. LNCS, vol. 13243, pp. 415–442. Springer, Cham (2022)
2. Casal, F., Rasga, J.: Revisiting the equivalence of shininess and politeness. In: McMillan, K., Middeldorp, A., Voronkov, A. (eds.) LPAR 2013. LNCS, vol. 8312, pp. 198–212. Springer, Heidelberg (2013). https://doi.org/10.1007/978-3-642-45221-5_15
3. Casal, F., Rasga, J.: Many-sorted equivalence of shiny and strongly polite theories. J. Autom. Reason. **60**(2), 221–236 (2018). https://doi.org/10.1007/s10817-017-9411-y
4. Enderton, H.B.: A mathematical introduction to logic. Academic Press, New York (1972)
5. Fontaine, P.: Combinations of theories for decidable fragments of first-order logic. In: Ghilardi, S., Sebastiani, R. (eds.) FroCoS 2009. LNCS (LNAI), vol. 5749, pp. 263–278. Springer, Heidelberg (2009). https://doi.org/10.1007/978-3-642-04222-5_16

6. Jovanović, D., Barrett, C.: Polite theories revisited. Technical report TR2010-922, Depatrment of Computer Science, New York University (2010). http://www.cs.stanford.edu/~barrett/pubs/JB10-TR.pdf
7. Marker, D.: Model Theory: An Introduction. Graduate Texts in Mathematics, vol. 217. Springer, New York (2002)
8. Nelson, G., Oppen, D.C.: Simplification by cooperating decision procedures. ACM Trans. Program. Lang. Syst. **1**(2), 245–257 (1979). https://doi.org/10.1145/357073.357079
9. Przybocki, B., Toledo, G.V., Zohar, Y.: characterizing sets of theories that can be disjointly combined. In: 53rd ACM SIGPLAN Symposium on Principles of Programming Languages, POPL 2026 (2026)
10. Ranise, S., Ringeissen, C., Zarba, C.G.: Combining data structures with nonstably infinite theories using many-sorted logic. In: Gramlich, B. (ed.) FroCoS 2005. LNAI, vol. 3717, pp. 48–64. Springer, Cham (2005). https://hal.inria.fr/inria-00000570, https://doi.org/10.1007/11559306
11. Tinelli, C., Zarba, C.: Combining decision procedures for theories in sorted logics. Technical report 04-01, Department of Computer Science, The University of Iowa (2004). ftp://ftp.cs.uiowa.edu/pub/tinelli/papers/TinZar-RR-04.pdf
12. Toledo, G.V., Zohar, Y.: Combining combination properties: minimal models. In: Bjorner, N., Heule, M., Voronkov, A. (eds.) Proceedings of 25th Conference on Logic for Programming, Artificial Intelligence and Reasoning. EPiC Series in Computing, vol. 100, pp. 19–35. EasyChair (2024). https://easychair.org/publications/paper/9KKC, https://doi.org/10.29007/6qkh
13. Toledo, G.V., Zohar, Y., Barrett, C.: Combining combination properties: an analysis of stable infiniteness, convexity, and politeness. In: Pientka, B., Tinelli, C. (eds.) CADE 2023. LNCS, vol 14132, pp. 522–541. Springer, Cham (2023). https://doi.org/10.1007/978-3-031-38499-8_30
14. Toledo, G.V., Zohar, Y., Barrett, C.: Combining finite combination properties: finite models and busy beavers. In: Sattler, U., Suda, M. (eds.) FroCoS 2023. LNCS, vol. 14279, pp. 159–175. Springer, Cham (2023) . https://doi.org/10.1007/978-3-031-43369-6_9
15. Toledo, G.V., Przybocki, B., Zohar, Y.: Being polite is not enough (and other limits of theory combination). In: Automated Deduction – CADE 30: 30th International Conference on Automated Deduction, Stuttgart, Germany, 28–31 July 2025, Proceedings, pp. 17–34. Springer, Heidelberg (2025). https://doi.org/10.1007/978-3-031-99984-0_2

A Circuit-Theoretic View of FO over Semirings

Timon Barlag[1(✉)], Nicolas Fröhlich[1], Teemu Hankala[2], Miika Juhani Hannula[2,3], Minna Hirvonen[1], Vivian Holzapfel[1], Juha Kontinen[2], Arne Meier[1], and Laura Strieker[1]

[1] Leibniz Universität Hannover, Hannover, Germany
{barlag,nicolas.froehlich,minna.hirvonen,holzapfel,meier, strieker}@thi.uni-hannover.de
[2] University of Helsinki, Helsinki, Finland
{teemu.hankala,juha.kontinen}@helsinki.fi, miika.juhani.hannula@ut.ee
[3] University of Tartu, Tartu, Estonia

Abstract. We study the expressivity and computational aspects of first-order logic and its extensions in the semiring semantics developed by Grädel and Tannen. We characterize the data complexity of first-order logic in terms of arithmetic circuits defined over a semiring. In particular, we give a logical characterization of constant-depth arithmetic circuits by an extension of first-order logic that holds for any semiring that is both commutative and positive. We show the result for non-uniform circuit families, meaning circuit families where there is no restriction on how computationally difficult it is to obtain any individual circuit.

Keywords: Semiring · First-order Logic · Computational Complexity · Circuit Complexity · Arithmetic Circuit

1 Introduction

In descriptive complexity theory, a cornerstone result equates first-order logic (FO), augmented with basic arithmetic predicates like successor, addition, and bit decomposition (often denoted FO+BITS), with the circuit complexity class uniform AC^0—constant-depth, polynomial-size circuits computable in logarithmic time. This equivalence, due to seminal work of Immerman from 1987 [22] (with independent contributions from Buss [13], as well as Gurevich and Lewis [21]), reveals a profound unity between logical expressivity over finite structures and parallel computation models. Its importance lies in providing a logical syntax for AC^0, enabling model-theoretic proofs of circuit lower bounds (such as computing the parity of a binary encoded input is not in AC^0) via Ehrenfeucht–Fraïssé games or locality arguments, and anchoring the entire descriptive complexity programme, where complexity classes like NC, P, and NP gain precise logical characterisations that bridge automata theory, logic, and circuit design.

P. Johann and R. de Queiroz (Eds.): WoLLIC 2026, LNCS 16757, pp. 111–125, 2027.
https://doi.org/10.1007/978-3-032-33486-2_8

Developments in semiring provenance [20] motivate extending the classical descriptive complexity framework—where FO = AC^0 captures decision problems over the Boolean semiring—to annotated databases. In semiring provenance, the tuples of a relation are annotated with elements of a semiring, which are then propagated to the satisfying tuples of a query, with the semiring operations interpreting the logical connectives and quantifiers. The resulting semiring values track "why" or "to what extent" the query answers hold.

While semiring semantics originated in database theory, it is now widely used and studied, for example, in description logics (see [9,10,14]) and in first-order logic and its extensions [7,12,16–18]. Despite the recent popularity of this approach, the computational aspects of these logics over general semirings have not yet been systematically investigated.

Our main result generalizes the aforementioned equivalence between FO and constant-depth circuits to positive and commutative semirings. It is worth noting that descriptive complexity results for algebraic circuits have also been established using metafinite logics (see [1,5,15]). Our aim, however, is to understand the computational counterparts of logics under semiring semantics, which differ considerably from the metafinite framework.

Organization and Contributions. We introduce the relevant notions for arithmetic circuits and define a version of first-order logic over a semiring K, denoted by $\mathrm{FO}_K^{=}$, including a treatment of built-in relations in the semiring setting. We then show that this logic captures exactly the problems defined by families of AC^0-circuits over the semiring K. This work introduces a circuit-theoretic point of view to the complexity analysis of the logic $\mathrm{FO}_K^{=}$ that was in [3] studied using generalized Blum–Shub–Smale machines over semirings. Related formalisms have also been studied previously: a variant without constant formulae was proposed in [4], building on semiring semantics for first-order logic (without constant formulae or comparison atoms) originally defined in [18].

2 Preliminaries

Semirings are structures that generalize the notion of rings by removing the requirement that each element must have an additive inverse. More formally, semirings are defined as follows.

Definition 1. *A* semiring *is a tuple* $K = (K, +, \cdot, 0, 1)$, *where* $+$ *and* $\cdot$ *are binary operations on* K, $(K, +, 0)$ *is a commutative monoid with identity element* 0, $(K, \cdot, 1)$ *is a monoid with identity element* 1, $\cdot$ *left and right distributes over* $+$, *and* $x \cdot 0 = 0 = 0 \cdot x$ *for all* $x \in K$.

We follow the common practice of writing ab instead of $a \cdot b$. A semiring K is said to be *commutative* if $(K, \cdot, 1)$ is a commutative monoid, and *positive* if it has no divisors of 0, i. e., $ab \neq 0$ for all $a, b \in K$, where $a \neq 0 \neq b$ and if $a + b = 0$ implies that $a = b = 0$. A semiring is *ordered* if there exists a relation $\leq$ that is reflexive, transitive, and antisymmetric (i.e., a partial order) such that for all $a, b, c \in K$ $a \leq b \implies a + c \leq b + c$ and $a \leq b \wedge 0 \leq c \implies ac \leq bc \wedge ca \leq cb$. The *natural order* $\leq_{\mathrm{n}}$ of a semiring K is defined by $a \leq_{\mathrm{n}} b \iff \exists c : a + c = b$. The natural order of a semiring is always a pre-order (meaning $\leq$ is reflexive and transitive). Moreover, if $\leq_{\mathrm{n}}$ is antisymmetric, then the semiring is ordered by it.

Important examples of semirings are the *Boolean semiring* $\mathbb{B} = (\mathbb{B}, \vee, \wedge, 0, 1)$ as the simplest example of a semiring that is not a ring, the *probability semiring* $\mathbb{R}_{\geq 0} = (\mathbb{R}_{\geq 0}, +, \cdot, 0, 1)$, and the *semiring of natural numbers* $\mathbb{N} = (\mathbb{N}, +, \cdot, 0, 1)$. Further examples include the *tropical semiring* $\mathbb{T} = (\mathbb{R} \cup \{\infty\}, \min, +, \infty, 0)$, the *semiring of multivariate polynomials* $\mathbb{N}[X] = (\mathbb{N}[X], +, \cdot, 0, 1)$, and the *Viterbi semiring* $\mathbb{V} = ([0, 1], \max, \cdot, 0, 1)$ that is used, e.g., in optimization.

Remark 1. Throughout this paper, we consider semirings that are commutative, positive, and nontrivial (i. e., $0 \neq 1$). These assumptions are required to ensure meaningful evaluation of first-order formulae under semiring semantics. For example, without commutativity the interpretation of conjunction could depend on the order of conjuncts, without positivity a disjunction of two true formulae might be false, and without nontriviality the interpretation of all formulae would be the same.

2.1 Arithmetic Circuits

Generally speaking, circuits are a model for parallel computation. They are particularly renowned for the plethora of complexity lower bounds, both in the realm of Boolean circuits and in the context of arithmetic circuits [23, 24].

Definition 2. *Let K be a semiring. An* arithmetic circuit *C over K (or K-circuit) is a connected, directed acyclic graph. Its nodes (also called* gates*) can be of one of the following types:*

- **Input gates** *are ordered, have indegree* (also called fan-in) *0 and contain the respective input values of the circuit.*
- **Constant gates** *have fan-in 0 and are labelled with elements of K.*
- **Arithmetic gates** *can have an arbitrary fan-in only bounded by the number of gates in the circuit. They can be labelled with either addition or multiplication of K.*
- **Output gates** *are ordered, have fan-in 1, outdegree 0 and contain the output values of the circuit after the computation.*

We call the number of gates in a circuit C the *size* of C and the longest path from an input gate to an output gate the *depth* of C. We also write size(C) and depth(C) to denote the respective values.

The function $f_C \colon K^n \to K^m$ computed by an arithmetic circuit C with n input gates and m output gates is defined in the obvious way: Initially, the constant gates are associated with their respective constant values and the input

$\overline{x} = x_1, \ldots, x_n$ is placed in the input gates. Then, whenever all predecessor gates of an arithmetic gate g have values, g computes the function it is labelled with, taking the values of its predecessors as arguments. Finally, once all arithmetic gates have values, the output gates take the values of their respective single predecessors and the values of the output gates $\overline{y} = y_1, \ldots, y_m$ are the output of the computation, i.e., $f_C(\overline{x}) = \overline{y}$.

A single circuit can only compute a function with a fixed number of arguments, which is why we call arithmetic circuits a *non-uniform* model of computation. In order to talk about arbitrary functions, we need to consider circuit families, i.e., sequences of circuits which contain one circuit for every input length $n \in \mathbb{N}$.

Definition 3. *Let $K = (K, +, \cdot, 0, 1)$ be a semiring. A K-*circuit family *is a sequence of K-circuits $\mathcal{C} = (C_n)_{n \in \mathbb{N}}$. The function computed by a circuit family $\mathcal{C} = (C_n)_{n \in \mathbb{N}}$ is the function computed by the respective circuit, i.e., for all $x \in K^+$ we have that $f_\mathcal{C}(x) = f_{C_{|x|}}(x)$.*

For a function $f\colon \mathbb{N} \to \mathbb{N}$, we say that a circuit family $\mathcal{C}$ is of size f (depth f) if the size (depth) of C_n is bounded by $f(n)$ for all $n \in \mathbb{N}$. We also write size($\mathcal{C}$) and depth($\mathcal{C}$) to denote the respective values.

Figures 1 and 2 depict examples of arithmetic circuits, one corresponding to a conventional Boolean circuit and the other computing a function over the reals.

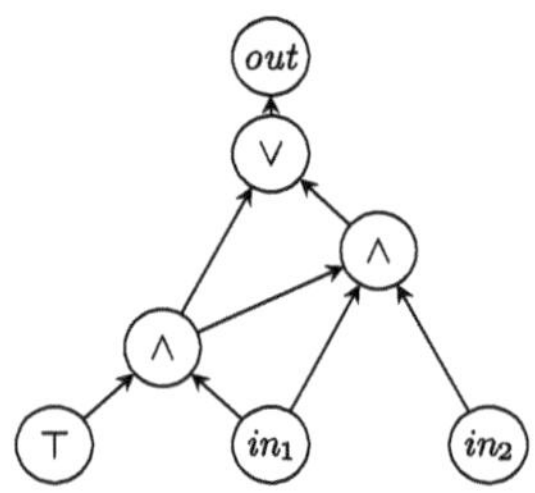

Fig. 1. Conventional Boolean circuit, computing the Boolean function $f(x_1, x_2) = (\top \wedge x_1) \vee ((\top \wedge x_1) \wedge x_1 \wedge x_2)$ equivalent to the function $f(x_1, x_2) = x_1$

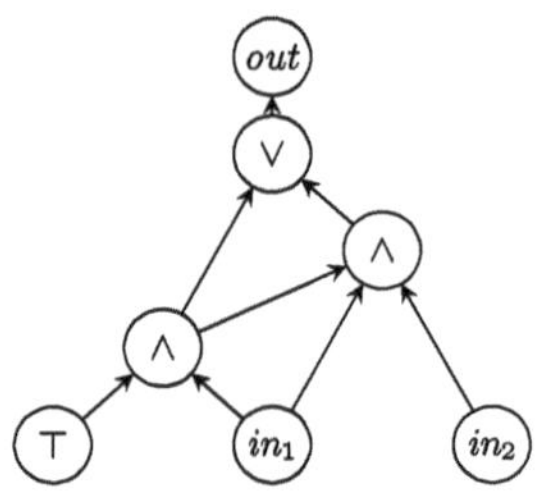

Fig. 2. Circuit over the semiring $\mathbb{R} = (\mathbb{R}, +, \times, 0, 1)$, computing the function $g(x_1, x_2) = (6 \times x_1) + ((6 \times x_1) \times x_1 \times x_2)$

To properly consider a circuit family $\mathcal{C}$ as an algorithm, some bounds for the computational complexity of obtaining the nth circuit when given n are required. Doing this would make them a so-called *uniform* model of computation. However, questions of uniformity lie outside of the scope of this paper. Accordingly, we restrict our attention to *non-uniform* circuit families, though we briefly return to the issue in the conclusion.

3 First-Order Logic with Semiring Semantics

We consider a variant of first-order logic that is interpreted over semirings, i. e. an interpretation of each formula of the logic is an element from a given semiring. The logic is extended with *constant formulae* and so-called *formula value comparison atoms*. A constant formula c is always interpreted as the corresponding element c from the semiring and a formula value comparison atom $\phi = \psi$ checks whether ϕ and ψ are interpreted as the same element of the semiring.

3.1 FO with Constant Formulae and Formula Value Comparisons

In this section, we define the syntax and semantics of $\mathrm{FO}_K^=$ and consider an example that illustrates the expressivity of the logic.

Definition 4. *The* syntax for first-order logic over a semiring K *(of vocabulary τ), is defined as follows:*

$$\phi ::= \; x = y \mid x \neq y \mid c \mid R(\bar{x}) \mid \neg R(\bar{x}) \mid \phi = \phi \mid (\phi \wedge \phi) \mid (\phi \vee \phi) \mid \exists x \phi \mid \forall x \phi,$$

where $x, y \in \mathrm{Var}$, $c \in K$, $R \in \tau$ and $\bar{x}$ is a tuple of variables so that $\mathrm{ar}(R) = |\bar{x}|$. For ordered semirings K, we extend the syntax by allowing $\phi \leq \phi$.

Note that the formulae of $\mathrm{FO}_K^=$ are defined such that they are always in negation normal form and any formula of $\mathrm{FO}_K^=$ without any constant formulae $c \in K$ or formula comparison atoms $\phi = \psi$ or $\phi \leq \psi$ is a first-order (FO) formula. The set of *free variables* $\mathrm{FV}(\phi)$ of a formula $\phi \in \mathrm{FO}_K^=$ is defined by extending the notion from FO in the following way: $\mathrm{FV}(c) = \emptyset$ and $\mathrm{FV}(\phi \circ \psi) = \mathrm{FV}(\phi) \cup \mathrm{FV}(\psi)$ for $\circ \in \{=, \leq\}$. A *sentence* ϕ is a formula without free variables, i. e., $\mathrm{FV}(\phi) = \emptyset$.

For a finite set A (called the model domain), a finite vocabulary $\tau = \{R_1, \dots, R_n\}$, and a semiring K, we define $\mathrm{Lit}_{A,\tau}$ as the set of *literals* over A, i. e., the set of facts and negated facts $\mathrm{Lit}_{A,\tau} = \{ R(\bar{a}), \neg R(\bar{a}) \mid \bar{a} \in A^{\mathrm{ar}(R)}, R \in \tau \}$. A *$K$-interpretation* π is a mapping $\pi \colon \mathrm{Lit}_{A,\tau} \to K$ that evaluates each literal as an element of the semiring K. A K-interpretation π is said to be *ordered*, if $A = \{a_0, a_1, \dots, a_{|A|-1}\}$ and τ contains a binary relation $R_<$ such that $\pi(R_<(a_i, a_j)) = 1$ if $i < j$, and $\pi(R_<(a_i, a_j)) = 0$ otherwise. An *assignment* s is a mapping $s \colon \mathrm{Var} \to A$ that associates each first-order variable with an element of A.

Definition 5. *Let $K = (K, +, \cdot, 0, 1)$ be a semiring, π be a K-interpretation, A be the model domain, and s be an assignment. The* semantics of a $\mathrm{FO}_K^=$-formula

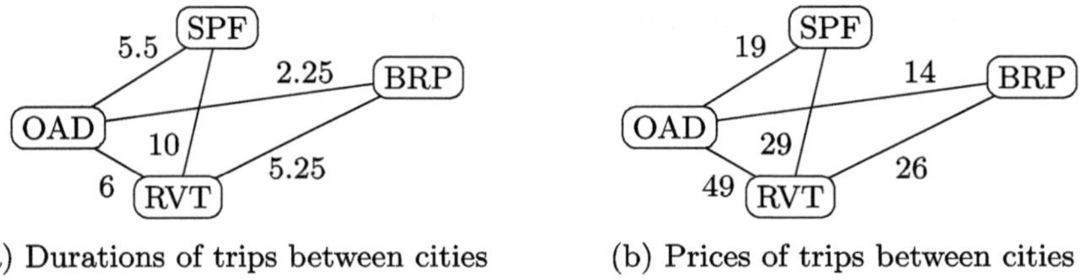

Fig. 3. Train network as a K-interpretation. For the sake of clarity, trip durations and prices are depicted in separate figures.

θ under π and s, *is denoted by* $[\![\theta]\!]_{\pi,s}$ *and defined as follows:*

$$
\begin{aligned}
[\![x \star y]\!]_{\pi,s} &= \begin{cases} 1 & \text{if } s(x) \star s(y), \\ 0 & \text{otherwise} \end{cases} && \text{where } \star \in \{=, \neq\} \quad [\![c]\!]_{\pi,s} = c \\
[\![R(\bar{x})]\!]_{\pi,s} &= \pi(R(s(\bar{x}))) && [\![\neg R(\bar{x})]\!]_{\pi,s} = \pi(\neg R(s(\bar{x}))) \\
[\![\phi \wedge \psi]\!]_{\pi,s} &= [\![\phi]\!]_{\pi,s} \cdot [\![\psi]\!]_{\pi,s} && [\![\phi \vee \psi]\!]_{\pi,s} = [\![\phi]\!]_{\pi,s} + [\![\psi]\!]_{\pi,s} \\
[\![\exists x\, \phi]\!]_{\pi,s} &= \textstyle\sum_{a \in A} [\![\phi]\!]_{\pi,s(a/x)} && [\![\forall x\, \phi]\!]_{\pi,s} = \textstyle\prod_{a \in A} [\![\phi]\!]_{\pi,s(a/x)} \\
[\![\phi \circ \psi]\!]_{\pi,s} &= \begin{cases} 1 & \text{if } [\![\phi]\!]_{\pi,s} \circ [\![\psi]\!]_{\pi,s}, \\ 0 & \text{otherwise} \end{cases} && \text{where } \circ \in \{=, \leq\}.
\end{aligned}
$$

If ϕ *is a* sentence, *we write* $[\![\phi]\!]_\pi$ *for* $[\![\phi]\!]_{\pi,\emptyset}$.

This definition only makes use of atomic negation, which is a standard approach in semiring semantics [20]. In this framework, $\pi(R(x))$ and $\pi(\neg R(x))$ are independent values representing the "evidence for" and "evidence against" a proposition.

The idea of a K-interpretation is that the semiring value 0 corresponds to "false" and all other semiring values to "true", i.e., a formula $\phi \in \mathrm{FO}_K^{\leq}$ is satisfied under π and s if $[\![\phi]\!]_{\pi,s} \neq 0$. Note that the negated versions $\phi \neq \psi$ and $\phi \not\leq \psi$ of the formula comparison operators are definable in $\mathrm{FO}_K^{\leq}$ by the formulae $(\phi = \psi) = 0$ and $(\phi \leq \psi) \leq 0$, respectively.

We say that a K-interpretation π is *model-defining* [18,19], if for all $R(\bar{a})$, we have $\pi(R(\bar{a})) = 0$ if and only if $\pi(\neg R(\bar{a})) \neq 0$. Sentences ϕ and ψ of $\mathrm{FO}_K^{\leq}$ are *K-equivalent*, written as $\phi \equiv_K \psi$, if $[\![\phi]\!]_\pi = [\![\psi]\!]_\pi$ for all model-defining K-interpretations. For logics $\mathcal{L}$ and $\mathcal{L}'$, we write $\mathcal{L} \leq_K \mathcal{L}'$ if for each sentence ϕ from $\mathcal{L}$ there is a sentence ψ from $\mathcal{L}'$ such that $\phi \equiv_K \psi$. The expressivity comparison relations $\equiv_K$ and $<_K$ are defined from $\leq_K$ in the usual way.

Example 1. Suppose A consists of the city codes SPF (Springfield), BRP (Bridgeport), RVT (Rivertown), OAD (Oakdale), and $\tau := \{T, P\}$. Consider the tropical semiring $\mathbb{T} = (\mathbb{R} \cup \{\infty\}, \min, +, \infty, 0)$ with its natural order. Note that since addition is interpreted as min, the natural order inverts the usual order of the reals. Define a $\mathbb{T}$-interpretation $\pi \colon Lit_{A,\tau} \to \mathbb{T}$ by assigning $T(x, y)$ and $P(x, y)$, for each pair of two different cities x and y, a number representing the duration and the price of a direct train between them, respectively, as in Fig. 3; if no direct train connection exists between two different cities x and y, $T(x, y)$ and $P(x, y)$ are assigned ∞. Additionally, we assign $T(x, x) = P(x, x) = 0$ for every city x, representing the fact that each city is reachable from itself without any time or cost. Each negated fact $\neg T(x, y)$ and $\neg P(x, y)$ can be assigned a number so that π is model-defining.

We can now define the formula $\phi := 12 \leq ((T(x, y) \wedge T(y, z))$,

which states that the trip between x and z via y takes at most 12 h. Note that since the semiring under consideration is the tropical semiring $\mathbb{T}$, we have that if ϕ is true, it is evaluated as 0 (the multiplicative identity of $\mathbb{T}$) and otherwise as ∞ (the additive identity of $\mathbb{T}$). Define then $\psi := \exists y(\phi \wedge (P(x, y) \wedge P(y, z))$.

The formula ψ evaluates as the price of the cheapest trip between x and z that has at most one transfer and takes at most 12 h. Lastly, define $\theta := \psi \leq P(x, z)$.

The formula θ states that the price of the direct connection between x and z is at most the price of the cheapest one-transfer trip that takes at most 12 h, i.e., in the case of cities x and z, taking a trip with a transfer does not reduce the cost when travel time of at most 12 h is desired. In our example, this is false for Rivertown and Oakdale, i.e., if s is such that $s(x) = \text{RVT}$ and $s(z) = \text{OAD}$, we have $[\![\theta]\!]_{\pi,s} = \infty$. On the other hand, for Springfield and Oakdale the formula θ is true.

In the above example, constant formulae and formula comparison atoms are used to express properties of connections in the train network using the tropical semiring. It is known that in the case of the Boolean semiring, constant formulae and formula value comparison atoms do not increase expressivity of first-order logic, i.e., $\text{FO} \equiv_{\mathbb{B}} \text{FO}_{\mathbb{B}}^{=}$ [4]. This is not a common phenomenon for semirings as for any semiring K with at least three elements we have $\text{FO} <_K \text{FO}_K^{=}$, meaning that the formula value comparison atoms strictly increase expressivity, even for constant-free $\text{FO}_K^{=}$-formulae [3].

3.2 Encodings of K-Interpretations

Any $\text{FO}_K^{=}$ sentence can be seen as a function from the set of K-interpretations to K. To make this fit in with our circuit model, which gets a tuple of K-values as an input, we define an encoding for K-interpretations, so that the function defined by an $\text{FO}_K^{=}$ sentence can be seen as a function from K^* to K.

In order to encode a K-interpretation in an unambiguous way, we need its universe A to be strictly ordered. This is not to be confused with an order on K; we do not require K to be ordered.

Definition 6. *Let A be a set with a strict total order, let τ be a relational signature, let $\text{Lit}_{A,\tau} = \{\ell_1, \ldots, \ell_n\}$, let K be a semiring and let $\pi\colon \text{Lit}_{A,\tau} \to K$ be a K-interpretation. Then we define $\text{enc}(\pi)$ to be the concatenation of the values assigned to each literal by π, i.e.,*

$$\text{enc}(\pi) := (\pi(\ell_1), \ldots, \pi(\ell_n)) \in K^n.$$

For technical reasons, we encode literals of relation symbols R of arity 0 as if they had arity 1, i.e., as $|A|$ copies of $\pi(R())$ and $|A|$ copies of $\pi(\neg R())$.

For a fixed signature τ, we need the encoding length of a K-interpretation π to determine the size of the universe A of π. This way, if a circuit gets $\mathrm{enc}(\pi)$ as its input, it also has $|A|$ available.

3.3 FO with Built-In Relations

To characterize circuit classes logically, we need to extend our logic by additional "built-in" K-relations that are not part of the K-interpretation. To that end we will slightly extend the syntax of $\mathrm{FO}_K^{\overline{=}}$ to $\mathrm{FO}_K^{\overline{=}}(F)$ for a particular set of function families F, where a function family $f = (f_n)_{n\in\mathbb{N}} \in F$ is a series of functions. We essentially want to allow additional K-relations that may depend on the size of the universe A, but not on A itself. We therefore treat ordered sets of the same cardinality as isomorphic to the first $|A|$ natural numbers and thus define the set F of function families accordingly. The set Arb_K is the set of all function families of the aforementioned kind (cf., e.g. [24] for the analogous definition of built-in relations in the standard Tarski semantics).

Definition 7. *Let K be a semiring. Then*

$$\mathrm{Arb}_K := \bigcup_{k\in\mathbb{N}} \{(f_n)_{n\in\mathbb{N}} \mid f_n\colon \{1,\ldots,n\}^k \to K \text{ for all } n \in \mathbb{N}\}.$$

We also need to extend the notion of a signature to allow to differentiate between built-in K-relations and those given by the input K-interpretation. To that end, we adopt an auxiliary vocabulary σ_F for each set of function families $F \subseteq \mathrm{Arb}_K$ consisting of a relation symbol P_f for each $f = (f_n)_{n\in\mathbb{N}}$ in F.

Definition 8. *Let τ be a relational vocabulary and let K be a semiring. Then for any $F \subseteq \mathrm{Arb}_K$ we define the syntax of $\mathrm{FO}_K^{\overline{=}}(F)$ τ-formulae by extending the grammar of $\mathrm{FO}_K^{\overline{=}}$ formulae by the rule $\phi ::= P_f(\overline{x})$, where $P_f \in \sigma_F$ and $\overline{x}$ is a tuple of variables such that $|\overline{x}| = \mathrm{ar}(P_f)$.*

The semantics of $\mathrm{FO}_K^{\overline{=}}(F)$ is defined in the obvious way for ranked (ordered) structures.

Definition 9. *Let K be a semiring, let $F \subseteq \mathrm{Arb}_K$, and let τ be a finite vocabulary. Furthermore let A be a strictly ordered set, $\pi\colon \mathrm{Lit}_{A,\tau} \to K$ a K-interpretation, and s an assignment. Then the semantics of $\mathrm{FO}_K^{\overline{=}}(F)$ extend the semantics for $\mathrm{FO}_K^{\overline{=}}$ by*

$$[\![P_f(\overline{x})]\!]_{\pi,s} = f_{|A|}(r(s(\overline{x}))),$$

where $P_f \in \sigma_F$, $\overline{x}$ is a tuple of variables such that $|\overline{x}| = \mathrm{ar}(P_f)$ and $r\colon A \to \{1,\ldots,|A|\}$ is the ranking function *on A, which maps each element of A to its position in the ordering on A.*

With this definition at hand, we are now able to define the set of functions definable by $\mathrm{FO}_K^{\overline{=}}(F)$ sentences.

In the following evaluation problem the semiring K, the set $F \subseteq \mathrm{Arb}_K$ and the $\mathrm{FO}_K^{\overline{=}}(F)$-formula φ are all fixed. The input π is encoded as $\mathrm{enc}(\pi)$, as specified in Definition 6.

Problem:	$\mathrm{FO}_K^{\overline{=}}(F)$-$\mathrm{EVAL}_\varphi$
Input:	K-interpretation π
Output:	$[\![\varphi]\!]_\pi$

To denote the set of all these function problems, we overload $\mathrm{FO}_K^{\overline{=}}(F)$.

Definition 10. *Let K be a semiring, and $F \subseteq \mathrm{Arb}_K$. Then*

$$\mathrm{FO}_K^{\overline{=}}(F) := \{\, \mathrm{FO}_K^{\overline{=}}(F)\text{-}\mathrm{EVAL}_\varphi \mid \varphi \in \mathrm{FO}_K^{\overline{=}}(F)\,\}.$$

4 A Circuit Characterization of FO Under Semiring Semantics

We move to our main result of showing correspondence of first-order logic and constant-depth circuits in semiring semantics. It is noteworthy that our result generalizes beyond model-defining K-interpretations.

If we want our circuit model to simulate the formula value comparisons of our logic, we need additional control structures. For this reason, we add binary relations to branch on in the following way.

Definition 11. *Let K be a semiring, let $R_1, \dots, R_\ell \subseteq K^2$ be relations and let $\chi_{R_i} \colon K^2 \to \{0,1\}$ be the characteristic function of each R_i. Then the class $\mathrm{FAC}_K^0[R_1, \dots, R_\ell]$ consists of all functions $f \colon K^* \to K$ computable by K-circuit families $\mathcal{C}$ such that $\mathrm{size}(\mathcal{C}) \in O(n^{O(1)})$ and $\mathrm{depth}(\mathcal{C}) \in O(1)$, where the circuits in $\mathcal{C}$ have additional binary gate types that compute the functions χ_{R_i}.*

If we do not have any relations R_i, we write FAC_K^0. The circuits of this class then compute only polynomials. Of particular interest for us will be the classes $\mathrm{FAC}_K^0[=]$ and $\mathrm{FAC}_K^0[=,\leq]$ (when K is ordered). The negated (in)equalities can be expressed in the same way as defined for the logic $\mathrm{FO}_K^{\overline{=}}$. In order to characterize these classes logically, we mention another useful property thereof: any function in FAC_K^0 or the aforementioned extensions can be computed by circuits that are essentially trees. The following lemma is a minor modification of a result about circuits over the reals [5, Lemma 26].

Lemma 1. *Let K be a semiring and let $f \colon K^* \to K \in \mathrm{FAC}_K^0[=]$, respectively $f \in \mathrm{FAC}_K^0[=,\leq]$ for ordered K. Then there exists a family of circuits $\mathcal{C} = (C_n)_{n \in \mathbb{N}}$ of size $O(n^{O(1)})$ and depth $O(1)$ computing f such that for each circuit $C \in \mathcal{C}$, all non-input gates have fan-out 1 and for each gate g in C, each input to g path has the same length.*

Theorem 1. *Let K be a semiring. Then for K-interpretations $\pi\colon \mathrm{Lit}_{\tau,A} \to K$, where A is strictly ordered it holds that $\mathrm{FO}_K^{=}(\mathrm{Arb}_K) = \mathrm{FAC}_K^0[=]$ for unordered and $\mathrm{FO}_K^{=}(\mathrm{Arb}_K) = \mathrm{FAC}_K^0[=,\leq]$ for ordered K.*

Proof. Let $O = \{=\}$ for unordered and $O = \{=,\leq\}$ for ordered K.
$\mathrm{FO}_K^{=}(\mathrm{Arb}_K) \subseteq \mathrm{FAC}_K^0[O]$: Given a $\mathrm{FO}(\mathrm{Arb}_K)$-sentence φ, the idea is to construct a circuit family that computes the function $\mathrm{FO}_K^{=}(\mathrm{Arb}_K)$-$\mathrm{EVAL}_\varphi$. This is achieved by structural induction on φ. For any $n \in \mathbb{N}$, we essentially built the nth circuit "top-down", i.e., starting at the output gate and continuing towards the input gates. This means that at each step of the induction, the constructed circuit computes f, provided that the predecessor gates of the currently constructed gate compute the same function as the subformulae which they will represent.

Let $\varphi \in \mathrm{FO}(\mathrm{Arb}_K)$ over the signature τ. For any length n of valid encoded K-interpretations π for τ, we are going to define a circuit C_n such that $f_{C_n}(\mathrm{enc}(\pi)) = \mathrm{FO}_K^{=}(\mathrm{Arb}_K)$-$\mathrm{EVAL}_\varphi(\pi)$. If φ contains k variables $x_1,\ldots,x_k$, we will do this for each subformula ψ of φ and any $(m_1,\ldots,m_k) \in A^k$. This means creating a circuit $C_n^{\psi(m_1,\ldots,m_k)}$ such that for any K-interpretation π, where $|\mathrm{enc}(\pi)| = n$, it holds that $[\![\psi[m_1/x_1,\ldots,m_k/x_k]]\!]_\pi = f_{C_n^{\psi(m_1,\ldots,m_k)}}(\mathrm{enc}(\pi))$. Here $\psi[m_1/x_1,\ldots,m_k/x_k]$ is the formula ψ, where each occurrence of x_i is replaced by m_i for all $1 \leq i \leq k$. The $m_1,\ldots,m_k$ are essentially used to keep track of the values "selected" by the quantifiers and we initialize them to be 0.

We proceed by structural induction on φ. W.l.o.g. let φ have exactly k variables. At the very top is the output gate, so $C_n^{\varphi(0,\ldots,0)}$ consists of the output gate in addition to the circuit as described by the following induction.

For any subformula ψ of φ, we proceed as follows.

1. Let $\psi = \exists x_i \xi$. Then $C_n^{\psi(m_1,\ldots,m_k)}$ consists of an addition gate with the predecessors $C_n^{\xi(m_1,\ldots,m_{i-1},a,m_{i+1},\ldots,m_k)}$ for all $a \in A$.
2. Let $\psi = \forall x_i \xi$. Then $C_n^{\psi(m_1,\ldots,m_k)}$ is defined as above, except that it has a multiplication gate at the top.
3. Let $\psi = \xi_1 \vee \xi_2$. Then $C_n^{\psi(m_1,\ldots,m_k)}$ consists of a sum gate with the predecessors $C_n^{\xi_1(m_1,\ldots,m_k)}$ and $C_n^{\xi_2(m_1,\ldots,m_k)}$.
4. Let $\psi = \xi_1 \wedge \xi_2$. Then $C_n^{\psi(m_1,\ldots,m_k)}$ is defined as above, except that it has a multiplication gate at the top.
5. Let $\psi = \xi_i \circ \xi_j$ for $\circ \in O$. Then $C_n^{\psi(m_1,\ldots,m_k)}$ is defined as above, except that it has a $\circ$ gate at the top.
6. Let $\psi = x_i \star x_j$ for $\star \in \{=,\neq\}$ and variables x_i, x_j. Then $C_n^{\psi(m_1,\ldots,m_k)}$ consists of a constant 1 gate if $m_i \star m_j$ and a constant 0 gate, otherwise.
7. Let $\psi = R(\overline{y})$ for $R \in \tau$. Then $C_n^{\psi(m_1,\ldots,m_k)}$ is the input gate representing the literal $R(\overline{y})[m_1/x_1,\ldots,m_k/x_k]$ in $\mathrm{enc}(\pi)$.
8. Let $\psi = \neg R(\overline{y})$ for $R \in \tau$. Then $C_n^{\psi(m_1,\ldots,m_k)}$ is the input gate representing the literal $\neg R(\overline{y})[m_1/x_1,\ldots,m_k/x_k]$ in $\mathrm{enc}(\pi)$.
9. Let $\psi = P_f(\overline{y})$ for $f \in \mathrm{Arb}_K$. Then $C_n^{\psi(m_1,\ldots,m_k)}$ is a constant gate that has the value $f(\overline{y}[m_1/x_1,\ldots,m_k/x_k])$, where $\overline{y}[m_1/x_1,\ldots,m_k/x_k]$ is the tuple of variables $\overline{y}$, where x_i is replaced by m_i for $1 \leq i \leq k$.

Table 1. Type associations

g	input	constant	$+$	$\times$	output	$=$	$\leq$
type	1	2	3	4	5	6	7

This construction ensures that the function defined by each subformula of φ is exactly the one of the respective subcircuit and thus the circuit $C_n^{\varphi(0,\ldots,0)}$ computes exactly the function $[\![\varphi]\!]_\pi$. Therefore, for each FO(Arb_K)-sentence ϕ, we have that $\text{FO}_K^{=}(\text{Arb}_K)\text{-EVAL}_\phi \in \text{FAC}_K^0[O]$ and thus $\text{FO}_K^{=}(\text{Arb}_K) \subseteq \text{FAC}_K^0[O]$.
$\text{FAC}_K^0[O] \subseteq \text{FO}_K^{=}(\text{Arb}_K)$: To be able to refer to properties of individual gates we associate gate types with numbers, as specified in Table 1.

Given a $\text{FAC}_K^0[O]$ family $\mathcal{C} = (C_n)_{n\in\mathbb{N}}$, the idea is to define a single sentence φ, such that $[\![\varphi]\!]_\pi = f_{\mathcal{C}}(\text{enc}(\pi))$. The sentence φ essentially describes how circuits in the family $\mathcal{C}$ are evaluated. It does this by making use of the Arb_K extension to $\text{FO}_K^{=}$. Since we have access to arbitrary functions that may depend on the size of the input K-interpretation, the interpretation of these functions can be chosen according to the number of input gates of the circuit. This way, φ will describe the entire circuit family. We will use these built-in functions to describe the gates of our circuit. In particular, they will give us information about gate types, edges, constant values and indices of input gates.

Let $C_n \in \mathcal{C}$ and let $q \in \mathbb{N}$ such that $\text{size}(C_n) \leq n^q$. As per Lemma 1, we can assume that each gate in C_n has fan-out 1 and that for each gate g, each path from an input gate to g has the same length. This essentially gives all of the circuits of $\mathcal{C}$ a layered form, such that one can talk in an unambiguous way about the depth of any individual gate, in the sense that it is the distance to an input gate.

Additionally, the fact that $\text{size}(C_n) \leq n^q$ allows us to encode each gate in C_n as a q long tuple of values in $\{1, \ldots, n\}$. This will enable us to effectively talk about the structure of C_n logically.

The sentence φ will have the signature $\{R^1\}$. From the Arb_K extension, for all $n \in \mathbb{N}$, we also make use of the functions $t_n \colon \{1, \ldots, n\}^q \to \{0,1\}^4$, $c_n \colon \{1, \ldots, n\}^q \to K$, $in_n \colon \{1, \ldots, n\}^{q+1} \to \{0,1\}$, $e_n \colon \{1, \ldots, n\}^{2\cdot q} \to \{0,1\}$ and $\textit{left} \colon \{1, \ldots, n\}^{2\cdot q} \to \{0,1\}$. Here

- $t_n(x_1, \ldots, x_q)$ yields the gate type in binary of the gate encoded by $(x_1, \ldots, x_q)$ as per Table 1.
- $c_n(x_1, \ldots, x_q)$ returns the value of the gate encoded by $(x_1, \ldots, x_q)$ if it is a constant gate and 0, if it is not,
- $in_n(x_1, \ldots, x_q, y)$ yields 1, if the gate encoded by $(x_1, \ldots, x_q)$ is the yth input gate and 0, if it is not,
- $e_n(x_1, \ldots, x_q, y_1, \ldots, y_q)$ returns 1, if there is an edge from the gate encoded by $(x_1, \ldots, x_q)$ to the one encoded by $(y_1, \ldots, y_q)$ and 0, if there is not.

We only need the additional function *left* if $\leq \in O$. Then $\textit{left}(x_1, \ldots, x_q, y_1, \ldots, y_q)$ returns

1, if the gate encoded by $(x_1, \ldots, x_q)$ is the left predecessor of the gate encoded by $(y_1, \ldots, y_q)$ and the gate encoded by $(y_1, \ldots, y_q)$ is a $\leq$ gate. Otherwise, *left* returns 0. It is worth to note that R, as the unary only relation symbol in τ, yields the individual elements of the input to the circuit. We make use of that fact when we characterize the input gates logically.

With all that at hand, we will now define φ by induction on the layers of the circuit, i.e., we start at depth 0 and move towards the output gate. We will do this by recursively defining φ_d for each $0 \leq d \leq \text{depth}(C_n)$. Here we use the relation symbol P_f for each of the aforementioned functions f, as described in Sect. 3.3. At depth 0, we have only input gates. Therefore $\varphi_0(x_1, \ldots, x_q) := \exists y\ P_{in}(x_1, \ldots, x_q, y) \wedge R(y)$. For depth beyond 0, the formula φ_d has the form

$$\varphi_d(x_1, \ldots, x_q) := \bigvee_{2 \leq i \leq 7} (P_t(x_1, \ldots, x_q) = \text{bin}(i) \wedge T_{i,d}(x_1, \ldots, x_q)),$$

where $\text{bin}(i)$ is the length 4 binary representation of i and where $T_{i,d}(x_1, \ldots, x_q)$ is a formula that yields the value of gate $(x_1, \ldots, x_q)$ if it is a gate of type i, e.g.,

$$T_{3,d}(x_1, \ldots, x_q) := \exists y_1, \ldots, y_q\ P_e(y_1, \ldots, y_q, x_1, \ldots, x_q) \wedge \varphi_{d-1}(y_1, \ldots, y_q).$$

The full definition of the formulae φ_d for $1 \leq d \leq \text{depth}(C_n)$ can be found in the arXiv paper [2]. Then it holds for the formula

$$\varphi := \exists x_1, \ldots, x_q\ P_t(x_1, \ldots, x_q) = (0101) \wedge \varphi_{\text{depth}(C_n)}(x_1, \ldots, x_q)$$

that $[\![\varphi]\!]_\pi = f_{C_n}(\text{enc}(\pi))$. Thus, for each $\text{FAC}^0_K[O]$-circuit family, there exists a sentence φ such that $\text{FO}^{=}_{K}(\text{Arb}_K)\text{-EVAL}_\varphi = f_{C_n}$. Therefore, $\text{FO}^{=}_{K}(\text{Arb}_K) \subseteq \text{FAC}^0_K[O]$ and putting it all together $\text{FO}^{=}_{K}(\text{Arb}_K) = \text{FAC}^0_K[O]$.

We remark that the formulation of $\text{FO}^{=}_{K}$ given in [3], and adopted in Definition 4, includes constants $c \in K$ in its syntax. These constants, however, are not needed to establish the previous result. In contrast, these constants were necessary for the complexity results in [3].

5 Conclusion

In this paper, we defined a first-order logic version in the semiring framework and gave a FAC^0_K circuit characterization for it. Our model is conceptually simple and mathematically robust, providing a clean correspondence between logical and algebraic perspectives. This result aligns with the classical correspondence stating that the languages definable in first-order logic are exactly those decidable by AC^0 circuits, i.e., $\text{AC}^0 = \text{FO}$ [6,22]. Furthermore, there is much work to be done with regard to arithmetic circuits over semirings. The result shown in this paper only pertains to so-called *non-uniform* circuit families, meaning circuit families, where there is no restriction on how computationally difficult it is to obtain any individual circuit. In general, this can lead to problems solvable by such circuit families, that are not computable with regard to other conventional computational models over semirings, such as BSS machines [8, 11]. In order to view a circuit family as an algorithm, a restriction on how hard it is to obtain any given circuit is required. Given the constructive nature of our proof, there is no doubt that it can be made uniform. The exact nature of that uniformity still needs to be examined, however. Additionally, larger circuit classes than FAC^0_K could be characterized, following, e.g., the characterization to the entire AC and NC hierarchies over integral domains [1].

Acknowledgements. The authors thank the anonymous referees for their valuable comments. The authors appreciate the project support by a Finnish-German co-operation Grant: DAAD (German Exchange Service, project id 57710940), Research Council of Finland (project id 359650). The second and eighth author appreciate funding by the German Research Foundation (grant id, 511769688, ME 4279/3-1). The fourth author appreciates support by the European Research Council (ERC) grant no. 101020762. The fifth author appreciates funding by the Magnus Ehrnrooth Foundation.

References

1. Barlag, T., Chudigiewitsch, F., Gaube, S.A.: Logical characterizations of algebraic circuit classes over integral domains. Math. Struct. Comput. Sci. **34**(5), 346–374 (2024). https://doi.org/10.1017/S0960129524000136
2. Barlag, T., et al.: Logic and computation through the lens of semirings (2025). https://arxiv.org/abs/2502.12939
3. Barlag, T., et al.: A complexity of logics with semiring semantics. In: Proceedings of the 23nd International Conference on Principles of Knowledge Representation and Reasoning (2026). to appear
4. Barlag, T., Hannula, M., Kontinen, J., Pardal, N., Virtema, J.: Unified foundations of team semantics via semirings. In: Marquis, P., Son, T.C., Kern-Isberner, G. (eds.) Proceedings of the 20th International Conference on Principles of Knowledge Representation and Reasoning, KR 2023, Rhodes, Greece, 2–8 September 2023, pp. 75–85 (2023). https://doi.org/10.24963/KR.2023/8
5. Barlag, T., Vollmer, H.: A logical characterization of constant-depth circuits over the reals. J. Log. Comput. **35**(6) (2025). https://doi.org/10.1093/LOGCOM/EXAE051
6. Barrington, D.A.M., Immerman, N., Straubing, H.: On uniformity within nc^1. In: SCT, pp. 47–59. IEEE Computer Society (1988)
7. Bizière, C., Grädel, E., Naaf, M.: Locality theorems in semiring semantics. In: Leroux, J., Lombardy, S., Peleg, D. (eds.) 48th International Symposium on Mathematical Foundations of Computer Science, MFCS 2023, Bordeaux, France, August 28 – September 1, 2023. LIPIcs, vol. 272, pp. 1–15. Schloss Dagstuhl - Leibniz-Zentrum für Informatik (2023). https://doi.org/10.4230/LIPICS.MFCS.2023.20
8. Blum, L., Shub, M., Smale, S.: On a theory of computation over the real numbers; NP completeness, recursive functions and universal machines (Extended Abstract). In: 29th Annual Symposium on Foundations of Computer Science, White Plains, New York, USA, 24–26 October 1988, pp. 387–397. IEEE Computer Society (1988). https://doi.org/10.1109/SFCS.1988.21955

9. Bourgaux, C., Ozaki, A.: Querying attributed DL-lite ontologies using provenance semirings. In: The Thirty-Third AAAI Conference on Artificial Intelligence, AAAI 2019, The Thirty-First Innovative Applications of Artificial Intelligence Conference, IAAI 2019, The Ninth AAAI Symposium on Educational Advances in Artificial Intelligence, EAAI 2019, Honolulu, Hawaii, USA, January 27 – February 1, 2019, pp. 2719–2726. AAAI Press (2019). https://doi.org/10.1609/AAAI.V33I01.33012719
10. Bourgaux, C., Ozaki, A., Peñaloza, R.: Semiring provenance for lightweight description logics. CoRR **abs/2310.16472** (2023). https://doi.org/10.48550/ARXIV.2310.16472
11. Bournez, O., Cucker, F., de Naurois, P.J., Marion, J.: Implicit complexity over an arbitrary structure: quantifier alternations. Inf. Comput. **204**(2), 210–230 (2006). https://doi.org/10.1016/J.IC.2005.07.005
12. Brinke, S., Grädel, E., Mrkonjic, L.: Ehrenfeucht-fraïssé Games in Semiring Semantics. In: CSL. LIPIcs, vol. 288, pp. 1–22. Schloss Dagstuhl - Leibniz-Zentrum für Informatik (2024)
13. Buss, S.R.: The Boolean formula value problem is in ALOGTIME. In: STOC, pp. 123–131. ACM (1987)
14. Calvanese, D., Lanti, D., Ozaki, A., Peñaloza, R., Xiao, G.: Enriching ontology-based data access with provenance. In: Kraus, S. (ed.) Proceedings of the Twenty-Eighth International Joint Conference on Artificial Intelligence, IJCAI 2019, Macao, China, 10–16 August 2019, pp. 1616–1623. ijcai.org (2019). https://doi.org/10.24963/IJCAI.2019/224
15. Cucker, F., Meer, K.: Logics which capture complexity classes over the reals. J. Symb. Log. **64**(1), 363–390 (1999). https://doi.org/10.2307/2586770
16. Grädel, E., Helal, H., Naaf, M., Wilke, R.: Zero-one laws and almost sure valuations of first-order logic in semiring semantics. In: Baier, C., Fisman, D. (eds.) LICS '22: 37th Annual ACM/IEEE Symposium on Logic in Computer Science, Haifa, Israel, 2–5 August 2022, pp. 1–12. ACM (2022). https://doi.org/10.1145/3531130.3533358
17. Grädel, E., Mrkonjic, L.: Elementary equivalence versus isomorphism in semiring semantics. In: Bansal, N., Merelli, E., Worrell, J. (eds.) 48th International Colloquium on Automata, Languages, and Programming, ICALP 2021, Glasgow, Scotland (Virtual Conference), 12–16 July 2021. LIPIcs, vol. 198, pp. 1–20. Schloss Dagstuhl - Leibniz-Zentrum für Informatik (2021). https://doi.org/10.4230/LIPICS.ICALP.2021.133
18. Grädel, E., Tannen, V.: Semiring provenance for first-order model checking. CoRR **abs/1712.01980** (2017). http://arxiv.org/abs/1712.01980
19. Grädel, E., Tannen, V.: Provenance analysis and semiring semantics for first-order logic. CoRR **abs/2412.07986** (2024). https://doi.org/10.48550/ARXIV.2412.07986
20. Green, T.J., Karvounarakis, G., Tannen, V.: Provenance semirings. In: Libkin, L. (ed.) Proceedings of the Twenty-Sixth ACM SIGACT-SIGMOD-SIGART Symposium on Principles of Database Systems, 11–13 June 2007, Beijing, China, pp. 31–40. ACM (2007). https://doi.org/10.1145/1265530.1265535
21. Gurevich, Y., Lewis, H.R.: A logic for constant-depth circuits. Inf. Control **61**(1), 65–74 (1984)

22. Immerman, N.: Languages that capture complexity classes. SIAM J. Comput. **16**(4), 760–778 (1987). https://doi.org/10.1137/0216051
23. Saptharishi, R.: A survey of known lower bounds in arithmetic circuits. a continuously updated git survey. https://github.com/dasarpmar/lowerbounds-survey
24. Vollmer, H.: Introduction to Circuit Complexity - A Uniform Approach. Texts in Theoretical Computer Science. An EATCS Series. Springer (1999)

Shadowy Institutions

Siddharth Bhaskar(✉) and Robin Kaarsgaard

Department of Mathematics and Computer Science, University of Southern Denmark, Odense, Denmark
{bhaskar,kaarsgaard}@imada.sdu.dk

Abstract. Order-invariant logic and similar "invariant logics" are of particular interest in descriptive complexity theory, as they capture important complexity classes below NP such as logarithmic space and polynomial time computation. However, it is unclear in what sense they form a "logic," as they lack a decidable syntax and compositional semantics. This inhibits the development of their model theory, where progress is slow and effortful.

We situate invariant logics in the theory of *institutions*, abstract category-theoretic constructions that axiomatize the usual relationship between signatures, sentences, structures, and satisfaction. Working within a nearly arbitrary institution, we provide a general definition of the device which induces a particular notion of invariant definability, which we call a *shadow*, and we show that shadows themselves form a "higher-order" institution.

As a considerable amount of model theory can already be developed at this level of abstraction, our work strongly suggests that institutions form the correct framework for developing the model theory of order-invariant and similar logics.

Keywords: Finite model theory · Descriptive complexity theory · Abstract model theory · Institutions · Order-invariant logic

1 Introduction

The descriptive approach to computational complexity affords first-class status to objects like *polynomial-time families of graphs*, treating them as a genuine collection of graphs instead a convenient fiction for a set of strings. The utility of this perspective was demonstrated by Ron Fagin's 1974 identification of nondeterministic polynomial time (NP) with existential second-order logic over arbitrary classes of finite structures [5]. However, no comparably universal characterization of any complexity class below NP has ever been found. Rather, a typical result is the identification of polynomial time (P) with least fixed-point logic, but only over *ordered* finite structures [8,10]. In general, logic below existential second-order is too weak to capture any reasonable notion of computation in the absence of a linear order or choice function.

P. Johann and R. de Queiroz (Eds.): WoLLIC 2026, LNCS 16757, pp. 126–136, 2027.
https://doi.org/10.1007/978-3-032-33486-2_9

Responses to this dilemma come in two flavors, broadly speaking. One is the "approach from below:" enhancing our logic with more and more features that capture the desired complexity classes over broader and broader families of structures (cf. the survey [3]). We adopt the alternative, that is, to keep our characterizations universal over all structures, but loosen what we mean by a "logic." This is the idea behind *order-invariant* logic (and related "invariant logics") where we consider formulas that use a linear order, but whose meaning is independent of the particular order chosen. Order-invariant logic then becomes meaningful over structures without a linear order: to evaluate a sentence, simply order the domain arbitrarily and proceed as before. In this reading, the characterization of P by least fixed-point logic over ordered structures is properly expressed as a characterization of P by *order-invariant* least fixed-point logic over *all* structures.

Nothing in life is free: the set of order-invariant sentences is undecidable, so our cheap universal characterization of P lacks any reasonable notion of syntax. However, we have gained something real: an undecidable syntax is no real obstruction to the formulation of certain model-theoretic questions, and the study of the expressive power and locality properties of invariant logics is an active field of research [6,7]. But in the words of Barceló and Libkin,

> Despite much effort, we still know relatively little about order-invariant properties, and results that we know typically require a very significant effort [...] One of the reasons that the progress in understanding order-invariance is rather slow is the lack of *logical tools* ([1], emphasis theirs)

It is unclear which tools we should even look for, because the ontological status of invariant logics is shaky. There is no general theory for what they are, or indeed in what sense they constitute a logic (beyond forming a "class of queries," cf. [9, Chapter 5]). This is exactly the problem we tackle in this paper. Drawing on the theory of *institutions,* categorical constructions that abstractly capture the notion of a logic, we show that the family of invariant logics over a given base institution form an institution in their own right, one we call the *shadow institution.*

Fleshing this out just a little bit, an institution axiomatizes the usual relationship between *signatures, sentences, structures,* and the *satisfaction* relation. So for example, there is an institution of first-order logic where we have a collection of signatures, and for each signature L, a collection of L-sentences, a collection of L-structures, and a binary satisfaction relation $\models_L$. In its corresponding shadow, the various notions of first-order invariance play the role of signatures. So for example if L is a first-order signature, we have a signature $(L, <)$ in the shadow whose set of sentences are the *order-invariant* first-order $(L, <)$-sentences, whose collection of structures are the first-order L-structures, and whose satisfaction relation was suggested above: expand the structure arbitrarily by a linear order, and evaluate using $\models_{(L,<)}$ in the base institution.

Situating invariant logics in the theory of institutions is very good news in the quest for logical tools, as a surprising amount of model-theoretic machinery can already be developed at this high level of abstraction [4]. Moreover, it seems to be the *right* level of abstraction: the basic definitions and results of invariant logics can be formulated quite cleanly, unburdened by the concrete syntax of any particular logical formalism. We are hopeful that the machinery we develop here will enable progress in a field which is, according to Barceló and Libkin, *notoriously difficult.*

Outline of this Paper. In Sect. 2 we motivate our formulation of shadows as a natural evolution of standard notions of invariance. Section 3 contains our main technical construction; viz., the construction of a higher-order "shadow" institution from a given basal institution. Section 4 contains some brief applications to definability theory: we formalize invariant definability relative to a given shadow and demonstrate how the machinery of the previous section yields some simple but useful tools for comparing definability classes, even at this level of abstraction. Finally, we discuss future directions.

2 Generalizing Invariance

Before we delve into category theory, let us outline a sequence of progressively more general notions of invariance, working within the default context of first-order logic for simplicity. The standard notion one finds in the literature is the following, where $\restriction_L$ denotes the L-reduct:

Definition 1 (Old definition of invariance [9, Chapter 5]). Let L and L' be disjoint signatures, $\mathcal{C}$ a class of L-structures and $\mathcal{Q}$ a class of L' structures. A $L \cup L'$-sentence φ is $(\mathcal{C}, \mathcal{Q})$-invariant if for any two $L \cup L'$-structures A, B with the same domain, if $A \restriction_L = B \restriction_L$ and $A \restriction_{L'}, B \restriction_{L'} \in \mathcal{C}$, then $A \models \varphi \iff B \models \varphi$.

This is perfectly adequate for defining, e.g., order-invariance, where $\mathcal{C}$ is the set of all finite L-structures and $\mathcal{Q}$ is the set of all finite linear orders. However it cannot accommodate notions of invariance in which $\mathcal{C}$ and $\mathcal{Q}$ interact; e.g., *traversal-invariant graph queries,* which refer to queries on ordered graphs that are invariant with respect to only *certain types of orderings* which cohere somehow with the edge relation. For this we need the following:

Definition 2 (Early modern definition of invariance [2]). Let $L \subseteq K$ be signatures, $\mathcal{C}$ a class of L-structures, and $\mathcal{P}$ a class of K-structures, such that the L-reduct of every structure in $\mathcal{P}$ is in $\mathcal{C}$, and every structure in $\mathcal{C}$ has an expansion in $\mathcal{P}$.

Then a K-sentence φ is $(\mathcal{C}, \mathcal{P})$-invariant if for any two structures $A, B \in \mathcal{P}$, if $A \restriction_L \simeq B \restriction_L$, then $A \models \varphi \iff B \models \varphi$.

This generalizes the old definition when K is taken to be $L \cup L'$ and $\mathcal{P}$ is taken to be the class of all simultaneous expansions of a structure in $\mathcal{C}$ and a structure in $\mathcal{Q}$.

To arrive at the current formulation, we note that a containment $L \subseteq K$ is a special case of a *signature morphism* $\pi : L \to K$, which gives a first-order

K-definition for each symbol in L. (In the case $L \subseteq K$, a symbol in L is simply defined by the same symbol in K.) Such a morphism induces a map from L-sentences to K-sentences (by replacing each L-symbol by its K-definition) and a map from K-structures to L-structures (note the reversal of direction!) where we interpret each L-symbol by the relation defined by its K-definition. It is the latter operation that generalizes the L-reduct in the case $L \subseteq K$, so we denote it by $\restriction_\pi$, and arrive at the following:

Definition 3 (Modern definition of invariance, this paper). Let $\pi : L \to K$ be a signature morphism, $\mathcal{C}$ a class of L-structures, and $\mathcal{P}$ a class of K-structures, such that $\restriction_\pi$ maps $\mathcal{P}$ into $\mathcal{Q}$ surjectively. Then a K-sentence φ is $(\pi, \mathcal{C}, \mathcal{P})$-invariant if for any two structures $A, B \in \mathcal{P}$, if $A \restriction_\pi \simeq B \restriction_\pi$, then $A \models \varphi \iff B \models \varphi$.

Modulo some accommodation for category-theoretic terminology, this is exactly Definition 6.

3 Shadows in an Institution

For a category **C**, $|\mathbf{C}|$ denotes the objects of **C**. In the following, we let **Set** denote the category of sets and functions, and **Cat** the category of (small) categories and functors.

Definition 4. An *institution* consists of

- a category **Sig**, whose objects are called *signatures,*
- a functor $\mathsf{Sen} : \mathbf{Sig} \to \mathbf{Set}$; for a signature L, elements of $\mathsf{Sen}(L)$ are called *L-sentences,*
- a functor $\mathsf{Mod} : \mathbf{Sig}^{\mathrm{op}} \to \mathbf{Cat}$; for a signature L, objects of $\mathsf{Mod}(L)$ are called *L-structures,*
- and a binary satisfaction relation $\models_L$ indexed by signatures L and taking a L-structure on the left and an L-sentence on the right. This relation satisfies the equivalence

$$A \models_K \mathsf{Sen}(\pi)(\varphi) \iff \mathsf{Mod}(\pi)(A) \models_L \varphi$$

for any signature morphism $\pi : L \to K$, L-sentence φ, and K-structure A; this is called the *satisfaction condition.*

The machinery of intuitions is not widely known in the model theory or finite model theory community; if this is your first time encountering it, it is useful to pause and check that this accords with your intuitions. For example, the Sen functor is *covariant:* if we have a map from signatures $L \to K$, this induces a map from L-sentences to K-sentences, for example by substitution. Similarly (and importantly) the Mod functor is *contravariant.* Think about defining the field $\mathbb{Q}$ as the field of fractions of the ring $\mathbb{Z}$: for each symbol in the language of fields we define it in the language of rings. This in turn gives us a map *in the other direction*, from rings to fields. We recommend [4] as a general reference for the theory institutions, in particular for motivation and examples.

As is common in categorical logic, we tend to think of Mod as a fibred category, with $\mathsf{Mod}(L)$ as the L-fibre. We fix an institution $\mathfrak{I}$ which is *closed under isomorphisms,* meaning that for any $M, N : |\mathsf{Mod}(L)|$ and $\varphi \in \mathsf{Sen}(L)$ if $M \simeq N$ then $M \models \varphi \iff N \models \varphi$. (Here $\simeq$ is the notion of isomorphism in $\mathsf{Mod}(L)$.) Henceforth, **Sig**, Sen, and Mod refer to the data of $\mathfrak{I}$, and whenever we refer to a "signature," we mean an object of **Sig**. Each of the following definitions are relative to $\mathfrak{I}$.

Definition 5. A *shadow* consists of

- signatures L, K, and a signature morphism $\pi : L \to K$,
- a nonempty subcategory $\mathcal{L}$ of $\mathsf{Mod}(L)$, and
- a nonempty subcategory $\mathcal{K}$ of $\mathsf{Mod}(K)$, such that the functor

$$\mathsf{Mod}(\pi) : \mathcal{K} \to \mathcal{L}$$

is essentially surjective.

We write a shadow as a triple, e.g., $(\pi, \mathcal{L}, \mathcal{K})$, with L and K understood.

Definition 6. Let $(\pi, \mathcal{L}, \mathcal{K})$ be a shadow and $\varphi \in \mathsf{Sen}(K)$. We say φ is $(\pi, \mathcal{L}, \mathcal{K})$-*invariant* if for any $M, N : |\mathcal{K}|$, if $\mathsf{Mod}(\pi)(M) \simeq \mathsf{Mod}(\pi)(N)$ then $M \models_K \varphi \iff N \models_K \varphi$.

Definition 7. Let $(\pi, \mathcal{L}, \mathcal{K})$ be a shadow, φ be a $(\pi, \mathcal{L}, \mathcal{K})$-invariant sentence, and $A : |\mathcal{L}|$. Define

$$A \models_{(\pi, \mathcal{L}, \mathcal{K})} \varphi$$

if for some (equivalently, for any) $M : |\mathcal{K}|$ such that $\mathsf{Mod}(\pi)(M) \simeq A$, $M \models_K \varphi$.

That this is well-defined relies of the fact that $\mathsf{Mod}(\pi)$ is essentially surjective; any structure A from $\mathcal{L}$ can be expanded to some M from $\mathcal{K}$ up to isomorphism.

3.1 Examples

Consider the institution of first-order logic where signatures are first-order signatures (and therefore sets). An important instance of shadows occurs when $L \subset K$, π is the inclusion map $L \to K$, $\mathsf{Sen}(\pi)$ is the natural inclusion $\mathsf{Sen}(L) \subseteq \mathsf{Sen}(K)$, and $\mathsf{Mod}(\pi)$ is the reduct to L. When $\mathcal{L}$ is the class of all finite L-structures, this is the setting of order-invariant or arb-invariant first-order logic from finite model theory.

Another important example that our framework subsumes is that of *embedded finite model theory.* Here L is a first-order signature, L' is a disjoint first-order signature, and $K = L \cup L' \cup \{\partial\}$, where ∂ is a fresh unary relation symbol. Typically $\mathcal{L}$ is the class of all finite L-structures, and there is a single infinite L'-structure U such that $\mathcal{K}$ is the class of all finite L-structures embedded in U. (So for any $A \in \mathcal{K}$, ∂ interprets the domain of the embedded finite L-structure.) The map $\varphi \mapsto \varphi^\pi$ is obtained by relativizing all quantifiers to ∂. The convention here is to call invariance *genericity.*

3.2 An Institution of Shadows

We now work towards the main construction: a new "higher-order" institution where shadows in the base institution play the role of signatures.

Definition 8. Let $(\pi, \mathcal{L}, \mathcal{K})$ and $(\pi', \mathcal{L}', \mathcal{K}')$ be shadows. Then a *shadow morphism* is a pair of signature morphisms $\sigma : L \to L'$, $\rho : K \to K'$ such that

- $\pi' \circ \sigma = \rho \circ \pi$ and
- There is a functor $M_\sigma : \mathcal{L}' \to \mathcal{L}$ satisfying the commutative diagram below, and there similarly exists a functor $M_\rho : \mathcal{K}' \to \mathcal{K}$.

$$\begin{array}{ccc} \mathsf{Mod}(L') & \xrightarrow{\mathsf{Mod}(\sigma)} & \mathsf{Mod}(L) \\ \uparrow & & \uparrow \\ \mathcal{L}' & \xrightarrow{M_\sigma} & \mathcal{L} \end{array}$$

Remark 1. Shadows with shadow morphisms form a category that we call *Shadow*.

Lemma 1. *Let (σ, ρ) be a shadow morphism from $(\pi, \mathcal{L}, \mathcal{K}) \to (\pi', \mathcal{L}', \mathcal{K}')$. Then*

1. $\mathsf{Sen}(\rho)$ *induces a map from $(\pi, \mathcal{L}, \mathcal{K})$-invariant sentences to $(\pi', \mathcal{L}', \mathcal{K}')$-invariant sentences, and*
2. *for any structure $M : |\mathcal{L}'|$ and $(\pi, \mathcal{L}, \mathcal{K})$-invariant sentence φ,*

$$M \models_{(\pi', \mathcal{L}', \mathcal{K}')} \mathsf{Sen}(\rho)(\varphi) \iff \mathsf{Mod}(\sigma)(M) \models_{(\pi, \mathcal{L}, \mathcal{K})} \varphi.$$

Proof. Towards the first claim, let φ be a $(\pi, \mathcal{L}, \mathcal{K})$-invariant sentence. Then $\varphi \in \mathsf{Sen}(K)$ so $\mathsf{Sen}(\rho)(\varphi) \in \mathsf{Sen}(K')$. Let $A, B : |\mathcal{K}'|$ and assume $\mathsf{Mod}(\pi')(A) \simeq \mathsf{Mod}(\pi')(B)$ as structures in $\mathcal{L}'$. Since functors preserve isomorphisms, we have

$$\mathsf{Mod}(\sigma)(\mathsf{Mod}(\pi')(A)) \simeq \mathsf{Mod}(\sigma)(\mathsf{Mod}(\pi')(B)).$$

Since functors preserve composition and $\pi' \circ \sigma = \rho \circ \pi$, we obtain

$$\mathsf{Mod}(\pi)(\mathsf{Mod}(\rho)(A)) \simeq \mathsf{Mod}(\pi)(\mathsf{Mod}(\rho)(B)).$$

By $(\pi, \mathcal{L}, \mathcal{K})$-invariance of φ, we have

$$\mathsf{Mod}(\rho)(A) \models \varphi \iff \mathsf{Mod}(\rho)(B) \models \varphi;$$

by the satisfaction condition,

$$A \models \mathsf{Sen}(\rho)(\varphi) \iff B \models \mathsf{Sen}(\rho)(\varphi),$$

which proves the first claim.

Towards the second claim, additionally let $M : |\mathcal{L}'|$. By essential surjectivity of π' there is a structure $A : |\mathcal{K}'|$ such that $\mathsf{Mod}(\pi')(A) \simeq M$. In the forwards direction, assume that

$$M \models_{(\pi',\mathcal{L}',\mathcal{K}')} \mathsf{Sen}(\rho)(\varphi).$$

Then $A \models_{K'} \mathsf{Sen}(\rho)(\varphi)$; by the satisfaction condition, $\mathsf{Mod}(\rho)(A) \models_K \varphi$; by $(\pi, \mathcal{L}, \mathcal{K})$-invariance of φ,

$$\mathsf{Mod}(\pi)(\mathsf{Mod}(\rho)(A)) \models_{(\pi,\mathcal{L},\mathcal{K})} \varphi.$$

But the left-hand side is identical to $\mathsf{Mod}(\sigma)(M)$, which is what we needed to show.

In the backwards direction, assume that

$$\mathsf{Mod}(\sigma)(M) \models_{(\pi,\mathcal{L},\mathcal{K})} \varphi.$$

Then for all $B : |\mathcal{K}|$ such that $\mathsf{Mod}(\pi)(B) \simeq \mathsf{Mod}(\sigma)(M)$, $B \models_K \varphi$. But $\mathsf{Mod}(\rho)(A)$ is such a structure; therefore, $\mathsf{Mod}(\rho)(A) \models_K \varphi$; by the satisfaction condition, $A \models_{K'} \mathsf{Sen}(\rho)(\varphi)$, and

$$\mathsf{Mod}(\pi')(A) \models_{(\pi',\mathcal{L}',\mathcal{K}')} \mathsf{Sen}(\rho)(\varphi);$$

as the left-hand side is isomorphic to M, we are done.

Definition 9. The *shadow institution* $\mathfrak{I}^\bullet$ of $\mathfrak{I}$ is given by the following data.

- *Shadow* is the category of signatures,
- the sentence functor $\mathsf{Sen}^\bullet : \mathit{Shadow} \to \mathbf{Set}$ takes an object $(\pi, \mathcal{L}, \mathcal{K})$ to the set of $(\pi, \mathcal{L}, \mathcal{K})$-invariant K-sentences and a morphism (σ, ρ) to the function $\mathsf{Sen}(\rho)$ from $(\pi, \mathcal{L}, \mathcal{K})$-invariant sentences to $(\pi', \mathcal{L}', \mathcal{K}')$-invariant sentences,
- the structure functor $\mathsf{Mod}^\bullet : \mathit{Shadow}^{\mathrm{op}} \to \mathbf{Cat}$ takes an object $(\pi, \mathcal{L}, \mathcal{K})$ to the category $\mathcal{L}$ and a morphism (σ, ρ) to the functor $M_\sigma : \mathcal{L}' \to \mathcal{L}$, and
- the satisfaction relation is given by $\models_{(\pi,\mathcal{L},\mathcal{K})}$.

The functoriality of both maps is straightforward to verify; the first one relies on part (i) of Lemma 1. Finally, the satisfaction condition is exactly part (ii) of the same lemma. This brings us to our first main result, viz.,

Theorem 1. *$\mathfrak{I}^\bullet$ is an institution.*

4 Definability

Associated with each shadow $(\pi, \mathcal{L}, \mathcal{K})$ is a notion of definability over $\mathcal{L}$:

Definition 10. A collection Q of L-structures is a *basic* $(\pi, \mathcal{L}, \mathcal{K})$*-invariant query* if $Q \subset \mathcal{L}$ and there exists a $(\pi, \mathcal{L}, \mathcal{K})$-invariant sentence φ such that for each $M \in \mathcal{L}$,

$$M \in Q \iff M \models_{(\pi,\mathcal{L},\mathcal{K})} \varphi.$$

One of the apparent disadvantages of the current approach to invariant definability relative to prior approaches (cf. Definition 1) is that order-invariance, for example, gives us a notion of definability *over all classes of structures* whereas basic $(\pi, \mathcal{L}, \mathcal{K})$-invariance only gives us a notion of definability over $\mathcal{L}$.

But in fact Definition 1 is too simple—and not just for the sake of the sort of abstraction we perform in this paper. It is too simple to handle extant logical descriptions of complexity classes; for example, of logarithmic space graph queries by *traversal-invariant* first-order logic. In this setting we consider sentences in the language of ordered graphs which are invariant with respect to not all linear orders, but only those (the 'traversals') which have a principled interaction with the edge relation [2].

The ease with which Definition 1 applies to any class of structures should therefore be understood as an artifact of a more primitive understanding of invariant definability. One way or another, we are forced to consider what $(\pi, \mathcal{L}, \mathcal{K})$-definability means over arbitrary classes of structures, not just $\mathcal{L}$. The natural way to do this is to pull back basic invariant queries along signature morphisms as follows. (This accords with the characterization of logarithmic-space queries over structures other than graphs in [2].)

Definition 11. Suppose L' is a signature and $\mathcal{L}'$ is a nonempty class of L'-structures. Then a collection Q of L'-structures is a $(\pi, \mathcal{L}, \mathcal{K})$*-invariant* $\mathcal{L}'$*-query* if $Q \subset \mathcal{L}'$ and there exists

- an morphism $\sigma : L \to L'$ such that $\mathsf{Mod}(\sigma) : \mathcal{L}' \to \mathcal{L}$ (in the same sense as Definition 8), and
- a $(\pi, \mathcal{L}, \mathcal{K})$-invariant sentence φ such that for each $M \in \mathcal{L}'$,

$$M \in Q \iff \mathsf{Mod}(\sigma)(M) \models_{(\pi,\mathcal{L},\mathcal{K})} \varphi.$$

Implicit in this definition is a philosophical claim, which is that **the correct definition of an invariant query depends not only on the sentences but also on the signature morphisms** of a particular logic. So, for example, to speak properly of order invariance, we also need to specify what morphisms we allow from signature to signature. One worries that in so doing we have made our work dubiously continuous with the past. While it is certainly possible to get "unnatural" definability classes, we show in Sect. 4.2 that reasonable choices of signature morphism do not change what we mean by "first-order order invariant definability." We expect that similar results apply in practice to other notions of definability studied in the literature.

4.1 Comparing Shadows

We are now positioned to ask, for given shadows $(\pi, \mathcal{L}, \mathcal{K})$ and $(\pi', \mathcal{L}', \mathcal{K}')$, a given signature J, and a given family $\mathcal{J}$ of J-structures, **what is the relationship between $(\pi, \mathcal{L}, \mathcal{K})$ and $(\pi', \mathcal{L}', \mathcal{K}')$-definability over $\mathcal{J}$?** The general problem is of central importance in finite model theory. We often are in a situation where one definability class easily is contained in another, but determining the reverse containment is hard. If it is true (and the classes are identified) we have a **collapse**; if it is false (and the classes are separated) we have **non-collapse**.

Since we can formulate the question of collapse in this abstract setting, it raises the question of the extent to which techniques for demonstrating collapse and non-collapse can be similarly lifted. We expect that this is a large and long-term project. In this paper we merely observe that Lemma 1 already generalizes one common simple techniques for comparing the expressive power of different shadows. (For legibility we abbreviate, e.g., $(\pi, \mathcal{L}, \mathcal{K})$ by π).

Lemma 2 (Corollary to Lemma *1***).** *The following each hold:*

1. *Suppose $(\sigma, \rho) : \pi \to \pi'$. Then the σ-inverse image of any basic π-invariant query is basic π'-invariant.*
2. *If π' can be decomposed into $\rho \circ \pi$, every basic π-invariant query is basic π'-invariant.*
3. *If we restrict the class $\mathcal{K}$ to $\mathcal{K}^\star \subset \mathcal{K}$, we increase the set of π-invariant queries.*
4. *Suppose that every $\sigma : L \to L'$ can be extended into a morphism $(\sigma, \rho) : \pi \to \pi'$. Then any π-invariant query over $\mathcal{L}'$ is already basic π'-invariant.*

Proof. (1) follows from the fact that if the π-invariant sentence φ defines the query Q over $\mathcal{L}$, then $\mathsf{Sen}(\rho)(\varphi)$ defines its pre-image along the map $\mathsf{Mod}(\sigma) : \mathcal{L}' \to \mathcal{L}$. (2) is a special case of (1) where L is identical to L' and σ is the identity. (3) is a special case of (2) where where K is additionally identical to K' and ρ is also the identity. Moreover it makes intuitive sense: we are asking a formula to be invariant over fewer structures, which means there are more such formulas.

For (4), suppose σ and φ witness that a query Q over $\mathcal{L}'$ is π-invariant. If σ can be completed into a morphism $(\sigma, \rho) : \pi \to \pi'$, then $\mathsf{Sen}(\rho)(\varphi)$ witnesses that in fact Q is basic π'-invariant.

One of the most frequent applications of Lemma 2 is showing that $(\pi, \mathcal{L}, \mathcal{K})$-invariance is subsumed by $(\rho \circ \pi, \mathcal{L}, \mathcal{K}')$-invariance for some $\rho : K \to K'$. (This is often the "easy direction" in many containments.) For example, let's work within the institution of first-order logic with finite models and sketch the argument that that every local order-invariant graph query is order-invariant. An *ordering* of a (finite simple undirected) graph is a linear order of its vertices and a *local ordering* is a linear ordering over each neighborhood, represented as a ternary relation $u <_v w$ (i.e., $u < w$ as neighbors of v).

To apply Lemma 2, let L be the language of graphs and $\mathcal{L}$ be the family of (finite simple undirected) graphs; K be the language of locally ordered graphs and $\mathcal{K}$ be the family of locally ordered graphs; K' be the language of ordered graphs and $\mathcal{K}'$ be the family of ordered graphs; and $\pi : L \to K$ be the subset map $L \subset K$. Define $\rho : K \to K'$ by defining $u <_v w$ in K as $u < w$ in K'. Then $\mathsf{Mod}(\rho) : \mathcal{K}' \to \mathcal{K}$ takes an ordered graph into a locally ordered graph by inheriting each neighborhood ordering from the global order.

Point (2) of Lemma 2 says that every basic $(\pi, \mathcal{L}, \mathcal{K})$-invariant query is basic $(\rho \circ \pi, \mathcal{L}, \mathcal{K}')$-invariant. (And thus every invariant query in the former is invariant in the latter.) But these are exactly the standard interpretations of "local order-invariance" and "order-invariance" over graphs, as $\mathsf{Mod}(\pi)$ and $\mathsf{Mod}(\rho \circ \pi)$ are simple reduct maps.

4.2 Traditional Order Invariance

In this section, we use Lemma 2 to show that every order-invariant query in our sense—the pullback of a basic order-invariant query from some *other* signature—is already basic order-invariant in *this* signature. (Of course, the answer will depend on what our base logic and signature morphisms are, but we mean "for most reasonable choices.") This shows that the present understanding of "order-invariance" is conservative relative to prior literature.

It suffices, by point (4) of Lemma 2, that any morphism $\sigma : L \to L'$ can be extended into a morphism $\rho : (L, <) \to (L', <)$ of the corresponding ordered structures. To talk about orderings, the models have to be sets of some sort. If the domain of the target $(L, <)$-structure is identical to the domain of the source $(L', <)$-structure, then the ordering defining $<$ in the former can literally be defined as the ordering in the latter. If the domain of the target structures is some cartesian product of the domain of the source, or some subset thereof, we may define the ordering in the target lexicographically from the ordering in the source. This can be done using a quantifier-free first-order formula.

In the most general formulation, the domain of the target is a *quotient* of some subset of some product of the source structure. (A typical example: constructing the rationals from the integers.) Here we do have to be a little careful: defining $(x_1, \ldots, x_n) < (y_1, \ldots, y_n)$ lexicographically, even for tuples in the domain of the target, may not respect the equivalence relation of the quotient. However, we can say that $(x_1, \ldots, x_n) < (y_1, \ldots, y_n)$ in case the least tuple equivalent to $(x_1, \ldots, x_n)$ is less than the least tuple equivalent to $(y_1, \ldots, y_n)$, where "least" and "less than" refer to lexicographic ordering on n-tuples.

Note that this does require existential and universal quantification. So there may be a world where we do increase the power of order-invariance, but it seems to require doing something unnatural, like having the morphisms be set-theoretically powerful (viz., the ability to take quotients) but definitionally weak (e.g., using quantifier-free logic).

5 Future Directions

The real promise of our work is in opening up a host of new avenues for building logical tools for generalized invariant logics. Here we list several natural directions:

- The Beth definability theorem implies that order-invariant logic over all structures collapses to first-order definability, since the class of all linear orders (unlike the class of all finite orders) is an elementary class. To what extent do Beth-like theorems entail collapse in the general institutional setting? (By a "Beth-like theorem" we mean something along the lines of "implicit definability implies explicit definability." These have been studied in the context of institutions, cf. [4, Chapter 10].)

- One of the broad themes of invariant logic is the study *locality principles*, cf. [6,7]; e.g., order-invariant first-order logic inherits Gaifman locality from first-order logic, but traversal-invariant logic does not. It seems likely that we can *formulate* locality principles in the institutional setting; to what extent do the techniques for reasoning about them lift as well?
- Along the same lines, the study of *games* is a major tool for the study of definability in finite model theory [9, Chapter 10]. To what extent can they be lifted to the institutional setting? Here even formulating them is probably challenging.
- Finally, there is a whole host of machinery known for relating and comparing different institutions. (E.g., institution morphisms and comorphisms plus endless variations on them, cf. [4].) What light do they shed on the relationship between a basal institution $\mathfrak{I}$ and its shadow $\mathfrak{I}^{\bullet}$?

References

1. Barcelo, P., Libkin, L.: Order-invariant types and their applications. Log. Methods in Comput. Sci. **12**(1), 9 (2016). https://doi.org/10.2168/LMCS-12(1:9)2016
2. Bhaskar, S., Lindell, S., Weinstein, S.: Traversal-invariant characterizations of logarithmic space. In: Amarilli, A., Deutsch, A. (eds.) The Provenance of Elegance in Computation - Essays Dedicated to Val Tannen. Open Access Series in Informatics (OASIcs), vol. 119, pp. 2:1–2:17. Schloss Dagstuhl – Leibniz-Zentrum für Informatik, Dagstuhl, Germany (2024). https://doi.org/10.4230/OASIcs.Tannen.2
3. Dawar, A., Pago, B.: A logic for P: are we nearly there yet? ACM SIGLOG News **11**, 35–60 (2024)
4. Diaconescu, R.: Institution-independent Model Theory. Studies in Universal Logic, Birkhäuser Cham, 2 edn. (2025). https://doi.org/10.1007/978-3-031-68854-6
5. Fagin, R.: Generalized first-order spectra and polynomial-time recognizable sets. In: Karp, R. (ed.) Complexity of Computation. SIAM-AMS Proceedings, pp. 47–73 (1974)
6. Grohe, M., Schwentick, T.: Locality of order-invariant first-order formulas. ACM Trans. Comput. Log. (TOCL) **1**, 112–130 (1998)
7. Harwath, F., Schweikardt, N.: On the locality of arb-invariant first-order formulas with modulo counting quantifiers. Log. Methods Comput. Sci. **12** (2016)
8. Immerman, N.: Relational queries computable in polynomial time. Inf. Control **68**(1), 86–104 (1986). https://doi.org/10.1016/S0019-9958(86)80029-8
9. Libkin, L.: Elements of Finite Model Theory, 2nd edn. Studies in Universal Logic. Springer (2012)
10. Vardi, M.Y.: The complexity of relational query languages (extended abstract). In: Proceedings of the Fourteenth Annual ACM Symposium on Theory of Computing (STOC '82), pp. 137–146. ACM (1982). https://doi.org/10.1145/800070.802186

Author Index

P. Johann and R. de Queiroz (Eds.): WoLLIC 2026, LNCS 16757, p. 137, 2027.
https://doi.org/10.1007/978-3-032-33486-2

MIX
Papier aus verantwortungsvollen Quellen
Paper from responsible sources
FSC® C105338

If you have any concerns about our products,
you can contact us on
ProductSafety@springernature.com

In case Publisher is established outside the EU,
the EU authorized representative is:
Springer Nature Customer Service Center GmbH
Europaplatz 3, 69115 Heidelberg, Germany

Printed by Libri Plureos GmbH
in Hamburg, Germany